The Bishop in Politics

– Loyal Friend. Bitter Foe –

Life and Career of

John MacEvilly

Bishop of Galway 1857-81

Archbishop of Tuam 1881-1902

LIAM BANE

Publishers: Westport Historical Society

Printers: Berry's Printing Works (Westport) Limited

© Copyright Liam Bane 1993

ISBN O 9514148 3 6

Contents

Page

Chapter

Archbishop John MacEvilly

MAYNOOTH COLLEGE CENTENARY CELEBRATIONS, JUNE 1895
Dr. MacEvilly is pictured sixth from the right, front row.

Palace — Residence of Archbishops MacHale and MacEvilly.

Old St. Jarlath's College, residence of Archbishop
MacEvilly before the death of Archbishop MacHale.

Butter knife belonging to Archbishop John MacEvilly of Tuam.
Donated by his grandniece, Mary Dunne, Louisburgh, Co. Mayo to Knock Folk Museum.

St. Jarlath's Cathedral, Tuam.

Introduction

BIOGRAPHIES OF NINETEENTH century Irish Catholic bishops, and studies of ecclesiastical affairs generally in that century, have, until recent times, received relatively little critical attention. Such works as have been done are not altogether satisfactory from the standpoint of modern historical research. Biographies such as Bernard O'Reilly's *John MacHale, His Life, Times and Correspondence,* published in 1890, or more general works such as D'Alton's *History of the Archdiocese of Tuam,* published in 1928, are useful as collections of information and as general guides and commentaries. Such works, however, rarely seek to offer an objective assessment of the church as a social institution, nor do they attempt critical judgement of the role of bishops as men of public affairs of their day.

The task of the modern historian has been greatly facilitated by the availability in recent times of much valuable source material, particularly collections of letters and private manuscripts. In the study of public figures such as bishops, the letter is an invaluable asset, superseding any amount of speculation, as nowhere else is the private man, the essential man, so revealed. The letter can provide the missing clue towards the interpretation of puzzling comment or behaviour, it can convey shades of feeling and critical attitudes that do not appear publicly, and at all times it furnishes the valuable background to public statements and actions. For these important reasons, I cannot subscribe to that point of view which would argue for the suppression of such material on grounds of it being private and personal. It is the availability of such material as the Kirby collection in the archives of the Irish College, Rome, that has made possible the more perceptive and analytical works of our times in this field, such as Norman's *The Catholic Church and Ireland in the Age of Rebellion – 1859-1873,* Larkin's controversial *The Roman Catholic Church and the Creation of the Modern Irish State 1878-1886, A History of Irish Catholicism* edited by P. J. Corish, or more recent episcopal biographies like *Croke of Cashel* by Mark Tierney. Into this category, too, come the published essays of C. J. Woods.[1]

With regard to the letters of John MacEvilly or to those relating to his life and career, I have been at once fortunate and unfortunate. First the debit side. Following the dispute between MacEvilly and Thomas MacHale, nephew of the archbishop of Tuam, the latter left for the United States, bringing with him a large slice of Irish history in the form of his uncle's collection of letters and manuscripts. This collection formed the basis of O'Reilly's biography of the archbishop but since then the collection has disappeared, and all attempts at tracing it have so far, unfortunately, failed. Also, John MacEvilly's own collection of letters, which one must presume so careful a correspondent would have kept, has disappeared from the Tuam diocesan archives. This collection was probably lost in the transfer of material from the old archbishop's palace in Tuam to the modern episcopal dwelling.[2]

For this bad fortune, however, I have been most adequately compensated. There are, first of all, the published collections, the letters of Paul Cullen collected and edited by Peadar MacSuibhne in five volumes, *Paul Cullen and His Contemporaries;* the calendar of Kirby letters compiled by P. J. Corish in *Archivium Hibernicum 1972-74;* the calendar of Croke letters compiled by Mark Tierney in *Collectanea Hibernica 1970-71.* Letters of MacEvilly in the Kirby collection in Rome, which have hitherto remained unpublished, have been made available to me through the good offices of Dom Mark Tierney O.S.B., Padraig O Tuairisc, M.A. of Tuam, and Fr Martin Coen, M.A. of Galway, all of whom have had access to the relevant archives in Rome, and two of whom, Coen and O Tuairisc, have at various times acted as archivists in the Irish College, Rome. I am further indebted to Dom Mark Tierney, who so readily granted access to his own personal collection of letters and documents, including some from the Propaganda archives in Rome and the Cashel diocesan archives. I have been most fortunate in being allowed access to the most valuable MacEvilly collection of all, that which is deposited in the Dublin archives. For this my gratitude goes to Fr Kevin Kennedy, former diocesan archivist. Other useful letters and documents that were made available to me were from the Galway diocesan archives, courtesy of Bishop Eamon Casey, and from the Elphin diocesan archives, courtesy of Bishop Dominick Conway. An t-Athair Reamon O Muiri, diocesan archivist at Armagh, sent me copies of the limited material relating to MacEvilly there.

The name of John MacEvilly is not one likely to strike a responsive chord in many minds today. Yet, I am certain that readers of this story will be quite amazed at the extent of MacEvilly's involvement in the affairs of his day. His lifetime ranges from O'Connell to Parnell and after, and his episcopal career encompasses the crucial second half of the nineteenth century. In our time, when the role of the catholic hierarchy in the nineteenth century is the subject of discussion, this study of MacEvilly raises, in one bishop's career, the important questions: What was the extent of episcopal influence in the last century? How great was the power of these men; how did they wield that power and what were the limitations on it? What, then, was their contribution to the modern Irish State?

It is my hope that this study of John MacEvilly, bishop of Galway from 1857 to 1881 and archbishop of Tuam from 1881 to 1902, will shed light on these vexed questions, pointing to some solutions and helping to separate the reality from the myth. John MacEvilly was an important man in his time and place and he chose to take an active part in the events of his day. He was the close friend of Paul Cullen, whose contribution to our history has not yet been fully analysed, and more importantly, MacEvilly was Cullen's agent in an area of the country where the archbishop of Dublin's influence was most diminished.

Another significant aspect of MacEvilly's career is that he governed in an area of the country which was most neglected by governments of the time. It is interesting to observe the manner in which he coped with the peculiar problems of the dioceses he ruled. He lived and worked through troubled times and he lived and worked in dioceses which were particularly turbulent. Because he was committed to certain lines of action, MacEvilly was faced with situations that created problems both for himself as bishop and for the church he served. How John MacEvilly responded to those situations, and why he made a particular response, are the basis of this study.

Besides those mentioned above, my thanks must go to the staff of the National Library, to the staff of the Royal Irish Academy and of the State Paper Office for their unfailing courtesy and help. This book is based on a thesis which was presented for an M.A. degree at U.C.G. in 1979. I am deeply indebted to Gearoid O Tuathaigh, professor of History at U.C.G., who was my supervisor, for his encouragement and invaluable guidance. I am also indebted to Maynooth College Trust for a generous grant towards the cost of publication, to Fr Michael Keane for his generosity and encouragement and to other contributors. I am grateful to Tom O'Donoghue for the loan of some valuable books and to my good friend, Noel Lyons, who had many helpful suggestions to offer. My family and friends were most helpful and supportive throughout. My sincere thanks to Jarlath Duffy, Elisabeth Farrell and the members of Westport Historical Society who are responsible for the publication of this book. Finally, thank you, Frances, for your patience and understanding.

Chapter 1

Early Life and Career

THE RURAL DISTRICT of Bunowen, in the parish of Louisburgh, lies at the foot of Croagh Patrick on the west coast of Mayo. It is nine miles from the town of Westport and it looks out on the sweep of Clew Bay. Here, on 15 April 1816, John MacEvily was born.[1] His parents, William and Sarah, are described as 'belonging to the respectable farming class.'[2] This does not tell us much, as the very fact that the MacEvillys had a bishop for a son would certainly have entitled them to the epithet 'respectable.' In all probability, the MacEvilly family was relatively well off in a time and place that knew great hardship.

John and at least one other brother, Jeremiah, attended St. Jarlath's College, Tuam. Like John, Jeremiah went on to study at Maynooth College, where he was ordained in 1853.[3] Another brother, Walter, was a prominent figure in the public life of Westport, serving on the Urban Council there in the late 1800s and the early years of this century.[4]

Certainly, long-living was a notable trait of the MacEvilly family. John's father, William, died in 1872 at the age of 86.[5] His mother, Sarah, had a remarkably long life. John speaks of a visit to her in 1881 and he gives her age then as 95.[6] William O'Brien also describes a visit to her, when she talked of having seen the French in 1798. 'She was flying from Killala in her father's car,' O'Brien recounts, 'when the "little men with the guns" jumped over the ditch and stopped them.'[7] Sarah MacEvilly died in 1886, having reached her hundredth year.[8] As far as I have been able to discover, there were eight children in all, five sons and three daughters.

Sometime in emancipation year, 1829, John enrolled at St. Jarlath's College. His uncle, Fr Boland, was parish priest of Kilbannon, outside the town of Tuam, and for a short time John attended the college as a day student. St. Jarlath's had been in existence since 1815, when it was founded by the archbishop of Tuam, Oliver Kelly, for the purpose of training students for the priesthood. It was supported partly by contributions of £2 per annum from each parish priest in the

MacEvilly home, Bunowen, Louisburgh.   (Photo: Frank Dolan, Westport)

diocese and partly by the subscriptions of fee-paying students.[9] In such colleges at the time, the emphasis was very much on the classics, in which the students were well read, but Healy, the writer of the history of Maynooth, reported that their knowledge of English and mathematics was defective.[10]

John MacEvilly worked hard and was an ambitious student. Having spent four years at St. Jarlath's, he entered Maynooth College in 1833.[11] At the end of their ordinary course of studies, some students were selected for further study at the Dunboyne establishment on the basis of their performance at examinations. This establishment was for many the first step towards a prominent career in the church.[12] In 1839, MacEvilly was sent for further study to Dunboyne. He spent three years there, making scripture his special study.[13] During those years, he had as fellow students Edward McCabe, later cardinal archbishop of Dublin, and Robert O'Keeffe, the tempestuous Ossory priest who, in his time, fought a series of legal actions against his own bishop and Paul Cullen of Dublin. MacEvilly appeared as an expert in canon law at the hearing of the case against Cullen.[14]

In 1840, MacEvilly was ordained priest by Archbishop Murray of Dublin.[15] Subsequently, he made two attempts to obtain a chair at Maynooth. In 1844, he was one of four candidates for the chair of theology, which went to Rev. George Crolly, and in 1845 he competed unsuccessfully for the vacant chair of rhetoric.[16] At that stage, he had established himself as professor of scripture and Hebrew at St. Jarlath's College, a post to which he had been appointed in August 1842 by his archbishop, John MacHale.[17]

John MacEvilly had grown up in an Ireland which was dominated by the person and personality of Daniel O'Connell, and the years of MacEvilly's youth coincided with those years when O'Connell was at the height of his fame and powers. As a boy, MacEvilly would have witnessed the struggle for catholic emancipation when the Catholic Association swept the country, with O'Connell establishing himself as the undisputed leader and idol of the people. It was not then surprising that MacEvilly should worship at the shrine as, for the young priest, O'Connell was 'the mighty leader who was made instrumental in the hands of Providence for achieving such moral conquests.' He described O'Connell as the man 'whose giant arm loosed the bonds and tore off the fetters from the paralysed limbs of Ireland.'[18]

One of O'Connell's achievements, and indeed one of his great strengths, was the politicization of the Irish clergy,[19] a task in which he was greatly assisted by John MacHale of Tuam. The priests of Tuam diocese were amongst the most politically aware and most politically active in the country. Such participation would certainly have been expected of a priest working in the town of Tuam, and John MacEvilly had an early introduction to political involvement when his archbishop gave his enthusiastic backing to the Repeal Movement.[20] The clergy of the diocese subscribed to the Repeal Association, among them John MacEvilly, who became a member in May 1843.[21] This was the year when Repeal fever was raging through the country. O'Connell was addressing huge crowds of people and hinting that the Repeal of the Union might be accomplished before the end of the year. These meetings were followed by banquets attended by local catholic lay leaders and members of the catholic hierarchy and clergy.[22] In June and July, MacEvilly was present at two such banquets given in O'Connell's honour at Galway and Tuam.[23]

The year 1843, however, marked the high point of the Repeal Association. Repeal engendered fiercer opposition and aroused greater passions than ever emancipation did; and after the debacle at Clontarf, when O'Connell called off the public meeting rather than run the risk of violent confrontation, the movement was on the wane. Whether it might have been revived is a moot point in the face of the catastrophe that followed. The *Tuam Herald* of October 1845 carried this ominous notice: 'There scarcely now remains a doubt that the potato crop will be more or less injured in every part of Ireland.'[24] As a young priest in the town of Tuam, John MacEvilly was in a position to witness at first hand the worst of the horrors that the Great Hunger brought.

A public meeting was held at Tuam in May 1846 for the purpose of appointing a relief committee. John MacEvilly was present;[25] and indeed in his lifetime, he was to become all too familiar with the workings of such committees. In the two years that followed, this committee could do little to relieve the awful distress and suffering in the town and district of Tuam. Again and again, Archbishop MacHale appealed publicly to Lord John Russell to come to the aid of the people.[26] By 1847, Tuam was the scene of the most appalling spectacles. In February, the *Tuam Herald* reported that people were being buried without coffins and that children were being left in the street.[27] Next month, the same paper wrote: 'The hearing of persons dying from want and destitution has now become as familiar to our ears as the striking of the clock.' Fever and dysentery were on the increase,[28] and as late as January 1848, the *Herald* recorded 'one of the most heart-rending spectacles we have ever witnessed.' The report referred to 'throngs of famishing people' in the streets, many of whom were so exhausted 'as to be unable to reach their destination.' Their destination was the workhouse where about 2,000 poor people had assembled in the hope of being fed. 'In all probability,' the paper forecast, 'there will be 3,000 applications for relief on Monday next.'[29]

The Famine was a disaster which obviously left a deep imprint on the consciousness of those who had lived through it and, in later times, MacEvilly often alluded to the sufferings of those years. When the worst horrors of the Famine had abated, the people had little interest in causes like Repeal and the movement itself was seriously split. Daniel O'Connell had died in May 1847 and his sons lacked the great personal gifts and charismatic appeal of their father. The dissenting wing of the movement was already set in another direction, culminating in the abortive revolt of Smith O'Brien in 1848. In general, the clergy remained loyal to the memory of O'Connell and to the remains of his Repeal Association. In July 1848, the clergy of the deanery of Tuam wrote a public letter to John O'Connell expressing their disapproval of the disbandment of the Repeal Association and the setting up of the Tenant League. John MacEvilly signed this letter,[30] and he also signed a memorial from the clergy of Tuam to Queen Victoria in August 1848 pleading for clemency for Smith O'Brien and the other political prisoners.[31]

MacEvilly's political training continued when he was involved in the formation of the Tenant Protection Society at Tuam in 1850.[32] His involvement here, and subsequent involvement with the Tenant League, are discussed elsewhere.[33] In August of that same year, he was present at the Synod of Thurles, where he had a taste of ecclesiastical politics.[34] The Synod was an event of some significance in Irish church affairs, marking the beginning of Paul Cullen's dominance of the Catholic Church in Ireland. MacEvilly was present as consulting theologian to MacHale and he also took part in the deliberations of the Synod, acting and voting on behalf of Bishop Browne of Galway, who was absent through illness. Here MacEvilly made first contact with Cullen, the man who more than any other was to influence his life and attitudes. We can take it that MacEvilly was deeply impressed and that here were the beginnings of that later friendship, when Cullen had MacEvilly's complete and unquestioning trust and confidence in all matters.

That was for the future and just then the Synod of Thurles laid bare the thinly disguised rift in the Irish hierarchy between the faction of which Cullen was to become undisputed leader and the more independent bishops, or 'intransigents,' represented by MacHale.[35] Following the Synod, however, the wounds were temporarily healed and the two factions were united for the moment through the unlikely agency of the British government. The announcement of the restoration of the catholic hierarchy in England in 1850 was made the occasion for a piece of anti-catholic legislation, the Ecclesiastical Titles Bill, which was carried in Parliament in 1851. The legislation, which made it a penal offence for catholic prelates to adopt territorial titles, was resisted strongly by the Irish bishops.[36] At a public meeting in Tuam, at which MacEvilly was present, a resolution was passed expressing opposition to 'the Penal Laws now in progress of enactment against the Roman Catholics.'[37] In April, the catholic clergy in Tuam met and passed a series of resolutions denouncing the Bill. Among the signatories was John MacEvilly, professor, St. Jarlath's College.[38] The Ecclesiastical Titles Act never became effective and the resistance, so firmly pursued, represented a victory for the intransigents in regard to their views about British administration in Ireland.[39]

The resistance offered by catholic M.P.s to the Ecclesiastical Titles Bill and the rise of the Tenant League were the principal factors in the formation of a new Irish party, pledged to pursue an independent line in parliament. The independent party had the support of MacHale and the Tuam clergy, and MacEvilly was actively involved in the canvass for the election of 1852. In April, he participated in a public meeting held at Tuam to promote the candidature of the clerical choice, Captain Bellew.[40]

Having taken a prominent part in the issues of the day, and still obviously enjoying his archbishop's favour, it was no surprise when MacEvilly was appointed president of St. Jarlath's in August 1852.[41] This post directly involved its holder in local politics, since the holder was automatically qualified to become a member of the town commissioners. The position of the Tuam town commissioners was unique among such bodies in Ireland, in that it had, since 1817, been controlled by catholics. This situation had arisen because no qualification was required in respect of property and members were chosen 'out of the better and more honest inhabitants of the borough.'[42] The revenues were derived from tolls and, in 1827, they were set for five years to the committee for building the new catholic cathedral.[43] Isaac Butt, in his pro-Union days, made much use of this fact in his speech opposing Irish municipal reform in the Mansion House, Dublin in 1840, and again when opposing the Irish Corporation Bill in the House of Lords.[44]

In January 1854, MacEvilly was one of the principal speakers at the banquet in Tuam to honour the leaders of the Tenant League. He delivered a major speech on the theme of the priest in politics and he staunchly defended the principle of independent opposition.[45]

In other fields too, MacEvilly was making his mark. In 1856, he had an English commentary on the Epistles of St. Paul published.[46] This was the first of a series of commentaries which were published periodically throughout his life until he had covered the entire New Testament, with the exception of the Apocalypse.[47] The commentaries did not advertise MacEvilly's style of writing but they were rather a proof of his industry and perseverance. D'Alton states that at no time did MacEvilly 'acquire much facility in expressing himself in readable English.'[48] This assessment is not altogether fair, as MacEvilly's later statements, while often ponderous in the fashion of the time, do exhibit a good command of the English language.

MacEvilly's writings, however, did add to his qualifications for elevation to the episcopacy. Academically, he was well qualified to be a bishop and he was a man who had taken a prominent part in local and national affairs. More significant than all of this, by the time the see of Galway had become vacant in 1857, MacEvilly had won the favour of Paul Cullen, who was the most important influence in the appointment of Irish bishops. Cullen supported MacEvilly's claims at Rome. The bishops of the province of Connacht had recommended Dr Thomas MacHale, the archbishop's nephew, for Galway. Cullen wrote to Tobias Kirby, who had succeeded Cullen as rector of the Irish College in Rome, saying that he considered Thomas MacHale 'not fit' and that 'Dr MacEvilly of Tuam would be better.'[49]

Not for the last time, Cullen's choice was Rome's choice and John MacEvilly was appointed bishop of Galway in February 1857 at the age of 39.[50] On 22 March, he was consecrated bishop by John MacHale at Tuam Cathedral, and the special sermon was preached by John Derry, bishop of Clonfert.[51] On his departure from Tuam, MacEvilly was presented with £350 and an ornate carriage, gifts from the townspeople.[52]

What kind of man was John MacEvilly? Physically, he was a strong, well-built man, of robust health and energy, which allowed him to live a full active life relatively untroubled by illness. He was reputed tough and uncompromising and certainly the picture that emerges is a serious, stern and austere man. He did not possess a very keen sense of humour, although in his letters there are traces of a dry, sarcastic wit. A disciplinarian, he expected total obedience from his priests and those who crossed him found a hard and stubborn opponent. He certainly had a capacity for hard work, as even his voluminous letter-writing shows, and it was his industry and application rather than any gifts of imagination or creativity that are demonstrated in his career. He was said to be an eloquent and impressive preacher, although it is difficult to know what precisely such a description means, given the general sycophantic tone of newspapers of the time in their appraisals of bishops. A fluent Irish speaker, he preached at least one sermon every Sunday in Irish.

MacEvilly was above all a man of cautious and conservative nature. He was shrewd in his reading of situations but often he found it difficult, almost painful, to come to definite decisions, and this facet of his character was highlighted after the death of his friend and counsellor, Cullen. A churchman of his time, he was not very adventurous or daring in thought, and his loyalty to Rome and its representatives was unwavering. He himself said: 'I always regarded as certain as anything in this world can be that Rome is always right.'[53]

Grave of William and Sarah MacEvilly, Kilgeever.   (Photo Frank Dolan, Westport)

Kilgeever Church.   (Photo: Frank Dolan, Westport)

Christening robe. (Courtesy Knock Folk Museum).

Chapter Two

Elections and Fenianism

TO A STUDENT OF John MacEvilly's career, it is strange indeed to see it written that he took no active or prominent part in politics, and this in newspapers which all his life reported his political involvement.[1] Of course, what is meant is that, in the popular view, MacEvilly was not a 'political bishop' as, say, MacHale or Cullen or Croke of Cashel so obviously were. It means that much of MacEvilly's political involvement was of a less spectacular kind, though no less effective for that, and that his manoeuverings were carried out in a private rather than in the formal public manner.

The prevailing clerical attitude towards political involvement, which had begun with O'Connell, was clearly elucidated by MacEvilly himself in a major speech which he delivered in Tuam in January 1854. Before the opening of parliament in that year, meetings were held in various places throughout the country in support of the policy of independent opposition, and in particular to support members who had remained true to their pledges.[2] At the Tuam meeting – which was attended by MacHale, G.H. Moore, Frederick Lucas and Dr Gray – MacEvilly, then president of St. Jarlath's, was replying to the toast 'the Irish Catholic Clergy' and made what Gavan Duffy called an 'exposition of singular ability on the relation of the clergy to public affairs in this country.'[3]

MacEvilly began by referring to the union that existed between priests and people. This relationship was to be for MacEvilly a touchstone right through his career by which he would judge particular political movements. If, as in the case of the Land League,[4] condemnation might result in strained relations between priests and people, MacEvilly would choose to remain silent rather than run the risk of what, on another occasion, he called 'the unnatural and suicidal severance in political matters between priests and people, which would be sure to end in the ruin of religion and civil society.'[5] In answer to the argument that the clergy should confine themselves to spiritual matters, MacEvilly, after roundly condemning those who proposed such arguments, declared first of all that the clergy had not renounced their rights as citizens and that they had a duty to resist every attack on the free exercise of their religion. In supporting such movements as Tenant Right, he argued, the clergy were merely vindicating and 'asserting the eternal principles of natural and revealed religion.'[6] In stating this, MacEvilly was advancing the common catholic theological argument of the time, namely, that all matters, even those which might seem to be strictly secular, were the concern of religion, even if that meant sheltering them under the umbrella of what was called 'natural religion.'

Such were the views of John MacEvilly in 1854, but were they the views of John MacEvilly who became bishop of Galway in March 1857? An important change had occurred. MacEvilly had 'switched sides' and, under Cullen's influence, was no longer the enthusiastic supporter of independent opposition. It was only as Cullen himself decided to become more directly involved in electoral politics that MacEvilly's participation also increased. Taking the lead from his mentor, MacEvilly involved himself in the promotion of the policies of 'justice for Ireland' and of the Liberal alliance.[7] The part played by MacEvilly in the various elections which took place during his time as bishop of Galway, and also his attitude to the clandestine political movement and ideas that went under the general name of Fenianism, can be examined.

THE 1857 ELECTION

The general election of 1857 was the first to be held in the wake of the defection of Sadleir and Keogh from the Independent Irish Party and the ensuing differences which that defection brought. From an ecclesiastical point of view, this election was interesting in that it was the first to be fought since the introduction of the Cullen-inspired statutes of 1854 aimed at limiting the activities of the clergy in politics. Probably what Cullen hoped to prevent was the more crude and obvious type of intervention by priests, such as had occurred in the 1852 elections.[8] No doubt he was in favour of the more subtle and private type of intervention, such as he himself practised in 1857 when he wrote to various members of the hierarchy, urging them to use their influence in the selection of candidates whose political views accorded with his own.[9]

Four members of Parliament were returned for Galway, two for the borough and two for the county. When MacEvilly arrived in Galway in March, the contest for the county was already well under way. The candidates were the sitting members, Sir Thomas Burke and Captain Bellew, both Catholics, and Sir William Gregory, husband of Lady Gregory. Bellew had the declared support of the archbishop and clergy of Tuam as well as Bishop Derry and the clergy of Clonfert.[10] The only evidence that MacEvilly played any active part in the election is the claim of Gregory, who later wrote that MacEvilly had said to him: 'If the consecration oil were not still moist upon me, you would see how I would exert myself for you.' Despite this, Gregory asserts, MacEvilly did in fact exert himself on his behalf and that there was 'thus the spectacle of two dioceses arrayed on the side of Bellew' and two on his own side.[11] Gregory was successful, being returned together with Sir Thomas Burke.

According to Whyte, the clergy at the 1857 election were as active as ever.[12] MacEvilly, however, reported that the Galway clergy had cheerfully complied with his recommendation to them 'to respect the sanctity of the day, Holy Thursday.' He was confident too that in the contest for the borough, the clergy were determined 'to keep aloof and to content themselves with simply recording their votes according to the dictates of their conscience.'[13]

THE 1859 ELECTION

In the previous election, MacEvilly's policy of non-intervention was in line with Cullen's policy. In this election Cullen withheld support from all candidates.[14]

By 1859, the Irish forces in parliament were in disarray and the policy of independent opposition was pressed by a diminishing few. The resulting disillusion among the Irish electorate meant less emphasis on the great national issues and more on the local issues. This combination of factors led to the election of such as John Orrell Lever, an English businessman who stood for Galway city.[15] One reason for Lever's success was that he had made Galway the terminus of a transatlantic shipping line. Another, and perhaps more important reason, was that he had the support of Peter Daly,[16] the influential Galway cleric who did not consider himself bound by any strictures which MacEvilly might place on the clergy. One of Daly's ambitions was to obtain the transatlantic packet for Galway. The Tories, now bidding for the catholic vote, included a proposed grant for the packet as part of their programme.[17]

THE 1865 ELECTION

When Paul Cullen decided to return to formal political involvement in 1864 with the founding of the National Association, he brought with him faithful disciples like John MacEvilly. While Cullen saw the new association as a constitutional counter to the influence of Fenianism, he must also by then have felt the need for an organisation which would promote the claims of catholics, particularly in the field of education and with regard to the question of the disestablishment of the church. The third great question, that of the land, was of course the one which concerned the laity immediately and vitally; and so it was added to the other two to form the triple programme of the new National Association, which had its first meeting in December 1864.

1865 was election year and MacEvilly devoted his Lenten pastoral to the topic of the National Association. He outlined its aims, calling for legal security for the tenants and for freedom of education in all its branches. He described the position of the established church as 'a badge of national disgrace' and 'utterly indefensible.' Disestablishment, he claimed, would lead to 'real equality between all classes of Irishmen.' The Association was entitled to the support of 'every man who loves his religion and country,' and he called on all, both cleric and lay, to join it as members or associates. He wrote in similar vein to Dr Kirby in Rome, commenting, 'To say we are yet emancipated is sheer folly.'

In June, MacEvilly confessed that he and the clergy were perplexed about the outcome of the election. Lever was again being strongly supported by Peter Daly and, in MacEvilly's view, it would be 'an eternal disgrace' to have Lever returned as member. According to MacEvilly, Lever had no chance whatever, 'unless they bribe the unfortunate venal freemen who form nearly the majority of our constituency.' The 'bribe' offered was the declaration by Daly that Lever had deposited with him a large sum of money to start a factory in Galway and also 'for another purpose.'

There was a vacancy in the borough caused by Lord Dunkellin's decision to contest the county seat. Two members of the National Association were candidates. MacEvilly reported to Cullen that one, Michael Morris, the attorney general and a Conservative, was a great favourite with the clergy but had not pledged himself fully to carry out the programme of the Association. The other candidate, Sir Rowland Blennerhassett, had been strongly recommended by various parties but MacEvilly would be slow to encourage him. He wrote that Daly's determination to support Lever was hampering them all, as it was 'a dreadful thing to see priest actively arrayed against priest.' But, 'until God changes his heart,' there was not much that could be done, he concluded pessimistically.[18]

Morris, along with Blennerhassett, was elected to represent the town of Galway, while Lever was a poor third.[19] On nomination day, a group of factory labourers had tried to take possession of the courthouse in Galway; and on polling day they had formed a body guard for Daly. According to the *Vindicator,* no friend of Daly, they would have prevented the freedom of election if they had not been removed by the police.[20]

MacEvilly immediately communicated the result to Cullen. MacEvilly himself had taken no part in the election as, in his estimation, none of the candidates had come 'up to our mark.' However, he stated, since 'a low Orange party,' supported by Daly, had attacked Blennerhassett because of his connection with the National Association, MacEvilly had advised those who were not members of the Association to vote against Lever, 'and they did so.' There was another reason too why MacEvilly did not participate actively in the election. Daly had started on a scheme of works for the people and MacEvilly was of the opinion that these works would cease whether Lever was returned or not. Thus, if he had been directly active in the defeat of Lever, and the works ceased, MacEvilly felt that Daly would rouse the people against the clergy and himself.

The return of Morris and Blennerhassett was contested by two of the losing candidates, Lever and Nicholas Stubber. The *Vindicator* had no doubt but that the real petitioner was Peter Daly and the paper attacked the priest viciously, accusing him of having used 'every effort, fair and foul' to return his own candidate. Although he was now over eighty, the article stated, Daly had fought 'like a man of twenty-five,' and now that he had been defeated, he was seeking his revenge. The petition which accused Morris and Blennerhassett of systematic bribery and corruption, was heard in March 1866 and was lost.

Country-wide, the 1865 election was not a success story for the National Association. In Galway, however, they had done well, having returned one fully-committed member, Blennerhassett, and a member, Morris, who was at least open to suggestion. While caution had been the keynote of MacEvilly's interest, he had been sufficiently interested to show that he was going to be a force with which future candidates would have to reckon.

THE 1868 ELECTION

The National Association, disappointing as its performance must have been to its supporters, was successful in at least placing firmly before the public the question of the established church. On this question MacEvilly had written: 'Disestablishment is a much more important measure than emancipation. Emancipation was never realised, never came home to people. Disestablishment will mean that we all can now meet on the common ground of Irishmen for the good of a common country.'

By the mid-1860s disestablishment was a grievance that could no longer be ignored. Earl Russell, who became prime minister in 1866, initiated the debate. In June, Russell's government fell and was replaced by a Tory cabinet under the Earl of Derby, who did not have a majority in the House of Commons. In this fragile position, the Conservatives made feelers towards the Irish catholic hierarchy. Michael Morris, now member for Galway and a supporter of the Tory administration, approached Cullen. Cullen decided that there was nothing to be gained from 'Mr Morris's friends.'

Meanwhile, the Irish bishops, anxious to avoid any measure that smacked of state control, had decided in favour of disendowment, which meant that the wealth of the established church would be taken over by the state and devoted to general charitable purposes, and that all churches in Ireland should become legally voluntary bodies. Catholic hopes received a boost when, at the end of 1867, Gladstone, who was committed to church disestablishment, became leader of the opposition. When the government was defeated in March 1868, on a motion of Gladstone's demanding disestablishment and a measure of disendowment, the stage was set for a general election.

18

The Irish catholic bishops under Cullen's leadership now set about achieving a Liberal majority and they began by selecting suitable candidates. George Morris, who had succeeded his brother Michael as member for Galway city, had supported the Derby administration and was therefore considered unsuitable. The question was how best to get rid of him. Cullen told William Monsell, Gladstone's man in Ireland, that he would write to MacEvilly about Morris, who he believed had great influence in the town. MacEvilly was obviously taken aback.

Obediently, however, MacEvilly set about the task of unseating George Morris. The first move was the formation in August 1868 of a 'Galway Independent Club,' under the patronage of the bishop and clergy, 'with a view to starting a Liberal candidate in Galway city'; and it resolved 'to accept no other candidate who will not pledge himself to adopt Mr Gladstone as his leader and promise to hurl from power the present no-popery administration.' A second, more decisive move, was made on 19 September with the publication of a series of resolutions from MacEvilly and his clergy which came to be known as 'the College House resolutions.' Of these, the one aimed directly at Morris, stated: 'We deem it our bounden duty at the approaching election of members for this borough to resist to the best of our power the candidature of any man who will not pledge himself both to support Mr Gladstone's resolutions against the Irish establishment, as set forth by him in the last session of Parliament, and to assist in hurling from office any, and every Ministry, which will refuse making the said resolutions cabinet measures.' In short, Morris was now challenged to declare himself publicly for Gladstone.

The *Galway Vindicator*, somewhat naively, expressed puzzlement at the purpose of this move: 'Of course his Lordship and our esteemed clergy would not counsel the people to vote for out-and-out supporters of Mr Gladstone' and recalled Gladstone's stand on the Italian question and his differing views on the education question. The *Freeman's Journal* did not have any such doubts about the bishop's intentions and, applauding Galway for having awakened 'from the trance which has paralysed her people for years,' called on Morris to declare himself or withdraw, to now 'elect between Orange rule and the policy of Mr Gladstone.'

At this opportune time, John Bridge Aspinall, recorder of Liverpool and a Liberal and catholic, arrived in Galway, offering himself as candidate and bearing a letter from Gladstone himself. The newcomer duly declared his complete acceptance of the resolutions of the bishop and clergy. The other sitting member, Sir Rowland Blennerhassett, also approved the resolutions. When no such approval arrived from George Morris, MacEvilly and the clergy met on 29 September and declared that silence in Morris's case was equivalent to a refusal to accept the resolutions, and consequently they had to declare him 'an unfit person to represent this Catholic borough.' They announced that they would meet again on 2 October to select another candidate.

In a letter headed 'To the Catholic people of Galway,' which he had published in the papers and placarded on the walls of Galway, Morris made his reply. He described his favourable voting record, and what he had considered to be his good relations with the bishop. As late as 5 September, the bishop had said to him that he did not think that Galway would be better represented. He would have then withdrawn had he known that he was to be opposed by the bishop and clergy. Finally, Morris declared that he had been elected to parliament by the people, not by College House. 'In no country or town in the kingdom,' he ended, 'has the existence of the catholic laity been ignored except in yours, and if the catholic city of the Tribes is satisfied to register the effects of the College House, I shall be no party to the process, even under the penalty of being described as an unfit person.'

In a reply of withering sarcasm and some fury, MacEvilly referred to what he called 'Mr Morris's third address.' MacEvilly claimed that he had in fact wished Morris every success until recently. What had happened to make him change his mind? His answer is less than honest and there is no mention of Cullen. MacEvilly told how Morris called on him on 5 September and solemnly promised not only to support the three great questions of the day but to vote against the Conservative ministry if they persisted in their views regarding the established church. However, said the bishop, in his first address of 7 September, Morris had made no mention of 'the three great questions' or of his solemn promise. Out came the second address, which, said MacEvilly, was still 'vague, amended or supplemented.' Then, Morris had made no answer to the resolutions but instead had issued his third address. The people of Galway would know how to answer that, MacEvilly declared, and he concluded, 'From the whole tone and supercilious bearing of some men . . . a stranger to this neighbourhood could arrive at no other conclusion, but that Galway was a family borough; that the whole gentry of the locality were men of some inferior caste, only destined and fitted to be so many attendant satellites of the illustrious and historic house of Morris.'

George Morris then announced his retirement from the contest. The *Galway Vindicator*, torn between its support for Morris and its loyalty to the bishop, regretted 'the misunderstanding' that had arisen, adding that 'a Catholic gentleman must always feel at a great disadvantage when he has a dignitary of the church for his opponent.' In contrast, the *Freeman's Journal*, calling it 'a great and glorious victory,' declared: 'Galway is awake, the catholic feeling of its people has been stirred, and they will no longer consent to be dragged at the wheels of the Orange ascendancy.'

In a letter to the papers which followed, Morris described MacEvilly's statement as 'a laboured attempt to become personal to me.' He went over the same ground, in more detail; and wondered again what had happened to the bishop from 5 September, when he stated Morris was the best representative, to the 17th when Morris became an 'unfit person?' Morris concluded: 'I admit I bear a homely Galway name. Two of the bishop's immediate predecessors also bore the Galway names of French and Browne. Relationship with the latter I had the honour to claim. I regret my name is not ''illustrious or historic'' and therein displeases the fastidious taste of Bishop MacEvilly.' Immediately on Morris's retiral, Lord St. Lawrence announced his candidature.

MacEvilly emerged from the whole affair of Morris's resignation with very little credit or honour. His concern more than anything else was to protect the real instigators, Cullen and Monsell, and so when challenged by Morris, he was forced to resort to half-truths and to substitute abuse for argument. Morris acted courageously in the matter and his stand shows that there were catholic laymen who were prepared to challenge their bishop publicly, however costly that action might prove in terms of their careers. The claim of the *Freeman's Journal* that Morris's retiral was a resounding victory over landlord ascendancy is hardly supported by the fact that Morris was replaced by Lord St. Lawrence, nephew of Lord Clanricarde, scarcely the most temperate of landlords. Obviously St. Lawrence himself had contacted Cullen, as MacEvilly wrote assuring Cullen that he would do all he could for the new candidate.

MacEvilly now took steps to prevent any division of the Liberal vote. At a meeting held in the sacristy of St. Nicholas on 31 October it was proposed that a scrutiny be held of the three remaining Liberal candidates – St. Lawrence, Blennerhassett and Martin F. O'Flaherty – to decide which two should stand. The three men were written to by Fr Patrick Cullen, secretary of the meeting. St. Lawrence and Blennerhassett agreed and appointed three supporters to represent them at the proposed scrutiny. O'Flaherty, however, was not so accommodating. In his letter of reply, he queried the manner in which the sacristy meeting had been convened and requested 'quiet private meetings as will afford honest men an opportunity of making their selection free from the taint or suspicion of a band of unprincipled intriguers.'

O'Flaherty did attend the scrutiny, held in the sacristy on 2 November, but only to register a protest. No further business was taken and all subsequent appeals to O'Flaherty to withdraw from the contest failed.

The election was the subject of the sermons in all the catholic churches of the town on Sunday, 8 November. MacEvilly addressed a crowded church, declaring that the question was pre-eminently a religious one and that in this country what were termed politics embraced the fundamental duties prescribed by either natural or revealed religion. Hence it was not only the right but the duty of the clergy to instruct their people in their duties in this respect. He declared that the legitimate influence of the clergy had been at all times 'the firmest bulwark of society. Estrange the people from the clergy and you estrange them from all legitimate authority at the same time.' The bishop then outlined the circumstances of the sacristy meeting of 31 October. He believed that St. Lawrence would prove 'the best man' and had words of praise too for Blennerhassett, but he could not support O'Flaherty because of his insulting letter and his refusal to undergo the scrutiny.

In the election which took place later in the month, St. Lawrence received 814 votes, Blennerhassett 793, O'Hara the Conservative 224. O'Flaherty polled 437, which was a respectable showing in the circumstances.

O'Flaherty then published in the *Galway Vindicator* a letter in which he made serious charges, along with correspondence to substantiate these. O'Flaherty put two queries to Fr Cullen: 1. Whether he had given a message to O'Flaherty two days before the election that his entire election expenses would be paid if he then retired? and 2. Whether Fr Cullen had on the following day, in the presence of three men, conveyed a further message that O'Flaherty, on condition of retiring, would be guaranteed the backing of the bishop and clergy and also of Lord Clanricarde at any future election? Fr Cullen replied to the first query that he had conveyed such a message, but without the knowledge of the bishop. O'Flaherty had refused the offer emphatically, Fr Cullen said. To the second query, Fr Cullen said that 'authorised by Rev. G. Commins on behalf of the bishop,' he had offered O'Flaherty the support of the bishop and clergy and the influence of the bishop with Lord St. Lawrence. O'Flaherty had replied that the offer had come too late because it was preceded by 'an active, organised and vicious combination to wound my character, both public and private, without mercy and without shame; in the pulpit – in the street – the drawing-room – the garrett and the cellar.'

To these charges, MacEvilly made no public response, being content to have published in the *Vindicator* details of gifts from St. Lawrence to various charities. It was hardly surprising that O'Flaherty should follow up these charges with a petition seeking to have the election declared null and void on the grounds of bribery and clerical intimidation. MacEvilly assured Cardinal Cullen that he had left nothing undone to conciliate O'Flaherty, affirming that, at St. Lawrence's bidding, he had authorised St. Lawrence's solicitor to promise O'Flaherty the 'perfect neutrality' of the clergy at a future election in return for withdrawal of the petition. But O'Flaherty was 'inexorable,' MacEvilly found, adding that he mentioned this to show that he himself was not the obstacle to a peaceful arrangement.

The trial of the petition opened at Galway in February 1869 before Judge Keogh. As far as MacEvilly was concerned, the most serious charges made against him were those by the two priests, Spelman and Cullen. Rev. Dominic Spelman testified that he had heard the bishop say to Fr Cullen on 18 November of the previous year that the administrators of the bishop's parish should necessarily adopt the bishop's political opinions and that if they did not wish to do so, 'let them call for a change of mission.' According to Spelman, Fr Cullen had asked if he were to consider these observations personal and the bishop had replied, 'Just as you please.'

Fr Cullen, whom MacEvilly once called 'a would-be Fr Peter,' had been secretary also of the meeting which had passed the College House resolutions. This position had been given to him, MacEvilly later claimed, 'to keep him on our side.' This obviously had not worked so well, as MacEvilly complained that Fr Cullen had 'joined the enemy' and, with Spelman, was 'all along betraying our secrets to O'Flaherty.' Fr Cullen's case in the trial rested on two points: firstly, that he had been compelled by the bishop to speak against O'Flaherty and secondly, that, as a result of his support of O'Flaherty, he had been demoted from parish priest to administrator.

On the first point, it was stated that a circular had been sent by the bishop to the clergy containing the outlines of their address to the congregations on the subject of the election. MacEvilly testified that he was present when Cullen was preaching and that Cullen had not used a word from the circular, and so he had ordered Cullen to go back and preach as instructed. On the second point, MacEvilly denied that the change in Fr Cullen's position had anything to do with the election, that he had intended changing the status of the parish but could not do so until Peter Daly's death. In the course of his evidence, MacEvilly also stated that if it were proved to him that any priest under his jurisdiction had refused the sacraments in consequence of the election, he would suspend that priest.

Judge Keogh in his summary held that the bishop and clergy did not transgress the boundary of discretion and duty. Complimenting MacEvilly on the 'frankness and fairness' of his evidence, he said that the bishops had the right to influence the electors in favour of their common representatives, provided that such influence was reasonable and legitimate, and he could find no evidence to suggest that it had been otherwise in this election. Keogh's part in the matter did not end with the judgement. One rather bizarre function that he had to perform before leaving Galway was to intervene to prevent a duel between O'Flaherty and Captain Blake Foster, a supporter of St. Lawrence.

Whether or not the influence exercised by MacEvilly was legitimate, it was certainly crucial to the outcome of the election. He had been deputised by Paul Cullen and Monsell to oust Morris, a sitting member, and the fact that he had been able to achieve this, given the popularity and influence of Morris in Galway, testifies to the power and influence of MacEvilly's own position at that time. The campaign also demonstrated the lengths to which MacEvilly was prepared to go to carry out the archbishop of Dublin's wishes in what they both believed to be the 'cause of right.' This may well be the explanation of the double standards that seem to be applied in MacEvilly's dealings with Morris and St. Lawrence. As to

O'Flaherty, once his refusal to submit to the scrutiny had been represented as an insult to the bishop and clergy, his chances of success were slender indeed.

THE 1872 ELECTION

By 1870 support for the Liberal alliance was already on the wane. Following on the formation of the Home Government Association by a group headed by Isaac Butt in that same year, home rule was fast becoming the new cry. The new movement did not have the support of John MacEvilly, due mainly, it is fair to say, to the fact that Paul Cullen withheld his support. Like Cullen, MacEvilly would not have been enamoured of an association which had as its leaders men who, like Butt, were protestant and former Conservatives. If anything more was needed to alienate MacEvilly, it would be the fact that the movement had from the beginning the support of John MacHale.

During 1871, two vacancies occurred in the county of Galway. The first was occasioned by the retiral of sitting M.P., Lord Burke. Two Liberal candidates presented themselves. One, Mitchell Henry, a wealthy merchant from Manchester and the owner of Kylemore Castle, had the backing of William Monsell, who wrote to MacEvilly in his favour. The second candidate was John Philip Nolan, a captain in the Royal Artillery and landlord at Ballinderry near Tuam. In their election addresses, both candidates declared their support for denominational education, the Pope and Home Rule.

As was now obligatory practice for any candidate entertaining hopes of success, both men made approaches to the catholic bishops of the constituency, seeking their favour. MacHale had refused to give any definite promise until both had also called on the bishop of Galway. MacEvilly was suspicious of such an action, since, he declared, it was the first time in his life MacHale had consulted one of his suffragans in such matters. Accordingly, reading the move as an attempt by MacHale to throw responsibility for any possible division on his suffragan, MacEvilly told Henry that he would support him if MacHale did, 'as it would be awkward to have us in opposite camps on such an occasion.' MacEvilly's conclusion was that if MacHale did not back out of it, he could see no difficulty for Henry, who also had the support of Lord Clanricarde.

Regarding Nolan, MacEvilly feared what he represented. If Nolan were to be the candidate, then the land would be the dominant issue in this election. MacEvilly, following Cullen, disliked the politics of the land because they were so potentially divisive. Issues such as education and disestablishment were 'safe' in that they found a broad base of support among the catholic community, landlord and tenant, gentry and peasant. Also Nolan's chief advocate was Peter Conway, parish priest of Headford. Conway was a Fenian sympathiser and intensely disliked by MacEvilly, who once described him as being 'like a mad dog biting at every person.'[21]

It was not surprising, then, that MacEvilly should support any move which would damage Nolan's candidacy. In fact, a most serious objection was raised by a Galway priest, John Dooley. On 15 February, the *Galway Vindicator* published a letter from Dooley in which Nolan was charged with having evicted fourteen families, consisting of ninety persons in all, from his estate at Portacarron, near Oughterard, in the years 1864 and 1866. Dooley gave a full list of those evicted, two of whom had since died at Oughterard workhouse, and he included a letter of corroboration from an evicted tenant, Martin Curran.

Nolan immediately issued a reply, which was placarded throughout the county. He quarrelled with Dooley about various details but the substance of the charge he admitted. He also declared that he was now prepared to submit the case to the arbitration of A. M. Sullivan and Fr Patrick Lavelle, as had happened in a recent case. Peter Conway wrote a letter in defence of his candidate. Conway's letter, however, was probably more harmful then helpful to Nolan, since it was mainly a scathing personal attack on Henry.

At the request of MacHale, Nolan then retired from the contest – 'very prudently' in MacEvilly's view. Henry was thus returned unopposed. On the day of the by-election, there was a dramatic intervention from Peter Conway. He came into the courthouse, accompanied by two laymen, and in a jurors' box washed his hands publicly, declaring that he was washing his hands out of 'the cursed county.' The *Galway Vindicator* took the gesture to mean that he would not interfere in future elections and commented wryly that it was 'a consummation devoutly to be wished.'

The court of arbitration to decide the Portacarron case met in Oughterard on Monday, 29 May. The three arbitrators – Sir John Gray, A.M. Sullivan and Patrick Lavelle – decided that the people should be restored to the land. Nolan accepted the decision; and in the later election, much was to be made of this Portacarron award.

The retiral of Sir William Gregory, who became Governor of Ceylon, caused the other vacancy in the county in 1871. On 1 August MacEvilly wrote to Cullen about a rumour that Sir Rowland Blennerhassett, a member for the borough, had received a government post in Germany. Blennerhassett had lost the bishop's support when he allied himself with the 'Old Catholic' breakaway group of Dollinger after the Vatican Council of 1870. His conduct, MacEvilly maintained, had raised 'a great cry against electing strangers' in Galway. He felt, however, that the local men could not be supported by the clergy and so, at this point, he had decided that the best policy was to keep aloof, which he said he was determined to do in the coming county election. MacHale, he reported, 'had taken up Nolan' although nothing practical had yet been done for the evicted Portacarron tenants.

Another Liberal candidate, Hyacinth D'Arcy, presented himself; and MacEvilly feared that the division of the Liberal vote would lead to the election of the Conservative candidate, Le Poer Trench, son of the earl of Clancarty, a notoriously harsh landlord.

MacHale's support for Nolan was publicly declared at the end of September. MacEvilly told how, on returning from a Maynooth meeting the previous August, Dr Gillooly of Elphin had brought him over to MacHale at Mullingar, stressing the necessity for unanimity at this election. To MacEvilly this meant that, as MacHale had already pledged himself to Nolan, he and Gillooly should do the same. MacEvilly had no objections to this, since it meant that the chief responsibility would rest with MacHale. Also MacEvilly felt that if he were to oppose MacHale or even remain neutral, he might be blamed in the event of Clancarty's son being returned. 'Dr MacHale, I am convinced,' wrote MacEvilly, 'would prefer to the success of a dozen of elections to place us in a wrong position and injure our influence over our own people.'

MacEvilly had reservations too about some of the resolutions adopted by the Tuam clergy, particularly two; one stating that they would use their influence '*under any circumstances* to prevent the return of Captain Trench,' and the other that the electors would not be interfered with in the event of a contest between Liberals. These two resolutions MacEvilly called 'perfectly contradictory,' and asked, 'How on earth could one use his influence *under any circumstances* to prevent the return of a Liberal.'

All of this matter-of-fact discussion about who should stand shows clearly that there was no debate in MacEvilly's mind about where the power of selection really lay. Indeed, he seems much more concerned about scoring points over MacHale and ensuring that MacHale should not score points over him. He was adamant that the responsibility for the selection should rest with MacHale, as in the event of defeat he would not lose face with the people. It is this consideration, more than the qualities of the candidate selected, that seems to be his primary preoccupation.

In December, a joint conference of the clergy of the dioceses of Tuam, Clonfert, Galway, Kilmacduagh and Kilfenora, issued resolutions supporting Nolan and expressing the hope that landlords would allow their tenants to vote according to their conscience. It was the first time, the *Galway Vindicator* reported, that any candidate had such unanimous clerical support in an election contest in Galway, and the paper declared that the clergy were 'the natural leaders of the people in politics as well as morals, as the people had not yet so far advanced out of the dark desert through which they had passed as to justify the clergy retiring within the sanctuary, leaving laymen to manage the political affairs of the nation.'

The landlords of the county answered this with a meeting of their own, held at Loughrea on 13 December. The chair was taken by Sir Thomas Burke, former

M.P. for the county, who declared that their purpose was to prevent 'Captain Nolan and humbug coming into the county.' References were made to clerical dictation and, naturally, the landlords adopted Trench as their candidate. It was this meeting which aroused MacEvilly's fury and decided him to give Nolan more wholehearted support than might otherwise have been the case. 'I felt myself,' he told Cullen, 'as placed between two evils, and I selected what I conceived to be the lesser.' He said the election would be a 'terrible fight' by the two great influences on the voter, priests and landlords.

The election campaign which followed was lively and sometimes bitter, and one in which the clergy played a very active part. Great meetings to rally support for Nolan were held throughout the county and always the platform was shared by prominent clergymen, such as Patrick Lavelle and Ulick Bourke, and letters of support from the bishops were read. In his letter to the Athenry meeting, MacEvilly declared that all his life he had striven for harmony between priests, people and landlords, and so he was greatly disappointed at the cry of 'priestly dictation' raised at the landlords' Loughrea meeting. If the people were severed from the priests, anarchy would result which would 'inaugurate the reign of communism' and the possessors of property would be the first to suffer. It was hard to believe that the landlords could be so blind to the 'great evil' which already had the continent of Europe in its grasp. Would the people of Galway be so mean-spirited, MacEvilly asked, as to co-operate in hurling from office a prime minister, whose chief offence in the eyes of many landlords was the 'granting of even a small measure of independence to the tenant classes of this country?'

In a letter to a meeting in Gort on New Year's Day 1872, MacEvilly denounced attempts to coerce tenants, declaring that the landlord who forced his tenant to vote contrary to his convictions was acting not only illegally but also very foolishly, in that the tenant might follow the example set by the landlord and himself resort to illegal methods. A resolution passed at this meeting stated that any catholic who would support Captain Trench must be deemed 'a recreant and renegade.' So committed now was MacEvilly that he told Moriarty of Kerry, who was seeking his help: 'We have so much hard work on hands to keep out a Tory of the deepest dye . . . that nothing can induce me to write a word or do an act politically that has not reference to the Galway election in which we must not be beaten.'

When D'Arcy eventually retired, or perhaps was persuaded to retire, it was a straight fight between Nolan and Trench, and when the victory went to Nolan with a majority of over two thousand votes, MacEvilly was triumphant. While others might view it as a success for home rule, MacEvilly had no doubt but that it was a victory for the priests. The return of a Clancarty to represent Galway would be viewed as a proof that 'the priests and people were disunited.'

No sooner was the counting completed than a petition was lodged, chiefly on the ground of 'undue clerical influence, causing spiritual intimidation.' The petition trial opened in Galway on 2 April before Judge William Keogh, who had tried the 1868 petition. Catholic bishops and clergymen attended regularly and in great numbers. MacEvilly was present throughout the trial, and reported to Cullen on its progress. Serjeant Armstrong, the prosecuting counsel, made serious charges against the clergy. MacEvilly was confident they would not be proved in regard to the clergy of Galway and Kilmacduagh, but had not the same confidence regarding the Tuam clergy. He feared that the 'barbarous uncontrollable' conduct of Fathers Conway and Loftus would lead to Nolan being unseated. Armstrong had endeavoured to make it appear that all the bishops were but satellites of MacHale, a charge, of course, that MacEvilly was determined to refute. MacEvilly also told Cullen that he had invited MacHale to stay with him during the trial but MacHale had declined.

Three days later, MacEvilly was of the opinion that Nolan would be unseated but that Trench would not get the seat. He confessed, however, that he would not regret seeing Trench seated as he feared that MacHale would otherwise encourage some 'wild candidate.' Indeed, he reported, there was a rumour that Butt himself would vacate Limerick and run in Galway, 'carrying out his Mazzini threat that his people will be returned in spite of the clergy.'

On the thirteenth day of the trial, MacEvilly appeared briefly to answer questions concerning documents. He was called for formal cross-examination on 27 April. In the course of his evidence, he said he was not aware of MacHale's offer of support to Nolan if he did not oppose Henry. He was of the opinion that Nolan would have been returned whether or not influence was brought to bear. He denied strongly that he was a satellite of MacHale's. He agreed that the exclusion of the clergy in elections might alienate them from the people, and that anarchy and communism would result with 'a fair sprinkling of the internationals over the country.' Asked if he were a supporter of the Liberal party, MacEvilly replied that he was when they deserved it.

Reflecting on his performance to Cullen, MacEvilly seemed pleased with himself and remarked that he had been most careful in his references to MacHale, not wishing it to appear that there was any bad feeling between them. It was impossible to say what the verdict might be, but the expenses 'would be ruinous to Nolan' if the verdict should go against him.

Some days later, MacEvilly was recalled for questioning concerning some decrees of Trent and Thurles. He was emphatic that public denunciation of laymen from the altar would not occur in any diocese with which he was connected. Privately, MacEvilly commented that personal denunciation was the theme of Conway's sermon every Sunday, and no action had been taken by MacHale. Judge Keogh, remarking that he was happy to hear the bishop of

Galway at all times, complimented MacEvilly on evidence which he said had been given in the 'frankest, most honourable and most creditable way.' The taking of evidence ended on 11 May. Whatever might be the result of the petition, in MacEvilly's view it would achieve some good by uniting the people and priests, and would make some priests more cautious in future.

On Monday, 27 May, at the end of a trial which had taken fifty days, Judge Keogh gave his verdict. Nolan was unseated and ordered to pay the costs. While the verdict itself may not have come as a surprise, the manner and content of the delivery were truly astonishing. In a speech lasting nine hours, Keogh launched a fierce tirade against the clergy and their part in the election, while eulogising the landlords and gentry. At times during his speech, Keogh walked back and forth, mimicking witnesses; at other times, he roared and screamed in rage, occasionally striking the desk with his clenched fist.

Of all the clergy concerned, MacEvilly came off lightest in Keogh's summary. According to the judge, the conduct of MacHale had been such that it made it impossible to speak of him with ordinary courtesy without 'polluting conscience,' while others of the clergy he called a 'rabble rout.' Conway was condemned for the 'clapper of his tongue, which must be infinitely more offensive to a rational creature than that dreadful lugubrious whistle which disturbed my rest for six weeks after I came into this town of Galway.' The landlords came in for special praise, as did Oliver Cromwell, who, in Keogh's opinion, was remarkable for 'majestic greatness of character, for splendid genius, for everything that ennobles a great man.' Finally, on the whole of the evidence, Keogh declared, there had never been 'a more astounding attempt at ecclesiastical tyranny' in the entire history of priestly interference in public affairs than was presented in this case, and he referred to those who voted for Nolan as 'mindless, brainless, coward instruments in the hands of ecclesiastical despots.'[22]

Although spared the edge of Keogh's tongue, MacEvilly was nevertheless named, along with MacHale, Duggan and several others, cleric and lay, in Keogh's report to the House of Commons for their 'organised attempt to defeat the free franchise.'[23] To MacEvilly, Keogh's speech was the 'most awful tirade' he had ever heard of against the clergy.[24]

The Keogh judgement provoked a storm of rage, protest and criticism throughout the country. 'It was,' said the *Freeman's Journal,* 'among the most extraordinary performances of the kind which has ever been placed before the public.' The paper announced the opening of the Galway vindication fund to help Nolan defray the expenses of the trial. Keogh was burned in effigy at Galway and a public meeting was held to denounce his insulting language. In the following weeks, there were meetings and statements of denunciation from Cullen and the Dublin clergy, MacHale and the clergy of Tuam, and from most of the dioceses of the country. The Galway clergy, with MacEvilly presiding, met on 12 June and several long resolutions were adopted expressing bitter indignation at the 'one-sidedness' of the judgement, the manner of its delivery and the language used by Keogh, and subscribing generously to the Galway vindication fund.

Keogh's report was duly presented to the House of Commons. He found that the archbishop of Tuam and the bishop of Galway were guilty of undue influence, but it was not proved that they actually sanctioned or took part in the denunciations of Trench. Keogh also submitted his findings to the court of Common Pleas; the government now had to decide what action should be taken against those complained of. MacHale and his suffragans then presented a petition to the House of Commons repudiating the charges and asking the House to initiate proceedings against them so that they should have the opportunity of clearing themselves. All this was played out to the background of meetings throughout the country. A great meeting in the Rotunda, Dublin, on 24 June resulted in a petition to Parliament calling for Keogh's dismissal.

Gladstone's government chose, however, to ignore all petitions and the storm of protest, and to prosecute criminally Duggan of Clonfert, twenty catholic priests, Nolan and his brother, and a number of laymen. These trials were held in February 1873, and Duggan and the clergymen, ably defended by Isaac Butt, were acquitted.

In the history of Irish election contests, the Galway by-election of 1872 is quite significant. It was a contest in which the landlords' candidate, Trench, was clearly pitted against the people's champion, Nolan, with the popular candidate winning an overwhelming victory. What is difficult to assess is just how significant to the outcome was the part played by the clergy. If the election is taken as a contest between the clergy and landlords, then the clergy won hands down. However, the clerical choice was the popular choice, and MacEvilly himself had stated categorically in court that Nolan would have won with or without the priests. There is no evidence that the clergy had directly influenced a single voter in his choice. Where clerical influence was effective was in the actual selection of candidates, as is borne out by the fact that candidates were careful to seek the support of the various bishops.

MacEvilly's conclusion was that the issue tried by Keogh had been essentially a religious one – the right of the clergy to use their influence for good on the people in the exercise of their civil rights.[25] 'Keogh's decision has shown the people that the clergy are interested in them,' he wrote to Rome. 'The Fenians had persuaded people to the contrary.'[26]

1874 ELECTION

One consequence of MacEvilly's having been named in Keogh's report to the House of Commons after the 1872 election petition trial was that he was banned from taking any active part in elections for seven years. It is interesting to watch

MacEvilly coping with this disability, and to observe his manoeuvres behind the scenes in the general election set for February 1874. In a long letter to Cullen some weeks before the election, he outlined the moves being made to ensure the selection of the candidate most favourable to catholic demands. For Galway Borough, MacEvilly was anxious to find a candidate to oppose George Morris, who had popular support. Lord St. Lawrence had not yet appeared, and there were fears that Blennerhassett or Francis Nolan, 'a very headless young barrister' and brother of Captain Nolan, might step in. When the time came, the clergy had no suitable candidate. 'I thought it better,' MacEvilly almost apologised, 'to advise the clergy – as they could not help it – to a course of abstention as regards George Morris.'[27]

The candidate that MacEvilly and the clergy would have liked to support for the borough was F. H. O'Donnell, a past pupil of Queen's College Galway and representative of the new type of candidate now emerging in Irish politics. O'Donnell had published an election address which included a letter from Cardinal Manning, endorsing him as a worthy candidate. MacEvilly, however, found it 'utterly impossible to carry him through this time' as the priests were not prepared, and O'Donnell's own relatives in Galway were not favourable to him. The bishop recognised that O'Donnell would be invaluable in parliament on the education question, about which MacEvilly himself was most concerned. He had hopes for O'Donnell on a future occasion as he felt that, should St. Lawrence be returned, he would be a member for only a short time, as his father was said to be 'in almost a dying state.'

MacEvilly then went on to treat of the position in Galway county. Trench had retired, and MacEvilly reported that 'a Mr Redington of Kilcornan, a most excellent young man' wanted to contest the county with Nolan, who, said MacEvilly, 'is universally disliked.' However, MacEvilly felt that the people would rally round Nolan anyway because of their hatred of Keogh. 'All I could do for him would be of a negative character.' MacEvilly stated, and, since MacHale would be for Nolan, it would not do to have 'bishop against bishop in public.'

MacEvilly followed this with another bulletin, in which he virtually apologised once more to Cullen for the candidature of George Morris. He explained that they were not prepared to risk defeat with a lesser candidate because 'if the priests were once beaten, their influence even in most important spiritual matters might suffer much.'

MacEvilly felt that Mitchell Henry was certain to be returned for the county. The bishop himself, however, was not too enthusiastic about Henry, complaining that the M.P. was helping out in Tuam and neglecting Galway. 'Some people here are not so much in love with him as they were,' MacEvilly commented. 'They think he has kept aloof from here to please Dr MacHale who would like to see

Galway borough affairs in confusion.' It is interesting to note in this remark the unspoken equation of election borough with diocese, with the consequent assumption that any confusion in election matters would reflect poorly on the bishop himself. Finally, MacEvilly concluded, 'the evener the balance between Whigs and Morris is kept, the better for Irish interests.'

O'Donnell did in fact stand for Galway borough but lost to George Morris and St. Lawrence. The death of the latter's father, as expected, meant the elevation of St. Lawrence to the peerage and, consequently, a vacancy in the borough.

Before the results of the county election were known, MacEvilly wrote to Cullen, declaring it a certainty that Mitchell Henry and Captain Nolan would be elected, which they were. MacEvilly commented: 'Keogh gave Nolan that place. No power on earth could influence them not to give Keogh and Co. a salutory lesson.'

Turning his attention to the coming election for the borough created by St. Lawrence's retiral, MacEvilly reported that O'Donnell was already canvassing and 'the priests have to almost a man joined in supporting him,' though 'wonderful efforts' were being made for his opponent by protestants, Queen's college people and 'aristocratic Catholics, who feel humbled that one from the ranks of the people should represent Galway.' The bishop concluded, '. . . although I am silenced by Keogh, I make no doubt O'Donnell will succeed, or rather the Catholic tenantry V the Queen's colleges, although I must regard it as a very dangerous game to send so young and penniless a man to parliament.'

In the election for Galway city which took place the following month, O'Donnell polled 579 votes against 358 for his opponent, Pierce Joyce, junior, of Mervue, Galway. 'Our triumph here was certainly a great triumph for the clergy and Catholic education,' MacEvilly announced, claiming that O'Donnell had been lost sight of in the whole affair. 'Every Protestant without exception was arrayed against us,' he continued. 'They and the Queen's college people gave Joyce a start of nearly 200 votes.' MacEvilly also stated: 'The gentry to a man is opposed to us. . . . Their idea is that the clergy should retire to the sacristy and say their prayers' – something which MacEvilly claimed the clergy would gladly do tomorrow if they could. 'But if they did,' he declared, 'it would be worse for the landlords, religion and society in this country.'

MacEvilly hoped that they would not be disappointed in O'Donnell for some of the clergy now had reservations about him. 'Had the conduct of himself and his backers, all healthy strong young men, been known, the clergy would have retired,' MacEvilly complained, as the Vicar General had found them on a Friday eating meat and fish at the hotel, 'and the servants and all connected with the hotel scandalised by them.' MacEvilly had told the clergy that they must let it pass, but the priests were indignant that men 'who were returned on high Catholic principles should act so unprincipled a part.' O'Donnell and his friends planned to have celebrations but were told by MacEvilly that if they were 'unnecessarily to interfere with the season of Lent,' he would denounce them. MacEvilly also had told O'Donnell that his 'great forte' was the education question, 'the only one the clergy here felt a deep interest in,' and that if he did not make that question 'his specialty,' it would be all over with him. All of this, the bishop was careful to point out, was meant for Cullen alone, as MacEvilly felt the cardinal should know 'the real state of things.' In general, the clergy thought it 'a very dangerous thing to give the people too much power,' MacEvilly stated. 'Those that cheer today may hoot tomorrow.'

As was now usual in Galway elections, there followed the inevitable petition, this time lodged by Joyce against O'Donnell's return. One of the stated grounds was that O'Donnell personally engaged as an agent the bishop of Galway, although O'Donnell knew that the bishop had, 'within seven years previous to such engagement,' been reported guilty of a corrupt practice. This charge, the Galway Vindicator said, was 'so ridiculously absurd' they wondered that any lawyer could have put forward such a statement. MacEvilly declared that he had kept 'perfectly aloof' and nothing had been spoken from the altar. 'Of course I never concealed my opinions or sympathies,' he went on, 'but surely, no law could prevent this.'

From a letter written some days later, it is clear that moves were made by Cullen to dissuade the Joyces from bringing the petition. MacEvilly thanked Cullen for his efforts, saying that Pierce Joyce, senior, was the man mainly responsible. Further, he claimed, young Joyce was the 'tool of artful men,' and the common opinion in Galway was that neither his father nor those 'with whom he has leagued' would let him see what their purpose was. '... There is no doubt but the Queen's college party and the Galway gentry, whose power is now ruined, are urging on Mr Joyce senior and acting on his vanity, in order to get some grounds under the present administration for passing a law altogether excluding priests from any share in elections.'[28]

Declaring that it was the catholic clergy who were really on trial,[29] the *Galway Vindicator* opened a defence fund for O'Donnell, starting with a subscription of £20 from MacEvilly.[30] Mitchell Henry contributed 100 guineas and professed shock and disgust at the 'insulting language' applied to his 'excellent and revered friend, the bishop of Galway.'[31]

MacEvilly wrote Cullen that O'Donnell had engaged Gerald Fitzgerald, a 'formidable counsel.' Speaking of Judge Lawson, MacEvilly said that, considering the judge's 'well known tendencies,' he felt sure O'Donnell would lose. MacEvilly was confident that the priests had never been so cautious and nothing discreditable could be proved against them. 'All that can be proved at best,' he declared, 'is that on asserting a principle – the principle of Catholic education – they might have acted over zealously.'

Every secular priest in the borough of Galway had been summoned, MacEvilly reported, but so far he himself had not been subpoenaed. However, he was told that O'Donnell's defence meant to do so. He was sure that Lawson would take no heed of what he had to say. 'This trial,' he wrote, 'is but a sequel of the Keogh affair in the county, and has for object, now that the influence of the priests with the people has been shown in returning O'Donnell, to destroy clerical influence in the borough.'

The petition trial opened in Galway on 18 May. The prosecuting counsel was again Serjeant Armstrong. The main thrust of his opening speech was that O'Donnell's cause had been adopted by MacEvilly, and the bulk of the clergy were under MacEvilly's control and bound to obey his commands. One of the witnesses, Major John Wilson Lynch, stated in evidence that he had asked Fr Dooley why the bishop and clergy were now supporting O'Donnell when they had supported Morris against him at the previous election. The explanation he received was that the bishop had heard he had incurred Cullen's displeasure for supporting Morris instead of O'Donnell at the general election, and that the bishop was now determined to support O'Donnell and return him to parliament.[32] MacEvilly was furious at this mention of Cullen.[33] Perhaps the most damaging evidence against MacEvilly was given by James Comyns, parish priest of Castlegar, who was determined to remain neutral in the contest as the Joyces lived in his parish. He stated in evidence that when he informed MacEvilly of his intention not to take any active part, the bishop became angry and spoke to him about neglecting the schools and about people not attending mass, although making no mention of the election.[34]

MacEvilly himself gave evidence on the fourth day of the trial. He stated that he had no communication from Cullen expressing displeasure at their failure to support O'Donnell in the late election and that he had nothing to do with O'Donnell's adoption by the clergy. He assured Cullen that he had refuted Wilson Lynch's evidence, and that nobody could have known of any communication from the cardinal, since he burned the letters 'on the spot.' The clergy had 'gone twice as far' in the 1868 election in support of St. Lawrence, MacEvilly wrote, but the people who had supported them then were now decrying them, as the real issue at this election had been the fight between Queen's College and the Catholic University. If there were another judge, MacEvilly had no doubt but that O'Donnell would not be unseated, and he concluded with the hope that he would never pass 'through such an ordeal again.'

MacEvilly was perfectly correct in his forecast of the outcome. Despite the absence of any hard evidence, Judge Lawson upheld the petition, declaring O'Donnell unseated and condemned to pay the costs. In his summary, the judge simply stated that he agreed with Armstrong that the bishop was at the bottom of the whole movement, that MacEvilly had secretly approved of all that was done, and that if the bishop had the slightest wish that the canvass by the clergy should not take place, then it would never have taken place. Also the judge said that the bishop knew perfectly well that when the vicar general and clergy canvassed, the public would understand that the proceedings had the sanction of the bishop.[35] Thus was MacEvilly condemned for things as they seemed to be, not as they had been proved in court. In his speech, Lawson implied that there were divisions between the secular and regular clergy of Galway in the matter of the election. This charge was stoutly denied by the heads of the various religious orders in Galway in a letter published in the *Freeman's Journal* the following month.[36] Lawson also reported the vicar general, Fr Dooley, and Rev. Martin Cummins to the House of Commons.[37]

The unseating of O'Donnell meant another election. This time the choice of the clergy was Dr Ward, who had been O'Donnell's election agent. MacEvilly reported to Cullen that the election had gone off quietly and that Ward would have an overwhelming majority, that Lawson would return him as 'Keogh returned Nolan.' Ward did win easily and the *Galway Vindicator* reported that the clergy took no active part, although it was well understood that they were most desirous of Ward's return.

So ended another turbulent Galway election, in which MacEvilly, although barred from active participation, still managed to control matters behind the scenes. It has been claimed that the 'new men' – candidates like O'Donnell – achieved a large degree of independence from bishop and clergy, and that this was a foretaste of things to come. The Galway contest of 1874 does not lend much support to this argument. Anyone reading MacEvilly's correspondence at the time cannot fail to notice his confidence that he and the clergy are in control of affairs. Also, MacEvilly does not hesitate to dictate terms to O'Donnell, telling the newly elected candidate that if he does not attend to the education issue in parliament, then 'it would be all over with him.'

This election too points up MacEvilly's ambivalent attitude to Butt and his home rule party. Certainly, MacEvilly was no supporter of home rule and he disliked Butt as a leader. While he privately opposed the holding of chapel collections for the party in his diocese, nevertheless, as on other occasions, MacEvilly was careful not to appear in opposition, particularly as he felt that any chance now of an education bill lay with Butt and his party.

After this election, MacEvilly confined his attentions to the education question and did not intervene in the politics of the day until a new force had arisen in the land, and stronger and more outspoken men seemed to threaten clerical influence with the people. Until the end of the decade and the stormy days of the land war, the bishop of Galway held his peace.

FENIANISM

In a reply to Cullen dated 11 April 1862, MacEvilly wrote assuring the archbishop of Dublin that he would be present at the coming bishops' meeting. Besides the other 'grave topics' which Cullen had mentioned, MacEvilly thought that the bishops should discuss 'the tendency of those brotherhoods, the chief object of which would seem to be to alienate the people from the clergy, to coerce the clergy themselves and diffuse unsound principles both relating to faith and policy under the sanction of *Quixotic* ecclesiastics.' This statement sums up MacEvilly's attitude to the IRB and its public front, the Brotherhood of St. Patrick. In general, he followed the Cullen line on Fenianism, seeing in the movement a threat to established order and arguing the futility of armed rebellion. MacEvilly's greatest fear of the movement, however, was that expressed here – that the Fenians might diminish the influence of the priests with the people. But, while firmly opposed to the secret oath-bound society and its policy, MacEvilly's condemnations were never as wide-ranging as Cullen's or as drastic as the famous Moriarty dictum consigning all Fenians to the infernal regions.

The 'Quixotic ecclesiastics' referred to by MacEvilly in the above quotation were his adversary, MacHale of Tuam, and those of his priests who sympathised with the nationalist movement. The particular problems created for Cullen by Patrick Lavelle's support for the Fenians and MacHale's refusal to discipline this Partry priest are dealt with further on.

In a pastoral published in October 1865, Cullen denounced Fenianism strongly, coupling it with 'Orangeism,' which, the archbishop argued, was the 'real parent of Fenianism.' Cullen returned to the theme of legitimate constitutional methods to seek reforms, condemning the use of armed force. MacEvilly, commenting on the pastoral, thought that 'the unhappy Fenians could read in it a father pleading for foolish and wicked children' – a most unlikely event. 'The enemies of our creed and country have felt the tables turned on them fearfully in the case of Garibaldi,' MacEvilly wrote. 'Indeed the whole pastoral was a complete table turning on such as did not duly appreciate your Grace's love of country.'

In this same letter, MacEvilly spoke of rumours that there were 'large numbers of unhappy Fenians' in the town of Galway. He observed that the priests could find no evidence of it, and he referred to the fact that no arrests had taken place. 'I suppose if they be here,' he concluded, 'they must sooner or later be discovered.' These remarks of MacEvilly testify to the accuracy of authors who have observed that the province of Connacht was the least well organised before the 1867 rising.

Writing to congratulate Cullen on his elevation to the cardinalate in July 1866, MacEvilly declared, 'I believe the Fenian movement is for ever dead. The monster fraud and swindle perpetrated by them on our poor deluded people is now patent to the entire world.' He noted that the *Connaught Patriot*, a Fenian publication, no longer contained offensive attacks on Cullen, and that it had nothing to say about his elevation to the cardinalate. 'The silence of the *Patriot* is in itself great praise,' MacEvilly observed drily.

Later that same year, Cullen wrote MacEvilly a letter in which the cardinal drew once more his favourite comparison, likening the Irish to the Italian situation. 'We have great noise here about the Fenians,' Cullen wrote, 'but I dare say the Orangemen are exaggerating things in the hope of getting martial law proclaimed. However that may be, it is certain that the Fenians are playing into the hands of our enemies – just as Napoleon is doing with Victor Emmanuel.'

In his reply, MacEvilly agreed with the thesis of government provocation. He felt that the government 'in league with the Orangemen' would 'shoot down the unhappy people' and that they would 'force on a crisis, as far as they can, just as it is well known they forced on for their own purposes in 1798.' At the same time, MacEvilly did not think that there was any 'general disposition' to join the Fenians. While there was a 'good deal of widespread discontent,' he was sure that the 'great mass' of the people were well aware that, even in the case of a Fenian success, 'which it is absurd to imagine,' the people would only be exchanging 'a bad for a worse state of things.' Of course, he went on, 'in all towns will be found at all times desperate characters prepared for any amount of outrages. Any one who would witness the state of our borough towns during the time of an election, can hardly doubt that an Irish mob is just like any other mob.' In conclusion, MacEvilly predicted: 'The whole affair will of course blow over, but owing to the panic it has created – I must say, a panic far greater than there are grounds for – it will have done mischief in the meantime.'

In February 1867, a police report to Dublin Castle stated that 350 Fenians had come to Galway and the surrounding area and that one thousand more would follow immediately 'and dispense themselves all over Ireland.' The report ended: 'All were of opinion that an outbreak was inevitable and not far off.' When the much-postponed Fenian rising did finally occur in March, the slender chances of success were rendered impossible through a combination of mismanagement, government informers and sheer ill-luck. Once again, MacEvilly recorded the death of Fenianism. 'The Fenian bubble has burst,' he told Kirby, and added that conditions and the harvest were so poor that the people were too broken to have any political views. Official reports of that same month from Galway state that there was 'no indication of any disposition to rise on the part of the Galway people.'

One outcome of the risings which did arouse widespread sympathy was the execution in November of the three men who came to be known as the Manchester martyrs. Many felt that the men had been convicted on scanty evidence indeed, and that their execution was a vindictive act on the part of the government. In many places throughout Ireland, special commemorative masses were offered. In Galway, a special mass was said in the Augustinian church without any prior notice to MacEvilly and much to his annoyance. He complained to Cullen that it had put him 'in a very false position with a very large mass of the deluded sympathisers with these people.'

The Franciscans too had prayed publicly in Galway for the Manchester martyrs and MacEvilly thought it 'really a bad state of things' that those who should be the '*cooperatores episcoporum*' should be 'striving to pander to popular prejudices and thus continuing to bring odium on the pastors of the people.' The offended bishop, putting religion 'altogether out of the question,' continued, 'this public display in favour of the poor Manchester men is the most foolish thing imaginable. It is hard to control a mob once excited, and those who pander to them, unless they join them in all their excesses, will themselves fare badly in the latter end.' The conduct of the friars, MacEvilly stated, had caused 'some characters who never go to the sacraments' to denounce him and the parochial clergy. He also reported a rumour that in one or two places in Tuam diocese the people had threatened to withdraw the supplies from the priests unless 'they had these Manchester masses.' Later, when it was safer to do so, MacEvilly did act in the case of the Augustinians, withdrawing faculties from the young priest who had said the mass. He also stated that before renewing the faculties of the chief promoter of the affair, he would insist on that man attending to the study of moral theology.

A mass for the martyrs was also celebrated at Ennistymon. On reading about this, MacEvilly wrote to the parish priest, Fr Sheehan, asking if it were done with the parish priest's 'sanction or authority.' Sheehan replied that it was not a requiem mass and that he himself had not attended. 'All the people here, young men and girls too, are red hot Fenians,' the parish priest hastened to explain. 'Without some such demonstration, they would give us a great deal of annoyance, and for peace sake we thought it better let them have their way.' The parish priest intimated that there was a hint that the supplies might be withdrawn. 'I might say there was moral compulsion,' he stated, ending with the promise that nothing of the kind would ever occur again without first consulting the bishop. Referring to Sheehan as 'an exceedingly odd character,' MacEvilly expressed his confidence that the aging parish priest would obey him. 'He has not a particle of Fr Peter in him' was the episcopal comment.[38] When relating Sheehan's case to Cullen, MacEvilly added these general observations: 'There is no doubt but the deepest dissatisfaction does exist, and that universally. If the government were only to redress the crying wrongs of the people, they would give a death blow to Fenianism in one month. The people themselves would banish them out of the country.'[39]

Fenianism proved to be more of a problem for MacEvilly in the dioceses of

Kilmacduagh and Kilfenora than had been the case in Galway. He had been appointed apostolic administrator of the Clare dioceses in 1866 and it was here that he first encountered the Fenian tactic of withholding supplies from the priests. The tactic, which MacEvilly had already adverted to as being used in Tuam, does seem to have had a measure of success, as in Ennistymon. Writing from Lisdoonvarna in the Kilfenora diocese in April 1869, MacEvilly stated that 'the place was alive with Fenianism.' He had removed the priest who was 'at the head of it,' a Fr Kemmy, administrator of Kilfenora, transferring him to 'the extreme point of Kilmacduagh near Loughrea.'[40]

As popular sympathy for the Fenian prisoners ran high during the late 1860s, the Amnesty movement grew in numbers.[41] It won the qualified support of Paul Cullen, who was prepared to seek amnesty as a humanitarian act. Cullen, however, was not prepared to support the national collection which the movement proposed to hold after Gladstone had granted amnesty to 49 of the Fenian prisoners in February 1869. The cardinal saw it as implicit approval of the politics of the prisoners and also feared it might prove embarrassing to a government seeking to introduce an ameliorative programme for Ireland.[42] Cullen therefore sent a letter to his clergy refusing permission for Amnesty collections.[43] MacEvilly concurred totally in all that Cullen had done and expressed.[44] Despite such episcopal opposition, the Amnesty Association persisted with the collection, and it was well supported.[45]

How wrong MacEvilly had been about the death of Fenianism he came to realise for, two years later, he told Kirby that Fenianism had taken deep root. 'The leaders are knaves,' he asserted, 'but many of their dupes are in good faith, influenced by hatred of England. They will however inevitably be led astray,' he predicted.[46]

Despite MacEvilly's hatred of Fenianism, he was circumspect in his public pronouncements. He was always aware of the damage that a Moriarty-like proclamation could effect in the relations between clergy and people. Thus, for the most part, MacEvilly carried his dislike of Fenianism privately. At a later time, this dislike was one of the chief motives for MacEvilly's opposition to the Land League; he was deeply suspicious of the League's Fenian connections. But the Land League was founded on a broader base of popular support and touched more surely the needs of the people. If MacEvilly had difficulty in maintaining the balance in regard to Fenianism between his public statements and his private views, the Land League was to force him to walk an even tighter rope.

Chapter Three

MacEvilly and MacHale

THE NAME OF John MacHale occurs again and again in the correspondence of John MacEvilly and almost always the famous archbishop, who was an idol of the people in his own time, is referred to in the most unflattering terms. There are occasions when MacEvilly's preoccupation with the neighbouring prelate borders on obsession, and the story of the relationship between the two men is one of unending hostility and rancour. It is not easy to say when this antipathy first arose, but that it did not exist from the beginning is clear. As a young priest under MacHale's jurisdiction, MacEvilly was a trusted lieutenant and a rising star in the diocese of Tuam. He was appointed a professor in St. Jarlath's College, the diocesan seminary, and he took an active and sometimes prominent part in religious and political affairs in Tuam. Significantly, he was *peritus*, or consulting theologian, to his archbishop at the Synod of Thurles in 1850,[1] and two years later he was appointed to the presidency of St. Jarlath's. At the great Tenant Banquet in 1854, MacEvilly sat with his archbishop at the guest table and was a principal speaker.[2] Nothing therefore in all of this suggests anything but the most cordial of relationships.

What was it then that killed this trust between the two men and led to a rift that grew worse until, at the end, MacHale would no longer allow MacEvilly into his presence? More than anything else the answer lies with Paul Cullen, appointed archbishop of Armagh in 1850 and Dublin in 1852. Just as the rivalry between Cullen and MacHale grew, so did the friendship between MacEvilly and Cullen; and it is fair to suppose that this above all else made MacEvilly the enemy of MacHale.

When did the Cullen-MacEvilly friendship begin? Again it is not possible to say precisely. There is evidence that certainly by the time MacEvilly became bishop of Galway in 1857, he was already known to and trusted by Cullen.

MacHale's biographer, Monsignor O'Reilly, identifies MacEvilly as the priest who informed Cullen of attempts made in Tuam to obtain signatures for a memorial drawn up against the archbishop in 1855.[3] Also, Cullen had supported MacEvilly for the vacant see of Galway in preference to Thomas MacHale, the archbishop's nephew and the choice of the Connacht bishops.[4] No sooner had McEvilly settled in Galway as bishop than he was writing in the most confidential manner to the archbishop of Dublin. From then until his death in 1878, Cullen was to McEvilly friend, confidant and adviser on all problems ranging from diocesan administration to national issues.

So too MacEvilly was useful to Cullen as informant on all matters relating to MacHale's activities in Tuam. Cullen wrote that he had no influence in Galway except with Dr MacEvilly.[5] Indeed it is doubtful if MacHale despised Cullen as much as he did MacEvilly, whom he must surely have seen as a spy in the camp. McEvilly in turn saw the hand of MacHale in all his troubles, and in most cases he was correct. 'Since I came to Galway,' MacEvilly once wrote of MacHale, 'he has left nothing undone to annoy and thwart me.'[6] The MacHale factor was present, for instance, in the first major internal dispute that MacEvilly faced, that with Galway priest, Fr Peter Daly, which is recounted in a later section.[7]

Indeed, there seemed to be no issues on which these two men could agree. Even in matters theological they differed and they were found on opposite sides at the First Vatican Council in 1870. More than anything else this Council would be remembered for its definition of the doctrine of Papal Infallibility. Paul Cullen of Dublin was pressing strongly for the definition and was recognised as a leader of the group known as the 'Opportunists.' He also had a hand in preparing the formula of definition which was finally accepted.[8] Needless to say, Cullen had the full support of MacEvilly, who addressed the Council for an hour and a quarter in favour of definition. MacHale of Tuam, together with Moriarty of Kerry, remained opposed to the end. However, at the Synod of Maynooth in 1875, MacHale did sign the joint pastoral enforcing the definition of infallibility as an article of faith.[9]

The other major points of disagreement between the two prelates were: Their differing views on Fenianism and the case of Fr Lavelle; the appointment of MacEvilly as apostolic administrator of Kilfenora and Kilmacduagh in Clare; and their last and greatest disagreement, the appointment of MacEvilly as coadjutor with right of succession in Tuam.

THE CASE OF FATHER LAVELLE

Patrick Lavelle was a priest of the Tuam diocese. As a professor at the Irish College in Paris, he had been involved in disputes with the rector and with Cullen. He was later appointed parish priest of Partry in County Mayo, where he was active in fighting against proselytism and rack-renting by the landlords of the area. A prolific writer of letters to the press, he was also a vice-president of the Brotherhood of St. Patrick, public front for the IRB, and was soon at the centre of a row between his archbishop, MacHale, and Cullen.[10]

Paul Cullen, as previously noted, set himself firmly against Fenianism. It was, therefore, a great affront, as he saw it, when Lavelle delivered an oration at the funeral of Terence Bellew MacManus in November 1861, especially as Cullen had forbidden any priest of his own diocese to attend.[11] So began a long saga as Cullen attempted to bring pressure on MacHale to discipline his Fenian priest and MacHale dallied and delayed, frustrating Cullen's efforts.

Early in 1862, Lavelle had lectured in Dublin on 'The Catholic Doctrine of the Right of Revolution.' In May, at a general meeting of the hierarchy, the bishops condemned secret societies as a whole. They also demanded that Lavelle resign from the Brotherhood of St. Patrick and apologise publicly.[12] Lavelle did write to Cullen, but his letter was a defence of his actions rather than an apology for them. On a visit to Rome, Cullen brought the matter to Pope Pius IX and the result was a mandate to MacHale ordering that Lavelle meet the demands of the bishops' meeting.[13]

Nevertheless, Lavelle continued to attend the Brotherhood and publicly to urge revolution.[14] MacEvilly wanted more rigorous action.[15]

Rome moved again and, in September 1863, MacHale was ordered by Propaganda to suspend Lavelle and have him retire to a monastery until he had proved himself repentant.[16] MacEvilly predicted that MacHale would comply 'in a stinted way ... promising obedience in words, as he always does and disobeying in acts, as he always does.' MacEvilly's predictions proved correct and, in December, he further reported that 'Fr Lavelle's last are worse than any of his former productions.'[17] These productions were articles believed to be written by Lavelle for *The Connaught Patriot*, a paper MacEvilly described as a 'malicious Garibaldian rag, which is sometimes heretical, sometimes schismatical and at all times personally offensive to the Head of the Church.' The paper, MacEvilly claimed, was 'the avowed organ of Dr M.'[18] In that same month, MacHale was again ordered by Rome to carry out the instructions previously given.[19]

By this time, a memorial in favour of Lavelle was being organised by MacHale for presentation to the Pope. MacEvilly described the document as 'a series of assertions put forward in a sensational style, every one of which is either a *suppressio veri* or an *expressio falsi.*'[20]

Lavelle himself had gone to Rome in January 1864 to plead his case.[21] MacEvilly feared that he might be let off lightly, which would only encourage 'every outrageous rebel to act as he pleases' and 'the last error will be worse than the first.'[22] Again MacEvilly was proved accurate. He reported that Lavelle had returned in triumph. Not only were Lavelle's articles appearing again in the *Connaught Patriot*,[23] but, in a manifesto on 5 March, he attacked Cullen's views

42

and once more defended his own position.[24] MacEvilly asked sarcastically who had deputed Lavelle to be the spokesman of the Irish people and he went on to allege that 'like many other pure patriots, he is not a loser by all this agitation nor do the unhappy people of Partry seem to be exclusively the gainers in the transaction.'[25] MacEvilly also declared that Lavelle was a 'mere tool' in the hands of others.[26]

On 29 April, MacEvilly, quoting a letter from Moran in Rome, informed Cullen that the Pope had ordered Lavelle's suspension to be renewed and MacHale to put this into effect.[27] In August, a meeting was held at the Mechanics' Institute in Dublin to protest Lavelle's suspension. A resolution was passed approving of the resistance offered by Lavelle to foreign tyranny.[28] There was also talk of withholding dues from the Dublin clergy, a course of action Lavelle publicly disapproved of, however.[29]

'Father Lavelle is suspended at last,' MacEvilly announced in a letter of 23 September, and the memorial in his favour was being abandoned 'for the present.'[30] Nevertheless, not long afterwards, MacEvilly maintained that Lavelle was still saying mass and administering sacraments, while claiming that the suspension had been brought about by false representations – 'the theology of the *Patriot*', said MacEvilly.[31]

In November, MacEvilly reported that the memorial was being revived again and that the majority were signing it 'from fear.' He remarked wearily, 'How hard it is for the Holy See not to be imposed upon by deceitful artifices.'[32] The memorial was forwarded to Rome at the end of 1864, signed by all except seven of the priests of the diocese. The document charged that Cullen was a dictator; that he had deceived Rome in this case; and that he had interfered more than once in the affairs of the diocese of Tuam. 'Of course, this memorial will open their eyes more and more at Rome,' MacEvilly observed hopefully.[33]

MacHale continued to resist the Cullen-inspired pressure from Rome and to stand by Lavelle. In fact, the archbishop appointed Lavelle parish priest of Partry in 1866.[34]

By January 1868, Lavelle was still active, and an article of his in the Irish *American* was, said MacEvilly, his 'most seditious document,' and again the blame was laid at MacHale's door. 'Of this, I have not the slightest doubt in my own mind.'[35] MacEvilly's attribution of such a motive to MacHale illustrates the low esteem in which he now held the archbishop.

The Lavelle battle ended inconclusively, though whatever victory there was went to MacHale, who, partly by evasion but mostly by sheer stubbornness, had kept Rome at bay and Lavelle in the ministry. MacHale's strong stand was due in part to his nationalist sympathies but there were other factors. One was the exception he took to what he considered to be unnecessary Roman interference in the internal affairs of his diocese, but probably the major factor was his dislike and resentment of Cullen and MacEvilly and his determination to resist them.

Patrick Lavelle was to reappear in MacEvilly's life when he took a very active part in Nolan's campaign in the election of 1872, as noted previously, and was the subject of a severe attack by Judge Keogh in his summing up at the conclusion of the petition trial.[36]

Lavelle's last public campaign was in the Mayo election of 1874, when he had a severe disagreement with MacHale on the question of support for the ex-Fenian, O'Connor Power.[37] On this turn of events, MacEvilly commented: 'These men are now falling out and justice will have its own.'[38]

It does seem that Lavelle's personal troubles multiplied in his later years. He was involved in a distasteful law suit,[39] his health was not good, and in particular he was beset by financial problems. In 1879, MacEvilly forwarded to Kirby a letter he had received from a parishioner complaining of Lavelle's 'falling sickness.' 'It is all the effect of drunkenness' was MacEvilly's diagnosis.[40] MacEvilly's last reference to Lavelle was in a letter to Kirby in 1882, when Lavelle was parish priest in Cong and MacEvilly archbishop of Tuam. 'Lavelle is an outrageous, defiant man.' said MacEvilly. 'He will not pay debts or observe the statutes.' All of this MacEvilly attributed to the fact that Lavelle had 'got too much liberty in the past.'[41] They remained enemies to the end, and no mention is made of the archbishop at Lavelle's funeral in November 1886.[42]

KILMACDUAGH AND KILFENORA

In 1863, John MacEvilly was commissioned by Propaganda to enquire into the state of the dioceses of Kilmacduagh and Kilfenora. The incumbent bishop, Dr Fallon, had a serious drink problem and the resulting maladministration was causing concern. MacEvilly made a visit to Lisdoonvarna the pretext for his investigation. He reported that he visited the bishop late in the day and found no evidence of drink. In fact, he found that Dr Fallon had recently been very active in administering confirmation in several parishes. MacEvilly was also shown a letter from MacHale, recommending Fallon to make himself more active in the diocese. The dramatic improvement in the health and performance of the bishop, MacEvilly was inclined to attribute to MacHale's letter, especially as this coincided with his own visit.[43]

Even before MacEvilly's appointment as bishop of Galway in 1857, the union of Galway with one or both of the other dioceses had been mooted. At the time, the proposed union was opposed by MacHale and Derry. As MacEvilly saw it, the real reason for MacHale's opposition was that such a union would lessen the number of MacHale's suffragan bishops. Now an added reason would be his opposition to MacEvilly personally.[44]

MacEvilly was, of course, most anxious that at least one of the two dioceses should be annexed to Galway. In his *relatio status* sent to Propaganda in 1862, he had put the case for the union.[45] Galway he considered a difficult diocese to administer because of its narrow territory. It would not be possible, for instance, to change ''an erring priest'' to an area where he would not be already known. Also the bishop of Galway had to contribute to many charitable institutions, yet his income was insufficient. Furthermore, reasoned MacEvilly, it would not promote the cause of religion that a place where the government had established institutions adverse to catholic interests should be ecclesiastically weakest in offering resistance. 'It is also impossible,' he argued, 'to establish a diocesan public opinion having influence for good among 17 or 18 priests. They must necessarily be guided by the influence of the very large diocese by whom they are surrounded,' and obviously MacEvilly did not think too highly of the influence of that very large diocese – Tuam. MacEvilly's proposed remedy was the union of Galway and Kilmacduagh, whenever either should become vacant, and the annexation to Galway of seven parishes belonging to the Abbacy of Cong, which he claimed were never canonically transferred to Tuam.[46]

Late in 1864, MacEvilly was worried by the rumour that a coadjutor was about to be appointed to Dr Fallon. This he attributed to MacHale's influence.[47] MacEvilly proposed a way out to the Holy See, namely, that the union need not take place just then but that the dioceses in question could be administered jointly.[48] Whether or not his suggestion was accepted, this was in fact what the Holy See decided upon, and in August 1866, Kirby informed MacEvilly he was appointed apostolic administrator of the dioceses of Kilmacduagh and Kilfenora. 'There were many difficulties which stood in the way of this settlement,' Kirby wrote, 'but the clear exposition made by Cardinal Cullen and the influence of that opinion with the Sacred College have thru' the divine mercy overcome every obstacle.' It would be as well to keep the matter quiet, Kirby cautioned, until the briefs of appointment had been received from Rome.[49]

The chances of keeping such a decision quiet were remote indeed, but MacHale was now left in the impossible position of fighting a decision which had already been taken. Nevertheless, he did fight it. That very same month, MacEvilly received a copy of a document forwarded to MacHale from the clergy of Kilmacduagh. They protested the annexation of their diocese and appealed to MacHale for aid. MacEvilly's informant, Mortimer Brennan, a curate at Ennistymon, told how three representatives of the clergy of Kilmacduagh attended a meeting of Kilfenora clergy, and that all present had signed the protest. Brennan himself, who had signed by proxy, put it down to 'disappointed ambition' and hoped his lordship would attribute his communication to the best motive.[50]

MacEvilly's instinctive reaction was to send copies to Cullen. He hoped Rome would take no notice of such a protest and stated that he was well aware that Dr MacHale and another – Derry, no doubt – were at the bottom of it. 'Nowadays,' said MacEvilly, 'it is usual for men to expect that if a lie gets a day's start, it will have done its work before the truth can overtake it.'[51] Cullen, as he was intended to do, conveyed the information to Rome.[52] He also reassured MacEvilly that the briefs were on the way and that their arrival would put an end to all speculation.[53] Similar reassurance came from Kirby in Rome.[54]

The letters of appointment duly arrived, much to MacEvilly's relief. MacEvilly disclosed his intention of calling together as quickly as possible the clergy of Kilmacduagh and Kilfenora and having the apostolic letters read to them.[55] In reply, Cullen advised him to take possession at once as delay might encourage those who were engaged in such matters.[56]

Dr Fallon retired to Mount Argus where he spent the remainder of his days.[57] Thus ended another unpleasant chapter in the MacEvilly-MacHale story, adding still further to the hostility and bitterness already existing between the two men.

The question of Kilmacduagh and Kilfenora arose again with the translation of MacEvilly to Tuam in 1881 when, at the following Connacht bishops meeting, other proposals were made for the dioceses. The final decision came with the bull of Leo XIII of June 1883, in which the union of the three dioceses, Galway, Kilmacduagh and Kilfenora, was made permanent.[58]

THE SUCCESSION ROW

John MacEvilly had taken such a keen interest in the affairs of Tuam diocese over a long period of years that it is fair to suppose that he saw himself as a likely successor to MacHale and a future archbishop of Tuam. John MacHale was equally aware of that possibility. It was this ambition on MacEvilly's part, and the attempt by MacHale to frustrate it, that caused the last and most bitter row between the two prelates, a row which centred on the question of a coadjutor for Tuam.

The question first arose in 1875 when MacHale, then in his eighty-fifth year,[59] wrote to Propaganda requesting a coadjutor. His request, however, was very specific for he asked that his nephew, Dr Thomas MacHale of the Irish College, Paris, be appointed (as he had when the See of Galway became vacant in 1857).[60] At the same time, MacHale contacted Cullen in an attempt to win him over to his side, asking for Cullen's 'valuable support.'[61] This first application of MacHale to Propaganda was refused on the grounds that the archbishop was still in vigorous health,[62] whereupon MacHale applied for a second time.[63]

Meanwhile, MacEvilly was airing his views on the matter to Cullen. That MacHale should get a coadjutor of his own choice 'would be perpetuating the seeds of discord,' was MacEvilly's verdict, 'which would bring forth evil fruit when we were all dead and gone.' A bishop was needed in Tuam who would carry out the 'unerring principles of the Holy See.' He pointed out that Dr MacCormack of Achonry and he himself had already written to Kirby about matters in Tuam, so that Propaganda knew the situation. 'It is hard to speak anything unpleasant of an old man,' he wrote attributing to himself nothing but the purest of motives, such as the good of religion and the salvation of souls. 'It is your Eminence's kind condescension at all times, which all the bishops appreciate, that emboldens me to speak.'[64] One would be forgiven for thinking that there was at least one other reason.

MacHale, in answer to his repeated request, was ordered through Cardinal Franchi, Prefect of the Propaganda, to hold an election in the usual way and submit three names to the Holy See.[65] By May 1876 this had not happened and MacEvilly maintained that the priests of Tuam, apart from a few, knew nothing of the instructions of Propaganda.[66] Cardinal Franchi wrote to MacHale in July that the wishes of the Holy See must be carried out and an election held as soon as possible.[67]

Thursday, 17 August, was the day appointed for the election. In his letter of convocation, MacHale informed the clergy that Thomas MacHale's name was being withdrawn at his own request on the grounds that he had not been accepted by the Holy See.[68] In the light of later events, this was an obvious ploy to save Thomas MacHale the indignity of being defeated on a vote, and then, if he did receive a number of votes, it could be claimed that he had been given them although not officially a candidate.

Perhaps even more important to the aged archbishop than the election of his nephew was the exclusion of his rival, MacEvilly. This the archbishop now attempted to achieve in the most blatant fashion. On the eve of the election, he addressed the assembled clergy, with the text of his address simultaneously published in the *Freeman's Journal*. He began, ironically enough, by remarking that in no way had he sought to influence the choice of the priests. Other bishops, he maintained, had not been so scrupulous. He went on to talk about MacEvilly without mentioning him by name. As a rule the pope did not appoint a coadjutor to an aged or infirm prelate without his goodwill and consent, because the church wished that peace and charity should reign among its members. This rule was even more pressing if the one to be appointed was already accustomed to exercising unrestrained rule over his own flock, and was even more dangerous in the case that 'the alienated feelings of the coadjutor became a matter of public notoriety.' These feelings could arise from 'different practical views of such important questions' as regards religion, the church and the welfare of the country. MacHale set forth other general reasons, then said if there were those who still wished to vote for a particular prelate, they were free to do so. They should know, however, that there were also special reasons for excluding such prelates which he would not fail to place before the sovereign Pontiff and the Sacred Congregation of the Propaganda, being convinced that 'a union shall not be celebrated disastrous to peace and charity and injurious to the best interests of religion in this diocese.' There were, he continued, priests of 'a high order of merit' from which they should make their selection while there was yet time, and he promised his ready approval to such a choice. Finally, in a not so veiled threat, he supposed that the pope 'who so ardently desires peace and concord among his children' would accept such a recommendation.[69]

It was an extraordinary performance, and, as in many of the archbishop's acts of this time, it is difficult to say how much he was influenced by his nephew, who, it was felt by many, was now the effective ruler of the diocese.[70] What is certain is that MacHale's action was proof enough for the Holy See that there would be neither peace nor harmony if MacEvilly was appointed. Cullen immediately sent a dispatch to Kirby commenting, 'This will create divisions and do harm,' and requested him to show it to Propaganda.[71]

MacHale's address did not succeed in its immediate aim and MacEvilly duly led the field in the election with 16 votes, four more than Thomas MacHale.[72] Reporting the result to Kirby, Cullen expressed the hope that MacEvilly would be appointed. 'He is a safe man and devoted to the Holy See.'[73] Cullen followed this three days later with another letter, suggesting that Propaganda should act promptly. 'Dr MacEvilly would be the best man,' he stated. 'He is a native of the diocese, knows everything and has the confidence of the majority of the clergy.'[74] Eminent recommendations indeed.

Once again, MacHale prepared to fight against the odds. He wrote Cullen, more in despair than confidence, that he was preparing to go to Rome to petition the Pope to grant him Thomas MacHale as coadjutor. The only other one, he said, who had received a considerable number of votes was the bishop of Galway, 'whom for well known reasons' he could never consent to accept. Yet again, he asked Cullen to support the appointment of Thomas MacHale, thus sparing him a long and tiring journey.[75] Three days later, he was writing again. He asked if perhaps Cullen had some objections to Thomas MacHale, in which case he would be glad to hear them.[76] This, of course, was MacHale's recognition of Cullen the bishop-maker.

Cullen replied that, since the matter was already in the hands of Propaganda, it would not be right for him to interfere.[77] When MacHale wrote back, again he brought up his proposed journey to Rome, where he would willingly go 'either to secure Dr [Thomas] MacHale's election or to exclude the bishop of Galway.' He was still hopeful that the journey would not be necessary.[78]

John MacHale's next move, in fact, was to approach Cardinal Franchi, who was on a visit to Ireland. MacHale handed the cardinal a letter in which he repeated his determination never to consent to the appointment of the bishop of Galway, and he hoped that this determination, often expressed, would be sufficient. MacHale also despatched his nephew to Rome to urge the appointment of either Dr Carr of Maynooth or Canon Ronayne of Ballinrobe.[79] MacHale's biographer, Monsignor O'Reilly, claims that MacHale himself should have gone to Rome as the 'impression everywhere produced by his venerable aspect' must have touched the heart of Pius IX.[80] It is most doubtful, however, if such a sight, pathetic as it must have been, would have been sufficient counter to Cullen's enormous influence in Rome.

Paul Cullen, during the last two months of 1876, wrote consistently to Rome, pressing for the quick appointment of John MacEvilly on the grounds that the Tuam diocese was badly in need of reform and attention, which he assured Rome MacEvilly would provide.[81] Cullen was joined by Gillooly of Elphin in promoting MacEvilly's claims. 'He speaks Irish which is almost indispensable in the diocese,' Gillooly wrote Cardinal Franchi, adding that MacEvilly was a man of 'singular energy and a prudent firmness.'[82]

Thomas MacHale's visit to Rome was not a success. According to his own account,[83] Rome considered various options, such as the appointment of a coadjutor who would not have the right of succession.

Finally, the matter was considered at a full meeting of the congregation of the Propaganda. It was decided to appoint MacEvilly, but that the appointment should not be made known or published during the archbishop's lifetime, and so matters would remain as they were as far as the public was concerned.[84] The decision, which was ratified by the pope, was difficult, if not impossible, to keep secret; already by December, rumours were abroad. Cullen wrote to Kirby to discover if the news of the appointment as published in the *Freeman's Journal* was true.[85] But Rome was not revealing anything just yet.

By March of 1877, Cullen did have news of MacEvilly's appointment and was hoping that it would soon be made public.[86] According to Bernard O'Reilly, such was MacEvilly's anxiety that he journeyed to Rome with Bishops Gillooly and MacCormack in the spring of 1877 to press his case.[87] This is not strictly accurate, since, conveniently as it happened, it was the time for the bishops' ad limina visits to Rome.[88] Certainly on his return home, MacEvilly was none the wiser as regards his appointment. In October, he was plainly worried by a rumour that MacHale was looking for an auxiliary. He requested Kirby to find out quickly if MacHale had made any such move.[89]

It does seem highly probable, though, that the visit of the Connacht bishops did have much to do with the charges of maladministration which Propaganda laid before MacHale at the end of the year. The charges were four-fold: firstly, lack of discipline among the clergy; secondly, the success of proselytisers in the diocese; thirdly, that priests were writing against each other in the public press; and lastly, that there were insufficient priests in the diocese.[90]

These charges were made by Rome as a prelude to the announcement of MacEvilly's appointment. Accordingly, Cardinal Franchi wrote to MacHale in December 1877, informing him of MacEvilly's appointment. The pope, who did not wish to offend MacHale, had the letter delivered through Fr Thomas Burke, the well-known Dominican preacher, who was friendly with MacHale.[91] Burke was to obtain MacHale's consent to the appointment, but this MacHale was determined to withhold.[92] MacEvilly now wrote to Cullen, telling him of Burke's fruitless visit to Tuam.[93] At the same time, he wrote Kirby, complaining about the state of Tuam and requesting power from the Holy See to tackle the problems.[94] To Cullen he confided that it seemed to him that Rome was afraid of MacHale. Whoever went to Tuam as coadjutor would have to be given independent faculties to achieve anything, MacEvilly thought.[95]

MacEvilly received his briefs of appointment as coadjutor with right of succession from Rome on 6 February 1878, together with a letter from Cardinal Franchi in which he was told that he would be left to govern his present dioceses until Tuam became vacant. MacEvilly, with the approval of Cullen, wrote to Tuam assuring MacHale of his willingness to assist him in any way possible.[96]

As time wore on, MacEvilly grew more impatient. Cullen, in particular, was the recipient of long letters of complaints of abuses in Tuam. Indeed it seemed that MacEvilly was now watching and waiting to report the smallest incident in that diocese. Often, one feels, he was prepared to exaggerate for his own purposes. He was annoyed that Rome would not intervene as he knew that MacHale of his own accord would never grant him the necessary faculties. He was still afraid that Rome might grant MacHale his request for an auxiliary and said that there was no parish priest in Tuam fit for that office – 'such of them as have ability, want piety, and such have piety, want ability and knowledge,' he averred. He alleged too that Fenianism was 'rife in the diocese' and gave instances of Fenian excesses going unpunished. Curates paid no attention to parish priests, he declared, 'in fact there is no government at all there,' while in Connemara, 'proselytism had incurably eaten into the hearts of the people.'[97]

Some weeks later, MacEvilly's complaints were becoming even more numerous and slightly hysterical. MacHale would never grant faculties, he repeated, and even if he did, he could not be trusted. 'In truth,' declared MacEvilly, 'from the first day I knew him, now nearly 38 years since, I know it to be his habit, to speak and write in the most dignified style in public and convey the opposite meaning through others supposed to be in his confidence . . . . Indeed, if he ever obeyed, it was when the mandate accorded with his own wishes.'[98] He also stressed that MacHale was no longer equal to the work of such a large diocese.

In May MacHale was ordered by the Cardinal Prefect to invite the bishop of Galway to begin work in the diocese.[99] MacEvilly, waiting impatiently, felt that this time MacHale would comply 'because . . . no man can publicly oppose Rome in this country.'[100] MacEvilly had underestimated his opponent. Not only did MacHale not comply but he took up the case anew with Leo XIII, who had succeeded Pius IX.[101] Cullen, who had been in Rome from February to June, was putting MacEvilly's case and seemed confident that he had succeeded when he wrote to Gillooly telling him of Propaganda's instructions to MacHale, and that if MacHale did not grant the necessary faculties within 30 days, the Pope would then grant them.[102]

Towards the end of June, MacEvilly called on MacHale at Tuam. MacHale denied that he had ever received the letter written by Simeoni, who had succeeded Franchi at Propaganda. MacHale then promised to write to the cardinal, a promise that MacEvilly was not too confident would be fulfilled. Cullen reported to Kirby that MacHale had refused to act, and he spoke of the aging archbishop's denial that he had received Simeoni's instructions. Then, obviously echoing MacEvilly, he wrote about MacHale. 'He is now perambulating his diocese, and giving a great show of energy, duly reported in the papers. I hope Propaganda will not allow their orders to be set aside.'[103]

Rome, indeed, was treading carefully, especially after MacHale threatened to appeal to the Irish nation. In MacEvilly's view, it was a bluff and he argued that MacHale thought Rome afraid of him.[104] Rome's next move was to enlist the services of the primate, Dr MacGettigan, archbishop of Armagh, who was commissioned by the pope to visit Tuam and induce the archbishop to submit. Archbishop Croke too was requested by Simeoni to lend a hand in the persuasion of the stubborn MacHale. MacEvilly did not think much of such moves, stating that the fact of sending persons to 'mollify him and treat with him' only confirmed MacHale in the conviction that Rome feared him. Fr Burke's 'ill-advised mission' had failed, MacEvilly pointed out to Cullen, and MacHale would treat the primate, a timid man, in the same way.

Dr MacGettigan, timid as MacEvilly had said and not at all relishing his task, sent MacHale the most careful of letters at the end of August, making arrangements for his visit to Tuam and informing MacHale in the most polite way of the purpose of his visit.[105] He duly visited Tuam and came away convinced that MacHale would never accept MacEvilly as coadjutor. He noted that MacHale had appointed his nephew vicar general of the diocese, the first the archbishop had ever had.[106] MacGettigan made his report to Rome, recommending that the question of a coadjutor be waived for the present.[107]

Rome, however, was not prepared to postpone the matter and, in January 1879, Simeoni asked MacGettigan to investigate the situation further, and this time to consult suffragan bishops before reporting back.[108] MacGettigan's report in February of 1879 declared that things were in a satisfactory state in Tuam, that there were no serious problems of discipline or proselytism, and that the archbishop was really in good health. He again advised that no change should be attempted as 'nothing but the most serious evils could result from forcing the Bishop of Galway into the church of Tuam, against the consent of the archbishop.'[109]

White Bear Hotel Harrogate
August 30 1873

My dear Sir [...]

Letter from Bishop MacEvilly to Cardinal Cullen.

Archbishop John MacHale.

How serious then were matters in the Tuam diocese? By far the greater part of the complaints was made by MacEvilly or by Cullen, whose source was MacEvilly, and MacEvilly is hardly an unbiased source. The one objective report, that of MacGettigan, had declared that there was no cause for alarm. There were of course other complaints made, such as those of the suffragan bishops but here, too, objectivity was at risk. Two of the suffragans in particular, MacCormack of Achonry and Duggan of Clonfert, were close personal friends of MacEvilly and were formerly priests of the Tuam diocese who had had their differences with MacHale. MacEvilly wrote, 'It is simply folly for any other bishops to give any advice to the Holy See about it, save the bishops of Clonfert and Achonry, who alone know of these crying evils.'[110] This really amounts to a plea to consult his friends and it is noticeable at least that he does not include the bishop of Elphin, Dr Gillooly. Gillooly, according to MacGettigan, did not subscribe to the view that there was chaos in Tuam and furthermore was annoyed at MacEvilly's impatience to take over.[111]

As regards the charges themselves, they would certainly seem to have diminished in seriousness by the time MacEvilly took over. He had complained that proselytism in Connemara was a problem of alarming proportions, yet when MacEvilly succeeded, there is no evidence he had to take any extraordinary measures to counter it. MacEvilly had complained that only the friends and relatives of the archbishop were being promoted in the diocese, and while there is some substance in this charge,[112] one of MacEvilly's first acts on succeeding was to promote his own brother to parish priest of Dunmore.[113] MacEvilly had complained of indiscipline among the priests and, in this area, it is possible that MacHale had lost some control since he was now approaching his ninetieth year and power had passed to his nephew, Thomas MacHale, who was not popular with the priests.[114]

As regards MacEvilly's charge that Tuam diocese was 'eaten up with Fenianism,'[115] there is really very little evidence to support this. Official reports of the time make scarcely any mention of Tuam diocese in regard to Fenianism.[116] But then, where Fenianism was concerned, MacEvilly was not one to draw distinctions. In 1879, he attributed the growth of the Land League in Mayo to 'the fact that Fenianism has been encouraged and patronised.'[117]

Upon the death of Cullen in 1878, MacEvilly enlisted the aid and sympathy of Cullen's successor, McCabe, who shortly after he took office had a meeting with MacEvilly at Kingstown in April 1879,[118] and from then on, McCabe joined MacEvilly in the attempt to force action from Rome. 'I have sound information that things are in a bad way there,' McCabe wrote Propaganda, no doubt quoting MacEvilly. 'The poor old Archbishop is, I suspect, an automaton in the hands of a party. The accounts of the work he is doing there are utterly absurd. They might possibly be credible if he were fifty instead of ninety .... If MacEvilly is not sent soon,' he warned dramatically, 'it will be too late.'[119] Never one to underplay his hand, MacEvilly told Kirby it would take 'generations of archbishops' to reform Mayo.[120] McCabe supplemented this with the information that proselytism in Connemara was very serious, that St. Jarlath's was heavily in debt and a 'nursery of Fenianism', and a rumour that the college would pass to Thomas MacHale on his uncle's death. 'Thomas MacHale is a good man,' wrote McCabe, 'but it is quite wrong that a private individual should hold public property.'[121]

In response to this pressure, Propaganda decided to move and risk the old man's wrath. In August MacEvilly had word from Kirby that he was being sent to Tuam and would receive shortly the relative document and all the necessary powers. Propaganda's action, however, was not at all as decisive as MacEvilly would have wished. Rome still left room for manoeuvre by granting MacHale one month in which to comply with the Pope's wishes by issuing an invitation to MacEvilly.[122]

If MacEvilly's efforts to have himself installed at Tuam were bordering on the desperate, so too were some of the attempts being made to prevent him. In one such attempt, seven parish priests of Tuam diocese sent a signed letter in Latin to Cardinal Simeoni. The priests referred to MacEvilly as 'untruthful in ecclesiastical matters' and they called him the 'public caluminator of the illustrious Archbishop of Tuam, John MacHale.' Making a formal request that MacEvilly be not appointed to Tuam, the priests declared that the bishop of Galway was foolish and stupid and that he had as friends 'laymen of heretical faith and depraved morals.'[123]

On the 1 September, MacEvilly went to Tuam to present himself, armed with a strong letter from Cardinal Simeoni.[124] He found Thomas MacHale 'polite and civil, but neither cordial nor co-operative.' Thomas MacHale told him that his uncle would not put any obstacle in his way but intended to resign. MacEvilly had received a great welcome from the priests and people, he stated, as 'Dr Thomas MacHale is not a great favourite.' In his opinion, if the Holy See had sent the strong letters two years before, all would be well.[125]

The beleaguered archbishop was down to his last card and he now proceeded to play it. He wrote to Simeoni, renewing his objections to the bishop of Galway who, he said, had always been 'openly and notoriously hostile' to him. Then came the archbishop's last shot –

> If in spite of all this, the Apostolic See wills to delegate to the bishop of Galway the faculties for performing certain functions in the diocese of Tuam, then I shall at once seriously think of resigning the episcopal office and dignity, for I will never be associated with the bishop of Galway. But in as much as the resignation of a bishop is a thing of very rare occurrence, mine will excite surprise both among the clergy and the people. It will then become necessary for me to give a public explanation of my act. In the documents which I shall then give to the public in connection with this

affair, I shall add nothing to the letters written by me, or in my name, to the Sacred Congregation. Historical truth and the necessity of my own reputation require that I should also make public everything in these letters which throw light on this momentous transaction.[126]

If the archbishop's threat was a bluff, as MacEvilly again maintained, Rome was not prepared to take the risk of calling it. It was certainly true that the archbishop's resignation would cause surprise, but how much more than that Rome did not wish to discover in the case of a man who had become a legend in his own lifetime and who, for many, had long been a defiant symbol of resistance to British rule in Ireland. Any action from Rome would be represented as a personal insult to a man who had given a long life of service to the church, but also at this particularly sensitive time, it would be seen as further proof of Rome's alliance with and blessing of English rule. Not all of the Irish bishops were as blasé about the implications as MacEvilly. Duggan of Clonfert, for instance, was fearful of the possible consequences and wondered if McCabe could prevent publication in the public press.[127] Rome, taking the archbishop at his word, decided not to risk a major public scandal. And so MacEvilly had to struggle on without his exclusive powers, for which he was to petition Propaganda so often.

One month after going to Tuam, MacEvilly reported to McCabe and Kirby that he had visited all the deaneries of the diocese, except Clifden, where he had heard matters were in a very bad state. As might be expected, his report was not encouraging.[128]

A month later, MacEvilly was worried at the story that Propaganda intended to appoint a bishop to Galway. He told Kirby there was no urgency and complained that he had 'not a penny' from Tuam.[129] To McCabe, he said that if they appointed another bishop and handed the man over to MacHale, they might as well sign his death warrant, as he would be given nothing. McCabe again supported him at Rome, and when the parish of Dunmore became vacant, MacEvilly applied for it as a means of meeting his expenses and also to give the priests 'much-needed example of how to run a parish.'[130]

By the end of the year 1879, MacEvilly was finding his situation in Tuam extremely difficult. He was ignored by the archbishop, his decisions had no standing and he had no power to effect any worthwhile changes. 'I must get a mandate to administer the diocese,' he told Kirby. 'MacHale will obey this, but nothing else.'[131] It may be an indication of the frustration he was experiencing but MacEvilly's stories were certainly becoming more colourful. There was a Fr Loftus, he told McCabe, who was brought before the magistrates for 'drawing a revolver to shoot a man.' Again he returned to his plea for exclusive powers, declaring, 'Up to this, I might as well have been in Botany Bay as in Tuam.'[132]

A week later, MacEvilly was writing again with the news that he had been given Dunmore parish.[133] But more and more, he was feeling isolated and powerless. McCabe once more pleaded for him at Rome. 'The position of the coadjutor of Tuam,' he informed Kirby, 'is almost untenable. He has no authority to interpose. The archbishop will not see him and all his suggestions are disregarded.' He ended with the pointed question, 'Can nothing more be done by Propaganda?'[134]

MacEvilly was now forced to apply to Rome for power to act in specific cases. He still repeated his request for full powers, particularly at this time when the priests were involved in the political agitation.[135] In March he reported that the archbishop was never seen by anyone as the nephew transacted all business. 'In the name of God,' MacEvilly cried, 'let something be done. For rely on it, if not, you will have lawsuits on lawsuits.'[136]

MacHale, aged and infirm though he undoubtedly was,[137] was determined not to yield and MacEvilly described his pathetic attempt to say three masses on Christmas morning – 'He goes to the cathedral leaning on his servant and ascends the altar steps . . . supported by a priest.'[138] By March 1881, MacHale was a 'perfect non-entity' and the nephew 'bungles everything,' according to MacEvilly. 'The clergy all hate Dr Thomas MacHale,' he wrote McCabe, 'and can't bear to receive any mandate from him.'[139]

The Cardinal Prefect informed MacEvilly that he had instructed Thomas MacHale to persuade the archbishop not to attempt performing functions he was unequal to; and also to ask the archbishop if he would consent to giving MacEvilly the diocesan collections and a permanent share of the diocesan revenues. Thomas MacHale told Rome that his uncle performed all his functions in 'admirable style.' He agreed to handing over the diocesan collections but did not offer any opinion regarding the division of the revenues.[140]

MacEvilly's long wait at last came to an end on the evening of 7 November 1881 with the death of John MacHale in Tuam.[141] Writing about the archbishop's death to Kirby, MacEvilly commented: 'It is now all over and Heaven knows all I suffered in silence to prevent scandal and exposure which was threatened. Since the poor old man's death I have acted as if he were *my greatest friend* and mean to do so till after the month's mind.'[142]

The bitter dispute and bad feeling which had marred the archbishop's last years were carried over into MacEvilly's reign. As one might expect, Thomas MacHale's position became impossible after MacEvilly's succession. At first, the nephew chose attack as the best form of defence and asked MacEvilly for the proceeds of the diocese of Tuam up to the following April or May. MacEvilly, now securely in the driver's seat, replied by demanding £300 a year for his services over the preceding two years, as he had done all the work while the MacHales 'received all the emoluments without the incidental expenses.' 'I suspect he will cry quits', was MacEvilly's prediction.[143] Thomas MacHale did indeed cry quits and returned to the Irish College, Paris.[144] Unfortunately for historians, one direct consequence of the MacEvilly-MacHale quarrel was that Thomas MacHale took with him all the letters and papers of John MacHale.

According to D'Alton, other MacHale relatives and supporters did not fare so well either. Fr John MacHale, a grand-nephew of the archbishop, was changed from St. Jarlath's to a curacy at Newport at his own request. He was later changed to Annaghdown before finally leaving the diocese altogether for Cleveland, U.S.A.[145] Ulick Bourke, parish priest of Claremorris, was one of MacHale's closest allies and the tension between MacEvilly and himself was always evident.[146] D'Alton also alleges that parish priests who had been friendly with MacHale would be admonished or sent a curate they did not want.[147]

The succession row was the explosive climax of a quarrel which had been brewing for many years. It was not, however, simply the personal confrontation of two stubborn men who had radical personality differences and essentially opposing points of view on the great questions of the day. It epitomised the struggle between the independent national church position, as represented by MacHale, and the centralised Roman church of Cullen and his disciple MacEvilly. The archbishop was ranged against a powerful trio in MacEvilly, Cullen and Kirby, rector of the Irish College in Rome and representative of the Irish hierarchy there. It was Cullen's special mission to bring Rome to Ireland, to organise and centralise the Irish catholic church and to win unquestioning obedience for Rome.[148] His greatest obstacle in accomplishing this was John MacHale, who clung tenaciously to his concept of an independent national church, with each bishop autonomous in his own territory. For Cullen to achieve complete success, MacHale had to be defeated, and in this task, Cullen had an invaluable ally in MacEvilly. There was never any doubt then as to which side Rome would choose.

The battle was not one which presented itself as crucial to an Irish peasant population struggling to exist, and that may be why the victory went to Rome and to all that Cullen represented. *De facto* the battle was over before the succession row took place, and the fact that MacHale was able to sustain his opposition to the very end is due, not to the strength of his cause, but more to the force of his personality and the appeal of his uncompromising nationalism as contrasted in the popular mind with the suspect 'castle' mentality of Cullen and MacEvilly.

Chapter 4

Administrative Problems

IT WAS AS AN administrator that John MacEvilly was best known and it was in the area of diocesan administration that his more lasting achievements were accomplished. The massive bulk of his surviving correspondence testifies amply to a man who was conscientious in the performance of his duties, as well as being orderly, most painstaking and hardworking. A range and diversity of administrative tasks faced a bishop of the time, excluding altogether involvement in the great political issues of the day.

THE CONFLICT WITH PETER DALY

Having spent eighteen years as rector of the Irish College in Rome, Paul Cullen became archbishop of Armagh in 1850. In 1852, he was translated to Dublin. Cullen was a man with a mission, and his ample skills and intelligence were employed in its achievement – the reformation of the nineteenth century Irish catholic church. Cullen had enormous influence at Rome and he used that influence in the appointment of bishops who would help in this task. By 1878, when he died, Cullen had accomplished much of what he set himself. There was a centralised, tightly disciplined Irish church, focussed on Rome and, in the process of that reformation, there had been a devotional revolution, which had switched the direction of Irish catholicism.[1] All of this had been achieved, in no small measure, through the devoted loyalty and unquestioning obedience of trusted lieutenants like John MacEvilly.

When MacEvilly went to Galway as bishop in 1857, he went there on the recommendation of Paul Cullen.[2] As Cullen's man, then, he was pledged to Cullen's mission, and nowhere perhaps was this mission more difficult than in the diocese of Galway. This was due to the unique position of the Galway diocese in the Irish church. Before it was created a diocese in 1830, Galway had been a wardenship.[3] The warden, who filled the role of bishop, was elected to his position, as indeed were the vicars or parish priests. This process, apart from involving priests in local politics, meant in effect that each parish priest was practical dictator in his own parish.[4] It would not be easy to impose the new discipline on men who had been so long accustomed to 'home rule.'

As early as July 1857, MacEvilly, having completed a preliminary survey of the diocese, was reporting to Cullen. Stating that there were parts of the diocese that had not seen 'the face of a bishop for the last 16 years,' MacEvilly continued: 'I must not . . . conceal from Your Grace that we have much to contend with against the lax notions as regards Episcopal Government and the blind obedience due to every thing emanating from the See of Peter, which might to some extent be traced to the Democratic or rather autocratic form of church government to which they were so long habituated. However, their condition must with all patience be left to time, divine grace, and I hope to the superintending care of our heavenly ''seat of wisdom.'' '[5]

From this report, it is evident that MacEvilly had grasped fully the extent of the problems that faced him. He had, however, other weapons in his armoury apart from those mentioned in the last part of his letter. Where the unquestioning obedience that he demanded was not forthcoming, he was quick to apply the law. If the imposition of ecclesiastical censures would achieve his end more quickly and more effectively, then he did not hesitate to use them. Yet, for all his grasp of the problems and his determination to remedy them, MacEvilly could not have foreseen that the very first challenge to his episcopal authority was to be the stiffest and most complex he was to encounter in his career as a bishop.

By the time MacEvilly came to Galway as bishop, Peter Daly had been ministering in the diocese for over forty years. Daly, who was ordained in 1815,[6] before MacEvilly was born, had built a considerable kingdom for himself, both spiritual and material. He was parish priest of two parishes in Galway town;[7] he had been at various times, and in some cases still was, chairman of the Town Corporation, chairman of the Gas Company, chairman of the Harbour Board and president of the Mechanics' Institute.[8] He had also acquired a huge personal fortune and was the owner of a large amount of property in the town. According to the *Galway Vindicator,* he had a rent-roll of over a thousand pounds a year. And he was, besides, owner and director of the Lough Corrib Steam Company.[9] All in all, Peter Daly was a large part of life in Galway.

The fact that a priest could rise to such a prominent position was partly due to the unique situation of the Galway diocese and partly due to Daly's own personality and talent. Daly was a man who had taken full advantage of his position and who had cultivated his contacts well. By all accounts, he was also a man of great energy, forceful personality and considerable business acumen.[10] From his letters and personal statements, the picture that emerges is that of an arrogant man, of overbearing manner and of remarkable, at times almost childish, vanity. He was also very stubborn and when this aspect of his personality found a match in MacEvilly, the ensuing conflict had to be lengthy and often bitter.

Obviously, a priest of Peter Daly's position and power must be a strong contender for the see of Galway. That Peter Daly was not appointed bishop inevitably meant problems for the one who was. It was clear from the beginning that Galway diocese was too small a place for this determined new bishop and his truculent parish priest. Scarcely had MacEvilly moved in than the battle was joined, a battle that was to continue with varying degrees of ferocity to Daly's death in 1868. The first shot was fired in December 1857, when MacEvilly had a letter from one Richard Lynch, telling of a visit to the local convent of Mercy to see his niece. While there, he was consulted by the Reverend Mother as to the steps the sisters should take to obtain from Daly a settlement of an account between the parish priest and the sisters. This referred to property and monies which Daly was holding in trust for the convent. If some immediate arrangement was not made, recourse would then have to be made to the courts of law. Lynch requested MacEvilly to intervene and so prevent an ugly law suit.[11]

MacEvilly entrusted the investigation to a parish priest, Laurence Leonard, instructing him to call on Daly to render an account.[12] Leonard then obtained from the sisters a list of the disputed properties[13] along with a copy of a declaration made in September 1852 and signed by Peter Daly, stating that the property had been bought by him the previous February in trust for the convent and paid for with the sisters' money, also held in trust.[14] Daly countered with denials, followed by threats of law proceedings.[15]

MacEvilly then informed Leonard that he could not refuse permission to the sisters to consult their solicitors.[16] At this point, Daly wrote to MacEvilly requesting a rest from his duties. The letter is worth quoting for the insight it gives into Daly's character: 'I most respectfully solicit your Lordship's indulgence under the following circumstances. I find my bodily health for some time so debilitated and my mind so depressed by anxieties and solicitudes which I am not aware of having caused by any blamable conduct that I find it absolutely necessary to seek a little repose and I am advised to avoid any cause of excitement as much as possible. I have been uninterruptedly engaged in the most arduous missionary duties for the last forty-five years and during that time have never until now sought any repose – I hope, therefore, you will kindly release me for a few months from some of the duties that require the application of the mind especially where study is required such as conferences and allow me to follow the medical's advice.'[17]

What Peter Daly was saying, of course, was that he had been a good and devoted clergyman for forty-five years and that he was now being persecuted for no cause that he could see. The shrewd MacEvilly knew just how to handle the request. He granted Daly leave of absence from conferences but as regards absence from the parish, a written application would have to be made each time; which he then effectively revoked by adding: 'Before granting present permission for leaving home, there are certain matters I wish to have arranged with you, after which I shall feel most happy to extend to you every indulgence and permission in my power.'[18] Thus Daly's escape route was blocked for the moment. This little exchange illustrates the type of subtlety and cunning that was to mark the conflict throughout, and with subtlety and cunning both contestants were amply endowed.

The contention was further aggravated when, on 2 April 1858, a letter from the parish priests of the town of Galway asked MacEvilly to procure a legal settlement of the property of Kilgill which Daly had purchased in trust for the priests and himself jointly. The purchase had been made from charitable funds subscribed by the people for masses to be celebrated annually for the repose of their souls. Daly had paid the priests the yearly rent arising from this property, 'share and share alike.' The property was, however, still legally vested in Daly himself, contrary to the decrees of the Synod of Thurles, which prescribed that all such charitable foundations should be properly secured in the names of a certain number of trustees. The priests were now requesting the bishop to see that this was done.[19]

Following an interview with Daly on the matter, MacEvilly wrote, demanding that he secure, in the manner prescribed in the statutes, all the ecclesiastical property in his possession, namely, the properties of Kilgill, Bodawn and the schools of the town; the property of the Magdalen Asylum and the House of Mercy transferred to Daly by Mr White of Clifden; the lease of the Custom House. MacEvilly also requested Daly 'in the name of religion' to leave the dispute between himself and the Sisters of Mercy to legal arbitration.[20]

At this stage, MacEvilly felt the need to consult an outside source and wrote a long letter to Paul Cullen, which concluded: 'Mr Daly is a man far advanced in life. If anything sudden were to befall him, his relatives would enter on the possession of the properties in question.'

In making his next move, MacEvilly was obviously acting on the advice of his mentor, Cullen. He wrote to Daly and produced the big guns: 'We therefore once more command you as Bishop of this diocese, in virtue of our Episcopal authority and under pain of suspension *ipso facto* which we are preparing to inflict on you in case of further contumacious resistance to our mandates.' Daly was given three days to comply with instructions and, should he fail to do so, then MacEvilly would proceed to 'the painful exercise of authority.' He asked Daly to remember his old age, 'when in the course of nature you are approaching that final term which is but the opening of God's irrevocable judgement and a never-ending eternity.' MacEvilly's final salvo was, 'Bear in mind that no one ever raised his hand against God's church and prospered.'[21]

To this mixture of threats, stern command and appeal to conscience, Daly replied the very next day: 'Your Lordship is one year in Galway and you threaten me with degradation and suspension unless within three days I declare I hold certain trusts which for a series of years I have openly avowed and faithfully discharged.' The embattled priest admitted to buying the estates of Bodawn and Kilgill and then named the bishop, the parish priests and himself as trustee in each instance. He stated that he would 'immediately direct a deed declaring these trusts to be duly made and executed according to law.'[22]

Daly, of course, had not fulfilled all the bishop's instructions and three days later MacEvilly issued his second canonical monition. Daly was once more given three days to comply fully.[23]

McEvilly reported back to Cullen, informing him of Daly's partial submission. 'I will send him a third monition tomorrow morning with a final warning that unless he comply within twenty-four hours I will suspend him,' MacEvilly announced confidently.[24] He had forwarded a detailed statement of the case to the Cardinal Prefect of Propaganda, as well as to Dr Kirby at the Irish College.

Five days later, MacEvilly was sending Cullen the latest news that Daly had submitted but only at the last moment. However, he felt that Daly was determined to prosecute in the case of the nuns and was hoping that Propaganda would direct Daly to leave the case to legal arbitration.

Nor were Daly's troubles confined to disputes with his bishop or clerics of the diocese. Daly was a fiery man who was given to angry outbursts at meetings of the public bodies on which he served. In one such outburst in December 1859, Daly attacked the press and especially the *Galway Vindicator*. When the editor replied in a strong leading article,[25] he was sued for libel by Daly. The case came to court in March 1860 and the verdict amounted to a moral victory for the *Vindicator*, as Daly was awarded sixpence damages and sixpence costs.[26] Obviously dissatisfied with the press coverage he was receiving, Daly bought his own newspaper, the *Galway Press*.[27]

The next clash between Daly and his bishop followed from complaints made by the curates of Daly's parishes who, in January 1860, claimed that Daly had not divided the Christmas collections, did not celebrate mass or hear confessions.[28]

MacEvilly then laid down seven conditions for Daly to follow. These were that Daly should celebrate public mass on Sundays and holidays, that he should preach, attend sick calls, repair Barna church, carry out the monthly settlement with his curates, pay the Bishop's mensal settlement monthly and follow the statutes of Thurles.[29]

The row between parish priest and bishop widened into the public domain when, in December 1861, MacEvilly received a report from the Harbour Board of instances of 'unbecoming' and 'abusive' language addressed by Daly, in public, to members of the Board. MacEvilly's immediate reaction was to send a copy of the report to Daly, entreating him 'in the first instance to withdraw at once from the Harbour and Town Commissioners' Boards' of this town. 'In God's name,' the bishop appealed, 'it is time you granted us some peace – which you did not give us since we came into the diocese.'[30]

To this Daly, no doubt feeling equally persecuted, made no reply. MacEvilly wrote a second letter.

Then ensued moves and countermoves, with this contest of wills taking on the complications of a chess game. Daly's next move, on 26 December 1861, was to appeal to Rome through a letter to MacEvilly.[31] On 2 January he attended a meeting of the Town Commissioners, acting as chairman. MacEvilly served him with a suspension on the 3rd and prepared a circular to this effect to be read from the altars on Sunday, the 5th. The parish church of St. Nicholas was thronged for the twelve o'clock mass. After the bishop's statement was read, Daly came from the vestry brandishing a copy in his hand, and the excited crowd called for him to be allowed to speak. He did so at great length, denouncing his seven complainants on the Harbour Board.[32]

This led to a day of street disturbances – from a 'drunken mob' managed by Daly, according to MacEvilly[33] – and the military was called in. Daly, through the Mechanics' Institute of which he was president, called a public meeting in Eyre Square for the following afternoon. The streets were again crowded and the church was, the *Freeman's Journal* reported, 'thronged almost to suffocation.' At the end of mass, MacEvilly, in full pontificals, addressed the people. He stressed their duty of obedience and the independence of Church authority to 'popular clamour'[34] and, without alluding to Daly, succeeded in dissuading all but a few hundred from attending Daly's meeting in Eyre Square.[35]

At the meeting a resolution was passed to petition the pope on Daly's behalf.[36] While MacEvilly made little of this, he was well aware that the essential battle would be fought in Rome. He was already keeping his allies informed, beginning with Cullen. 'One thing is certain,' he told Cullen, 'that if the Roman authorities restore Fr Peter after the gross and publicly scandalous conduct he had been guilty of, every good Catholic here will sustain a shock from which they will never recover.' The letter that MacEvilly wrote to Kirby in Rome was even more detailed than his account to Cullen. He also warned Rome of what might happen in the event of Daly being pardoned. In his efforts to discredit Daly totally at Rome, he stated that Daly, 'although he was worth £15,000,' was the only priest who did not contribute to the diocesan fund collected in sympathy for the pope. He again listed Daly's misdemeanours, this time adding a good deal of colour. He stated, for instance, that Daly had spent a full day in court evicting tenants and that, at one of his balls, religious subjects like the Madonna, the divine infant and the immaculate conception were made 'the subjects of ribald and impure jests.' Finally MacEvilly was careful to impress on Kirby that if Daly were to triumph, no bishop could remain in Galway.[37]

On 12 January, MacEvilly again wrote to Cullen. Daly had placed tables at the doors of churches on that Sunday to obtain signatures for his memorial for Rome. MacEvilly had decided not to oppose this as he did not see 'what good or harm it could do.' MacEvilly also argued that the 'whole question of education in Ireland' was involved as Daly was 'the avowed Patron of government education of the worst system and in all its branches.'[38]

The *Freeman's Journal* was of the opinion that support for Daly was on the increase. Their correspondent reported that on Friday, 10 January, a meeting of sympathy with Daly was convened at the Mechanics' Institute in Galway. Here it was resolved that a memorial be sent to the pope, requesting Daly's restoration 'as the adviser and guide of the people in temporal as well as in spiritual matters.'

On 17 January, Daly wrote to MacEvilly, again requesting the necessary letters in order to go to Rome and prosecute his appeal. He informed MacEvilly that he would be leaving for Rome on the following Monday and he hoped to meet MacEvilly there.[39] Daly did leave, bringing with him the signed memorial[40] but without any letters from MacEvilly.[41]

While MacEvilly had no intention of proceeding to Rome, he despatched another long epistle to Kirby, requesting he lay it before the Cardinal Prefect of Propaganda. MacEvilly conceded that Daly had done much good, but, he quickly retracted, 'he has done much harm too.'[42]

Paul Cullen was exerting his great influence at Rome in favour of his friend, the bishop of Galway. He wrote to the Prefect, Cardinal Barnabo, repeating much of what he had been told by MacEvilly. He added that Daly was now about seventy-four years of age but 'full of energy.' Although Cullen himself had always been friendly with Daly, he felt it his duty now to warn Barnabo about him.[43]

The Roman dice was well and truly loaded against the parish priest. On 15 February, MacEvilly had a telegram from Cardinal Barnabo, stating: 'Daly starts for Galway, information and instructions by post.' The letter from the Cardinal Prefect which followed explained that Daly had been refused an audience by the pope. The suspension and irregularity incurred were still in force and MacEvilly was being granted faculties to remove them.[44]

Daly was making his way home all right but hardly in a penitential spirit. He might have lost the battle at Rome but the war was far from over. He wrote to MacEvilly from London, informing the bishop that he would be in Galway on Wednesday night, 24 February, and would call on him on Thursday morning to hand him a letter from the Cardinal and 'to request that peace and reconciliation which I so much desire.'[45] MacEvilly wrote to Daly's Dublin address, warning him against encouraging any public display on his return and telling him that, if any such occurred, MacEvilly would lay the case before the Holy See again with a request that they would never restore him.[46]

To this Daly replied from the Imperial Hotel, Dublin. He regretted that the bishop's letter did not 'correspond in spirit' with that which the Cardinal Prefect dictated to him in Rome 'as the means of peace.' Daly then stated that he had purposely kept secret the time of his return in order to avoid 'any popular excitement.'[47] Daly duly arrived back in Galway on 26 February to a quiet town.[48] MacEvilly told Cullen that Daly had come to see him on Thursday morning, 27 February, with a brief letter from Cardinal Barnabo. 'He thought he should be restored on the spot,' said MacEvilly, who had then read out to Daly the conditions of his restoration as intimated by the Cardinal. The longer Daly could be kept without being restored, MacEvilly thought, 'the better terms will be got from him.'[49]

The saga of Daly's restoration began on 6 March when MacEvilly sent him a list of eight conditions which would have to be fulfilled. Daly's reply to this had an air of long-suffering innocence and endurance. The Cardinal Prefect had indeed induced him to write a humiliating letter, assuring him that this would be the end of 'the miserable affair.' The Cardinal would now see he was mistaken. 'You are resolved in continuing it,' Daly charged the bishop. MacEvilly restated his position and demanded acceptance of the conditions.[50]

That the bishop's patience was now wearing very thin is evident from a letter he wrote to Kirby on 8 March. He began with a vicious attack on Daly and declared that Daly would resist not only St. Peter but St. Paul also 'and as many more of them.' Daly had come back 'far worse than when he left,' MacEvilly complained. From the time he reached Paris on his return, MacEvilly maintained that Daly had sent 'a flood of letters' claiming a victory in Rome.

In Daly's opinion, the conditions being imposed on him were 'contrary to nature, reason and religion' and he told MacEvilly that the mandates of the bishop were not those of the Holy See. Rather, he said, they were 'simply the interpretation' which MacEvilly had put on the instructions from Barnabo. Daly prayed for 'grace to show' during the remainder of his life 'the same example and edification' he had shown from the beginning of his ministry 'for nearly fifty years up to the present awful trial.'[51]

On 10 March, Daly appealed to Rome against the imposition of the conditions.[52] Kirby, however, had been working hard for MacEvilly there. He had spoken with Cardinal Barnabo and had submitted a full statement to Propaganda. 'All will be well,' he assured MacEvilly. 'They will write a letter directly to Fr Daly . . . and it will be sent in one to your Lordship.' The Cardinal would insist on the conditions, Kirby stated, and, fearing that this might lead to a possible schism, he issued this advice: 'The great point now, as it occurs to me, is to try and so manage him as to prevent him from defying the Holy See itself, an excess which from his violence there may be some reason to apprehend.' Kirby assured MacEvilly that God would reward him for all he had suffered 'from this terrible man.'[53]

The promised letters duly arrived from Rome. 'I hardly think he will yield, his indomitable pride is such,' was MacEvilly's comment to Cullen. And indeed, Daly was not yet prepared to submit. The priest restated to MacEvilly his earlier position, namely, that he had been induced by the Cardinal to write a letter which he had been told 'would terminate the unfortunate affair.'

It was MacEvilly's move. He simply pointed out to Daly the instructions from Rome. A settlement, however, was closer than MacEvilly had anticipated for Daly was anxious to be restored before Easter Sunday. The settlement came about through the mediation of two Jesuit priests, Fathers Haly and Ronan, but not easily and not without attempts by Daly to modify MacEvilly's conditions. On Easter Sunday, 20 April, Daly went to the parish church of St. Nicholas and there read his public submission. The *Galway Vindicator*, reporting on the 23rd that Daly had left town to make a retreat at Milltown Park in accordance with the terms of the submission, declared: 'We have now done with this to us very painful matter.'[54]

Although another battle had been won, the conflict continued. MacEvilly and Peter Daly had disagreed about schools before and, in 1863, when MacEvilly made a determined onslaught on the Galway Model school,[55] full hostilities were renewed.

MacEvilly prepared a short pastoral on his new project for catholic secondary schools, to be read in all the churches on 4 January 1863. Daly had publicly 'flung it aside,' MacEvilly wrote Cullen, and furthermore was 'telling people to continue sending their children' to the state school. MacEvilly commanded Daly 'under pain of *ipso facto*' to read the letter. Daly then did, 'very quietly and made no remarks' and so, said MacEvilly, he had 'to some extent repaired the scandal.' Nevertheless, MacEvilly remained convinced that, his instructions to the contrary, Daly told parents not to withdraw their children from the condemned schools.

A month later began the next serious and protracted row between bishop and parish priest, and one which brought the archbishop of Tuam into the dispute. MacEvilly had requested information from Daly which was not forthcoming. After waiting several weeks, MacEvilly issued three commands. Firstly, Daly was to forward before 19 August a 'distinct reply' to the letter requesting information on the Model schools. Secondly, Daly was commanded to observe the mandate of March 1862 regarding 'attendance at meetings of the Mechanics' Institute, Trades Unions, etc.' Thirdly, Daly was ordered 'to have removed from the chapel of Barna before next Sunday the quantity of lime deposited there' by his directions. The postscript was the sting in the tail: 'You will observe the above under pain of suspension *ipso facto*.'[56]

Daly's reply was immediate and evasive, but displayed a new strategy for dealing with MacEvilly when he ended by writing: 'You threaten me with suspension *ipso facto*. I hereby, my Lord, appeal from it to the Metropolitan Dr

MacHale with whom I will lodge this appeal tomorrow and I cite your Lordship to his tribunal.'[57]

A swift two days later, MacEvilly received a note from MacHale,[58] simply stating that Daly's appeal had been lodged, that the archbishop would take the earliest convenient opportunity of judging the case, and that he would give MacEvilly and Daly notice of the day which he would have selected for his decision.[59] MacEvilly replied: 'Had your Grace been fully aware of the circumstances, I feel assured you would have declined receiving the appeal. The most important position of the case which you mean to judge, having been already decided by the supreme authority of the Holy See on an appeal directly and immediately made to it, passing over all other Tribunals, by the Rev. Peter Daly.' Having stated his basic defence, namely, that the affair was not MacHale's business, MacEvilly went on to comment on his three commands to Daly. He attached a letter explaining the conditions of Daly's restoration of April 1862, pointing especially to the condition forbidding Daly's attendance at the Mechanics' Institute. Commenting on Daly's claim that the bishop could not prevent him exercising a civil right, MacEvilly said: 'Has he not a civil right to marry a wife, open a shebeen house, form a stock company etc.' MacEvilly, not daring to attribute any malice to the intervention of the archbishop, repeated that if MacHale had known the facts of the case, he would never have accepted Daly's appeal.[60]

Daly now played for time by confusing the issues as much as possible, denying to MacHale that he had signed the promises under pain of suspension. 'Is there no remedy for a persecuted priest in the church of God?' he bewailed.[61]

Statements and counter-statements ensued, including those of the two Jesuits who had mediated in Daly's previous dispute with the bishop until, quite suddenly, on 15 September, MacHale wrote the following to MacEvilly: 'Having made due enquiry with the case of Rev. Mr Daly's appeal regarding which I communicated with your Lordship on the 17th ultimo, and being now, in a great measure, possessed of the different views on both sides, I beg to intimate to your Lordship that I will on next Friday, the 18th, give my decision on the subject.'[62]

MacHale's decision had the appearance of impartiality in stating that Daly should have obeyed mandates one and three, namely the commands to supply information on the schools and to remove the lime from Barna church. The important issue, of course, was contained in the second mandate, and here MacHale wrote: 'It will be for the Holy See to pronounce whether the Mechanics' Institute be such an obnoxious society as that suspension *ipso facto* should attach to a clergyman for taking any share in their proceedings, and again . . . whether the penalty is incurred before the definitive sentence of the judge is pronounced.'[63]

The case against Daly was, once again, appealed to Rome and, to this end, MacEvilly was vigorously gathering all available evidence damaging to the parish priest. On 3 October for instance, MacEvilly had a letter from a Fr Roche informing him of Daly's presence at a ball in the home of Lord Walscott at Oranmore on 23 September 'to the great disedification of all Catholics present. Lord Wallscot's family, I needn't say, are all Protestant,' Roche ended.[64] This information was straightaway transmitted to Kirby as, here again, Daly had violated a promise he had made on his previous restoration not to attend balls or dancing.[65]

For Cullen, MacEvilly had further colourful details of Daly's appearance at the ball. 'He went there fully dressed in his Roman costume and continued enjoying the dancing until two o'clock in the morning.' MacEvilly went on, 'I am informed that Dr MacHale and Fr Peter are determined to urge against me the interference with Fr Peter's civil rights, as if a Priest could not be prevented from exercising his civil or any other rights when by doing so he gives scandal.'

The case dragged on into 1864 with both sides presenting evidence at Rome. Once again the decision of Propaganda went in MacEvilly's favour, the pope assenting on 6 June.[66] Even this did not end the contention. Once Rome had pronounced against him, Daly returned to his best weapon: obfuscation.

In October, Daly finally asked for, and MacEvilly supplied, the new conditions on which he was to be restored – again. These included a letter of apology to be published in the *Freeman's Journal*, a proposed draft of which MacEvilly also supplied. MacEvilly said he required no personal apology of any kind, adding piously: 'We value your soul, just as much . . . as we do that of any other Priest under our charge. As we are all engaged in the same ministry, may we all reach the same happy end.'[67]

The happy end was not yet at hand. Daly rejected the conditions as 'accumulating a load of insults on an old priest.' A reflex action perhaps, for, on 11 November, MacEvilly wrote to Cullen that the priest had capitulated. 'Poor man, he is a most wayward character,' the bishop commented.[68] Before this day ended, MacEvilly was writing to Cullen again, proving the point. Daly, it seems, had changed his mind and 'refused every single condition imposed upon him.' To Daly, the frustrated and angry bishop wrote on 25 November, 'What then can you mean, or what is it you want, by sending us so long an epistle on irrelevant topics so often refuted already, we cannot, for the life of us, conjecture. All we have to say of it is that . . . we cannot for a moment acquiesce.' MacEvilly announced that he had appointed administrators of Daly's parishes.

Daly delayed replying until 8 December. 'In view of the sacred time so near and hoping to obtain some of the blessings of the Saviour's visit to his people,' Daly began, 'I venture to approach your Lordship, soliciting the kindly consideration of a parental mercy.' Promising to publish the letter of apology, Daly then proposed conditions of restoration for himself. MacEvilly answered this by insisting on three further conditions.[69]

Negotiations continued through the mediation of others and, on 12 December, Daly did indeed submit. MacEvilly wrote to Cullen on 15 December: 'Fr Peter has consented to all the terms required of him. So here at last we have peace. He will publish the apology in the *Freeman*.'[70] The statement was yet a little premature for Daly vacillated over the apology.[71]

The saga of Daly's second restoration ended when, at last, the *Freeman's Journal* of 24 December carried the following letter from Daly:

> I deeply regret and deplore that any acts of mine should have placed me at variance with my Bishop. I bow to the decision of the Holy See with regard to the censure lately incurred by me. I solemnly declare it to be my belief that none can interfere in ecclesiastical matters save those who have received authority from the vicar of Christ. I regret sincerely that any act of mine should have given rise to a contrary opinion. I firmly hope and resolve to live and end my days in these sentiments and in peace with all.[72]

Although this letter was far from what was required by MacEvilly initially, the bishop did restore Daly on Christmas Eve 1864.[73]

Restored Daly might have been, but repentant he was not. 'Fr Peter was never so bad,' MacEvilly stated in February 1865. The Bishop complained of Daly's 'astounding' conduct at the relief committees; of his urging 'some character to strike for higher wages than we could give'; of his attending a Protestant funeral service; of his not attending the annual diocesan retreat. 'I don't believe he was ever in worst disposition than he seems to be at present. It is a bad sign to see the patient reject the medicine.'[74]

Peace did come finally, but only with the death of Peter Daly. That long, eventful and latterly troubled life came to an end on 30 September 1868. In a carefully worded obituary, the *Vindicator* reported that the priest had sent for his bishop and a reconciliation had taken place.[75] 'Poor Fr Peter Daly died,' MacEvilly informed Cullen, 'I hope a good death.' MacEvilly still had complaints to make, mainly that Daly had left his affairs in a 'very uncertain way, having made no will until two days before his death.' The bulk of Daly's great estate had gone to his friends, with 'not a farthing for . . . masses.' MacEvilly told Cullen that at the end he had called on Daly 'repeatedly' and that Daly 'seemed very grateful.'[76] Kirby's comment, on hearing the news, was: 'Poor Father Daly! May God have mercy on his soul. I hope your Lordship will now enjoy a little peace, after all your past sufferings.'[77]

The conflict with Peter Daly represents a significant test case in the struggle between the old autocratic church and the new, disciplined and centralised church of Paul Cullen. The case was unique in the amount of time and energy expended. It was unique, too, in the personalities involved. In his day, Peter Daly was an unusual clergyman, possessed of exceptional wealth and influence. A stubborn MacEvilly was determined to impose his will and the new regime on his priests, and a stubborn Daly was equally determined to resist. This made for a

Father Peter Daly

conflict that was as intriguing as it was dramatic, yet it went beyond the two men directly involved. It became another extension of the MacHale-MacEvilly antipathy, of the MacHale-Cullen struggle, and of MacHale's running battle with Rome. It was a contest that MacEvilly felt he had to win if he was to wield the kind of authority in Galway that he wished. It was, however, a contest that he could scarcely have lost, given the support and firm backing of Paul Cullen, the voice of Rome in Ireland, and Tobias Kirby, the voice of Cullen in Rome.

If MacEvilly learned no other lesson from the Daly affair, he had learned the effectiveness of suspension and, during the remainder of his career, it was a weapon he was not slow to use.

PROSELYTISM IN GALWAY AND TUAM

When MacEvilly became bishop of Galway in 1857, it was a small diocese of fourteen parishes and twenty-one secular priests. The town of Galway was well staffed besides by members of the religious orders.[78] According to accounts, the diocese was also in a state of disarray, mainly owing to the fact that MacEvilly's predecessor, Browne, was a poor administrator and was largely under the control of Peter Daly. Due to the peculiar origins of the diocese, the parish priests retained a large degree of control in their own areas.

Perhaps because of the lack of supervision and certainly because of the poverty existing there, areas of Connemara became the centres of activity of preachers and bible readers. One particularly prominent area was Oughterard, where a mission station had been established in 1850[79] and was causing concern. Cullen, for instance, when archbishop of Armagh, had reported to Rome that nearly one hundred children were attending protestant schools in Oughterard.[80]

The new bishop was quick to take action, sending a mission to Oughterard. In July 1857, he wrote: 'There is not a vestige of the accursed system of souperism existing amongst them, even in Oughterard, which most certainly could have been lost to the Church of God were it not for the glorious mission of the Vincentian Fathers.' He stated that there was not a single proselytising school now open. As if to show the extent of his victory, MacEvilly added that even the rector's gatekeeper and family were received 'into the church and admitted to confirmation.'[81]

The problem at Oughterard, however, does not seem to have been solved so easily, because exactly one year later MacEvilly felt the need to make a public appeal in the form of a letter to the *Galway Vindicator*. He wrote that two years before a site had been purchased at Oughterard for the purpose of establishing a convent of nuns to combat the activities of the bible societies. A few hundred people, MacEvilly admitted, had 'in the day of suffering and trial received the bribes of food and clothes and money.' While proselytism had been defeated and the bible schools abandoned, the establishment of the new convent school was the greatest necessity and MacEvilly was thus appealing to the people to support the project generously.

Oughterard was still troubling MacEvilly as late as 1866. He thought that the problem had arisen there originally because of the lack of catholic schools. MacEvilly said that he had placed there 'a most active clergyman' but he complained that the spirit that existed in the village itself – 'the relics of heresy' – was far from 'being as Catholic in tone as it ought to be.' The bishop, however, seemed pleased with the results of his efforts and he wrote: 'Thank God, at present, Oughterard is free from proselytism.'[82]

It was generally accepted by catholics that proselytising activities went on in institutions such as prisons, schools, orphanages, and in particular the dreaded workhouse. Irish antipathy to the workhouse, and the refusal to grant outdoor relief, rendered the Poor Law Act of 1838 almost useless in meeting the huge demands of the hungry years. As well as that, the bishops felt that they did not have sufficient control over the chaplaincies of the workhouses.

That the catholic bishops were concerned about possible proselytising in Irish workhouses is evident from their efforts to obtain reforms in the Poor Law system in the early 1860s. The attack was spearheaded by Paul Cullen, who gathered detailed evidence for the Select Committee set up in 1861 to examine the operation of the Poor Law. Despite Cullen's efforts, the Committee's report did not recommend any major changes.[83] On the local front, MacEvilly wrote to William Gregory, M.P. for Galway county, asking him to support a bill in Parliament which was proposing changes in the system in 1863. The endeavours of the bishops were unavailing and the despised system remained a bone of contention for the remainder of the century.

As a counter to what he saw as the proselytising attempts of the workhouses, MacEvilly became involved in the provision of industrial schools in Galway. He presided at a public meeting in the town in March 1871 'to inaugurate a subscription for the establishment of an Industrial school for boys'.[84] St. Patrick's Industrial school opened at Salthill on 24 September 1871 with an enrollment of 31 homeless boys.[85]

In 1873, however, MacEvilly wrote: 'The whole concern, I am sorry to say, has been a failure under the monks of St. Patrick, whom I was principally instrumental in having appointed to take charge.' Besides being £700 in debt, MacEvilly now felt the school should be run by someone with experience 'in managing a reformatory.' The boys had come from several workhouses, such as Cork, Tipperary, Birr and Galway and, said MacEvilly, 'they reveal a state of workhouse immorality that is truly shocking.' The Brothers, 'than whom there cannot be better men,' had begged of MacEvilly to accept their resignation as they were overworked, having other schools to manage.[86] In November the school came under new management.[87]

In the diocese of Kilmacduagh and Kilfnora, of which he became apostolic administrator in 1866, MacEvilly had to deal with cases of suspected proselytism, and also in the nearby parish of Lough Coutra; chiefly problems concerning schools.

There were areas of Tuam which had witnessed some of the greatest suffering in the years of the Great Famine. The diocese also lacked schools due to MacHale's opposition to the National system. These two facts, the poverty and lack of schools, made the diocese an obvious target for the activities of non-catholic missionaries in the 1850s.

The areas where most activity was concentrated were Achill and Clifden. Edward Nangle, one of the most notorious of these preachers, had been at work in Achill Island since 1834[88] but it was not until the 'hungry years' that he registered any success. The number of converts increased so dramatically during 1847-1853 that his efforts seemed to be unusually successful.[89] While hunger was a great incentive to conversion, nevertheless by the late 1850s, Nangle's mission was in sharp decline.[90] In 1872 the Orphan Home at Achill was closed and its few inmates sent to Clifden. In 1879, Nangle's biographer spoke of the 'almost total collapse of all missionary work.'[91] Ten years later, MacEvilly was able to speak of Achill as a place 'where nearly a million of money was spent on proselytism with hardly any perverts.'[92]

In Clifden, there were two serious attempts at 'evangelising' the native population. From 1836 to 1847, Hyacinth D'Arcy, the son of John D'Arcy who was Clifden's creator, and Anthony Thomas worked to build up an evangelical team in the Clifden union. They were encouraged initially by Archbishop Trench and later, Thomas Plunkett, who became protestant bishop of Tuam in 1839. Hyacinth D'Arcy inherited a heavily encumbered estate from his father in that same year[93] and when he lost that estate in the Encumbered Estates Court after the famine, D'Arcy elected to stay among the people to preach the protestant gospel.[94] According to Bowen, D'Arcy was well loved by the catholic people of the area.[95]

In 1849, D'Arcy's efforts were supplemented by those of the veteran preacher, Rev. Alexander Dallas, and the Irish Church Mission.[96] Undoubtedly their efforts met with some success but on balance it does seem that the number of converts claimed by the preachers was greatly exaggerated.[97]

MacEvilly's accounts of proselytism in Connemara are not altogether trustworthy either. There is a distinct difference between accounts written before his succession to the See of Tuam, when they were alarmist, and those written afterwards, when mention of proselytism is significantly absent. As early as 1867, Alexander Dallas admitted that his mission had achieved little lasting success.[98] Yet, some ten years later, MacEvilly complained to Rome that proselytism had 'incurably eaten into the hearts of the people.'[99] Archbishop

McCabe of Dublin, obviously basing his report on information received from MacEvilly, told Rome in 1879 that the parish priest of Clifden had admitted that there were '450 perverts' in the central part of his parish alone. 'There are no Catholic schools,' McCabe stated baldly and inaccurately, expressing fears that the damage in Connemara was 'almost irreparable.'[100]

Such reports were without doubt much more concerned with obtaining action from Rome in the matter of MacEvilly's coadjutorship of Tuam than they were with the success of proselytism in Connemara. While Clifden did have a stronger protestant colony than was usual in Galway towns,[101] the number converted from catholicism must have been small. The evidence given by MacEvilly himself is revealing. On a visit to Clifden in 1887, he congratulated the people on having withstood all attempts at proselytising. 'Between bribes, hunger and privations of every sort on the one hand,' he stated, 'and the usual threats of eviction by some proselytising landlords on the other, many a wretched Irish mother, out of false feeling of love for her starving children, trampling upon the duties of conscience, handed them over to these selfish harpies.' Other mothers, however, MacEvilly declared, had allowed their children to die rather than 'taste of the polluted bread of proselytisers.' He congratulated the people on the successful struggle which they had sustained against 'the enemies of the faith, a struggle more severe, more prolonged and more momentous in its issue than the bloody combat of Clontarf.'[102]

There can be no doubt but that in areas such as Achill and Clifden there were exchanges of faith for food and shelter and that proselytism was taking place in some schools and orphanages. Equally, there can be no doubt but that in the years of MacEvilly's episcopacy, and certainly by the time he came to Tuam, attempts at proselytising had disappeared among a less desperate people and a more vigilant catholic clergy.

PRO BONO PUBLICO

The efforts of John MacEvilly to achieve denominational education at all levels are dealt with in greater detail later.[103] The education question topped his list of priorities and, if there could not be an exclusively catholic system, then he was prepared to settle for a compromise situation. Only in the case of the Queen's Colleges did he adamantly withhold support. In his outlook on the question, MacEvilly differed – yet again – from his metropolitan, John MacHale, who strongly opposed any compromise with state education at any level. MacHale saw the National system of education, founded in 1831, as the beginnings of state control over all aspects of Irish life.[104] The archbishop even made it a reserved sin for pupils who attended the Tuam National schools and for their parents.[105] An alternative system had thus to be provided.[106] However, in a diocese like Tuam, which embraced some of the most deprived areas in the country, it was not financially possible to sustain a widespread independent system satisfactorily.

When MacEvilly succeeded as archbishop, he set about remedying the situation. Primary schools were placed under the National Board, thus securing for them monetary grants and recognition for examinations. Priests were instructed to apply for schools to be built in their parishes and, where it was necessary, application was made for grants for renovation. It was claimed that within ten years of MacEvilly's coming to Tuam, the number of primary schools was actually doubled and the number of children on the rolls similarly increased.[107]

As with schools, MacEvilly encouraged the building and renovation of chapels, churches and presbyteries throughout the diocese. He was anxious too that the church should gain ownership of sites wherever possible. He himself set a headline by purchasing the fee of the archbishop's palace and the presbytery. He also bought out the fee of the ground of Tuam cathedral, which had previously been vested in trustees. He then undertook the renovation of the cathedral.[108]

In one case, the building of a church led to serious divisions among the local community. This was in Castlebar where, in 1872, John MacHale had laid the foundation stone for a new church. There was no contract and it was decided to build the church as funds became available. Despite collections in the town and America, building had to be abandoned because of a shortage of funds.[109] The unroofed shell stood for almost twenty years, with no attempt being made either to demolish or complete it.

In 1891, the parish priest, Patrick Lyons, decided that a new church was a matter of urgency. He also decided, on the advice of architects, that the abandoned church would be too costly to complete and that the foundations were faulty. He proposed building on a new site. In February, an advertisement appeared in the local paper requesting the parish priest to 'take steps towards the erection of a new church.' The advertisement was signed by many of the professional and business men of the town.[110] The following week, the parish priest invited tenders for the work.[111]

At this stage, the storm erupted. A number of people publicly announced their opposition to a new church and called for completion of the abandoned building, or the MacHale church as they called it. In their view, Lyons was acting on the instructions of MacEvilly, who, they claimed, was determined that his predecessor should not have a memorial.[112] Lyons answered this criticism in a letter to the papers, saying that the MacHale church would cost £17,000 to finish. He stated further that MacHale had merely laid the foundation stone of the church and had not intended it as a memorial.[113]

The controversy raged in the columns of the local press. The *Connaught Telegraph,* centred in Castlebar, took the part of the church authorities and launched the most slanderous attacks on the opposition.[114] Lyons now wrote a second letter, denying that he was under orders from MacEvilly not to complete the MacHale church. His only instructions were 'to build a church for the people.'

'This I am doing,' the parish priest fumed, 'in spite of the impotent malice, gross misrepresentation and arrogant dictation of a few monomaniacs.'[115]

The opposing group refused to be cowed and the two factions clashed in what the *Connaught Telegraph* described as 'scenes of irreligious rascality and fierce tumult.' *The Telegraph* blamed the MacHale church supporters, referring to them as 'excited and James-inflamed.' A public meeting was convened by the leader of the opposition, Michael Quinn, at the abandoned site. The meeting was well attended. It was resolved to request the archbishop to permit Lyons to continue work on the unfinished building. It was pointed out that £7,000 had already been spent. Also, according to the architect hired by the opposing group, completion would cost £9,000. This architect also declared the foundations to be sound. 'I hope now,' said one of the spokesmen, 'that the rev. gentleman will now listen to the logic of facts, and recognise that the voice of the people is the voice of God.'[116] Lyons held a meeting at the presbytery to which representatives of both sides were invited. The parish priest had by then reduced his figure for completion to £12,500, while the protesters were still insisting on their figure of £9,000. The meeting adjourned without coming to any definite conclusions.[117]

Another meeting failed to bring any agreement. The protesting group was now demanding that a committee of the people be formed to supervise the project and that Lyons be merely an adviser. There were, the parish priest declared, 'rules and regulations' of the church forbidding such committees. Lyons pressed ahead with the collection for the new church.[118]

On a visit to Castlebar in September 1892, MacEvilly referred to 'the scandal in connection with the Parish Church.' He said that he was afraid to speak his mind fully on the subject but, in his official capacity, he would say 'fearlessly' that it was 'a disgrace to the Parish, a disgrace to the country, a disgrace to the nation and a disgrace to humanity.'[119] It was as well MacEvilly chose not to speak his mind fully.

Although resistance continued, it diminished with the passing years.[120] The new church was completed in 1901. When MacEvilly went to Castlebar for the consecration in October, he praised Lyons for his perseverance in the face 'of very great difficulties and obstacles,' and these, he concluded piously, 'will be remembered only that they may in a spirit of Christian forgiveness be buried in utter oblivion.'[121]

The affair of the Castlebar new church was an example of popular protest against a clerical decision which had been taken without proper consultation with the people. The parish priest had consulted with the professional and monied classes of the town as he wanted a guarantee of finance from them. He had alienated the less wealthy and less educated class, who proved themselves most able and most vocal. Still, in their public statements, these men were always careful to utter sentiments of respect for their parish priest and church authorities.[122]

The reverse certainly was not true. Finally, it could be said that even though now ten years dead, John MacHale was still causing problems for John MacEvilly.

One other aspect of MacEvilly's career that should be mentioned was his attempts to cure one of the greatest social ills of nineteenth century Ireland – the drinking problem. MacEvilly was a constant and consistent advocate of temperance. He was an early supporter of the Sunday closing movement in England. Thus in June 1867, he wrote to Dr Spratt, leader of that movement, pledging his support and urging that the closing time for all licensed premises run from 6 p.m. on Saturday to 6 a.m. on Monday. He also suggested possible diversions for the working classes on Sundays, 'so as to make their withdrawal from the public houses less felt.'[123]

Again in 1874, MacEvilly renewed his efforts, publicly pledging his support to such societies as the long-named Association for Stopping the Sale of Intoxicating Liquors on Sunday.[124] Later that year, he took his campaign a step further when on Sunday, 25 October, he issued a circular to be read in all churches of Galway, Kilmacduagh and Kilfenora:

> In consequence of the dreadful scandals and loss of souls (not to speak of countless temporal misfortunes) arising from Sunday drinking, we hereby prohibit all catholics under our spiritual control from selling spirituous and intoxicating liquors on Sundays . . . . Should any person, having no reverence for God or charity for his neighbour, violate this prohibition, we hereby withdraw, after this announcement, from all confessors in the diocese, faculties or jurisdiction for absolving such persons, including employers and employed.[125]

The sale of liquor on Sunday was thus made a reserved sin, a category that in most western dioceses would have included the illicit brewing of alcohol.

This stern edict, illustrating once again MacEvilly's belief in the censure as a means of obtaining obedience, seems to have achieved a degree of success. The *Galway Vindicator* declared that the bishop's order had been almost implicitly obeyed,[126] while MacEvilly himself later stated that his 'diocesan Sunday law' had been crowned with success beyond 'our most sanguine expectations.'[127]

In 1877, MacEvilly founded the Galway Temperance Society with himself as patron.[128] In his Lenten pastoral of that year, he again referred to the success of his diocesan law but he regretted that there were some who had disobeyed. He hoped before long that 'other more potent agencies than the dictates of conscience' would be brought to bear 'on those few who are amenable to no moral law or religious restraint.'[129]

Whether or not the episcopal warnings and condemnations had sobering effect we do not know. In MacEvilly's favour, he was not an empty preacher as he himself became a total abstainer. At his death, the *Freeman's Journal* said: 'His Grace was all his life a great temperance advocate and almost rivalled Fr Mathew himself in his indefatigable and successful efforts to stamp out the fatal vice of drunkenness within the limits of his diocese.'[130]

KNOCK AND THE NUN OF KENMARE

In the evening of 21 August 1879 at the village of Knock, Co. Mayo, in the diocese of Tuam, a number of people claimed to have seen visions at the gable of the local church.[131] The claim, though sensational, was not unique in the rural society of the time. Understandably, official church reaction was one of extreme caution. In October, Archbishop MacHale set up a commission to investigate the alleged apparitions.[132] Evidence was taken from fifteen people, and, in March 1880, the commission reported that in their view the testimony taken was 'trustworthy and satisfactory.'[133]

MacEvilly was then coadjutor of Tuam and had his own problems, mainly that of establishing himself in the diocese against MacHale's opposition. His first recorded reactions, given in February 1880, were suitably cautious. He told Kirby: 'So far as I am concerned, I neither assent nor dissent.'[134] By June, MacEvilly still had not made up his mind. He expressed again to Kirby his fears that the whole thing might turn out to be a 'fiasco.'[135] MacEvilly never did move from this position of neutrality. He did establish a commission of doctors to investigate reported cures,[136] but it found no evidence to support the claims of supernatural agency in any of the cures examined.[137] Officially, that was as far as MacEvilly was prepared to go, and he held his silence on the question of Knock to the end of his days.

Among those attracted to Knock was Sister Mary Francis Clare or, as she was popularly known throughout Ireland at the time, the Nun of Kenmare. She became the central figure in a strange chapter of incidents.[138] If the problems of Daly, proselytism and alcohol were the legacy of the past, MacEvilly also found himself defending the new orthodoxy and conformity against threats which were portentous. More particularly, the archbishop came up against an independent, charitable woman, interested in giving Christian witness through social action. Added to these differences, there was the cultural distance that must have existed between the polished, articulate Englishwoman and the gruff, canny, conservative Irish prelate.

After a visit to Knock, Sister Clare decided that she would like to found a convent and school there. She wrote to MacEvilly, outlining her plans to combat emigration by educating the poor girls of the district in domestic skills and crafts. MacEvilly thought her ideas 'admirable' and 'entitled to every consideration and practicable encouragement.'[139]

On 23 November 1881, MacEvilly granted Sister Clare permission, in writing, to found a convent of her order at Knock, on condition that 'ample pre-existing funds' be provided both for building and staffing the foundation.[140] This letter was published in the *Freeman's Journal* of 2 December, together with one from the Nun appealing for funds.

However, McCabe of Dublin had contacted MacEvilly about questions arising over the canonical position of Sister Clare, whether she did have permission to transfer from Kenmare to Knock and found a convent. A convoluted series of events then occurred as the Nun sought to clarify her position, through bishops Higgins of Kerry and Leahy of Dromore, to MacEvilly's satisfaction. What became clear during this was that MacEvilly no longer wanted her in Knock, although his reason was not made clear to the Nun.

In a letter to McCabe of 26 December, MacEvilly states:

> I share largely in Your Grace's fears regarding the party in question. I am now sorry I ever put a pen to paper in their regard and did not observe more caution from the beginning. I was influenced from a desire to have a good school where a school is badly needed.

In the illwill that followed, with the Nun still attempting to establish her right to be in Tuam, MacEvilly went as far as to refuse her the sacraments in the diocese and again, she claims, 'no reason was assigned.'

On the advice of some priests, Sister Clare next moved to Claremorris, and from there went ahead with her plans for Knock. She began collecting funds and opened a school where local girls were taught 'practical home industry.' She also started a kindergarten.

Matters had thus gone awry for the bishops. The Nun was not going to move away 'quietly.' While it is obvious that the bishops wished for Sister Clare's unconditional departure, what is not obvious is why they wished this so strongly and, since they were not prepared to reveal their real motives, their actions have the appearance of clumsy intrigue. It may well be that the bishops' case was not sufficient to justify taking more direct action and that Sister Clare, a forceful personality, would not be moved otherwise.

The Nun began her convent building in Knock. By the time the structure was ready for roofing, however, her once-friendly relations with the parish priest, Archdeacon Cavanagh, had deteriorated badly, and MacEvilly refused to intervene.[141] On 1 November 1883, Sister Clare left for Dublin and from there tried by various means to come to some arrangement with MacEvilly whereby she could continue her work 'in peace.' MacEvilly, for his part, prevented her from seeing McCabe and then from taking her case to Rome, but did sanction a visit to England to see Cardinal Manning. Upon Manning's advice, she wrote to MacEvilly for a canonical transfer for herself and associated sisters to Nottingham diocese and, not surprisingly, she received his prompt and gracious permission.[142] (Again, the anomalies arise; as to how, for instance, MacEvilly could have transferred jurisdiction which he was complaining that he did not have).

After the Nun's departure, there remained the problem of what to do with the

Church of the Rosary, Castlebar.

funds and property at Knock. The settlement of this became as complex and disputatious as all previous matters pertaining to Sister Clare, Knock and MacEvilly. Eventually, the Nun went to New York to collect funds for her Nottingham project.[143] While there, she established a foundation in Jersey City but was refused permission by Archbishop Corrigan, the coadjutor, to start a similar institution in New York. This led to a confrontation and, shortly after, she left her order – the Poor Clares – and later left the catholic church.[144] MacEvilly, in a letter to Kirby on 5 May 1889, refers to the 'apostacy of Mary Francis Clare.'[145]

Undoubtedly, the Nun of Kenmare was an able, articulate woman possessed of a strong, direct personality. Perhaps in some respects she was a woman born out of time; possibly her political and social opinions and attitudes were an embarrassment to men of conservative attitudes like MacEvilly and McCabe; or even, as MacEvilly seems to imply, that she was unreliable and given to visions and voices. At no point was any one of the Nun's accusers prepared to state exactly why it was they wished to be rid of her. Whatever the reason, one thing that does emerge clearly is that the Nun of Kenmare was treated very shabbily by her ecclesiastical superiors.

From the evidence she presents, one can sympathize with the Nun when she states in her book: 'It is precisely this unfortunate policy of condemning people without allowing them any chance of being heard, of knowing who are their accusers, which brings such discredit on the Roman church.'[146]

Chapter 5

The Education Question

IF THE EDUCATION question became one of the foremost political issues of the latter half of the nineteenth century, this was due in no small way to the importance attached to it by the Irish catholic hierarchy in general and by their leader, Paul Cullen, in particular. That MacEvilly gave the question the same priority as his master and friend is shown by such pronouncements as 'There is no other question which so intimately affects the faith of today as the question of education';[1] and later when he wrote that he knew of 'no other question which is so peculiarly *our* question, as nothing else so directly affects the souls of men and the salvation of generations yet unborn.'[2]

Basically, the bishops were demanding a catholic education for catholic children and objecting to a mixed system whereby children of all religious denominations attended the same schools, receiving only their religious instruction separately. Their demands referred to all three levels of education, and so the three essential points of episcopal policy were: the correction of the National system, the setting up of catholic intermediate schools, and the granting of a charter for the catholic university.[3]

PRIMARY EDUCATION

In 1858, the Report of the Royal Commission on Intermediate Education recommended the setting up of a non-denominational system of intermediate education, and this report galvanised the bishops into action. The government proposals were quickly dropped. This initial success prompted the bishops to a more thorough examination of education in all its branches, and a comprehensive policy was forged during 1859 from a number of contributing events and publications.[4]

The bishops met in Dublin on 8 August 1859 for their first wide-ranging discussion. Regarding National education, two points of view arose. One, urged by Archbishop John MacHale, was to condemn the National system *in toto* and withdraw all children from the schools. The other, represented by Leahy of Cashel, was to bear with the system while pressing for a denominational system. It was the latter view that found favour with most,[5] MacEvilly included. MacHale was instructed to draw up a memorial for presentation to the lord lieutenant, Lord Carlisle, while the resolutions of the meeting became a joint pastoral to the Irish people,[6] and called for their support.

In November, the bishops had a reply from chief secretary Edward Cardwell. The principle of mixed education was upheld but the government was prepared to consider changes within this framework.[7] Cullen prepared another memorial for Cardwell, forwarded in March 1860 and signed by all the bishops except MacHale.[8] To boost it further, the memorial was also signed by nineteen M.P.s.[9] 'I cheerfully adopt every word of it,' was MacEvilly's comment.[10]

In August and again December, Cardwell offered further changes,[11] all of which the bishops considered insufficient. In April 1861, they repeated their demand for a denominational system.[12] Again nothing came of it.

When Cullen launched his National Association in 1865, it included, along with the questions of the land and church disestablishment, the education question. In December of that year, the four archbishops went to London for an interview with Sir George Grey, the then home secretary, and subsequently, in January 1866, once more presented memorials on education.[13,14] Grey replied promptly to that on university education but delayed his reply to the memorial on primary education until May.[15] He concluded that state support given to a denominational system would deprive the country of the advantages of the existing system, which had proved successful. MacEvilly remarked sarcastically that Grey did not seem to realise that the people of Ireland were catholic when he spoke of the advantages they would forfeit by the introduction of the denominational system, and he wondered by what standard they had measured the boasted success of the National system, as the people had no alternative.

In August of 1867, a royal commission was appointed to inquire into primary education in Ireland, under the chairmanship of Lord Powis.[16] The bishops co-operated, with Cullen and others giving evidence.[17]

The commission's report appeared in June 1870. In the religious area, the most controversial recommendation was that which allowed one catholic and one protestant school in districts where there were two or more schools. In this way some National schools would become denominational.[18] Gladstone intended to introduce legislation based on the Powis report but, owing to the strong anti-catholic feeling prevailing in England in 1871, this was not possible.[19]

Once again, meetings and petitions to parliament were organised countrywide to support catholic demands. Nevertheless, by February 1873 Gladstone had decided there was nothing more he could do regarding the National system and that he would 'leave each bishop free to take his own course on his own responsibility.'[20] In other words, he was prepared to let matters of primary education proceed exactly as they had been proceeding.

As the years passed, the bishops had less to say about the disadvantages of the National system. In 1888, MacEvilly, now archbishop of Tuam, delivered a speech in Castlebar in which he outlined the episcopal view. The bishops would tolerate the National system until in time a denominational system was established. In the diocese of Tuam, MacEvilly stated, the system was denominational in practice. Why then, he asked, is the principle not granted? Children of other denominations would be accepted in their schools and their faith would not be tampered with. Catholics and protestants were all 'children of the same soil' who should labour together for the common good. 'But,' the archbishop was careful to distinguish, 'when the distinctive interests of religion are concerned, there can be no compromise, no attempt to blend together elements utterly incompatible.' Then, warming to his theme, he added, 'There can be no association of light with darkness – of Christ with Belial.'[21]

The bishops were content with making the occasional noises about the necessity of establishing the principle, while at the same time being careful not to create too much of a scene lest they lose anything of what had been gained.

In February 1892 a Conservative government, pursuing a policy of conciliation in Ireland, introduced the National Education (Ireland) Bill which was designed to end the payment of school fees and to increase teachers' salaries. The Bill also sought to establish compulsory education in the bigger towns and cities. MacEvilly reported that the bishops were very uncomfortable over the question of compulsory education and that he himself expected 'no good but mischief in the long run' to come from it.[22] Despite this and other opposition,[23,24] the Bill was pushed through parliament and became law on 27 June. At least it did satisfy the teachers, whose lot it improved considerably.[25]

From the early 1870s, guided by their new organiation, the I.N.T.O., the National teachers had begun to agitate for increased pay and other benefits.[26] The situation was remedied to some extent in 1875 when the government raised salaries, while halving its contribution towards results' fees and proposing that the other half come from local rates. This made the bishops suspicious that the managerial system was under attack as such a proposal could lead to the transfer of management from the local pastors to school boards.[27]

Grievances such as security of tenure also touched on the managerial system. This was remedied partly by the 'Maynooth Resolution' of 1894, but some teachers began demanding a greater say in the running of schools. MacEvilly warned against what he called 'the syren voice of agitators' in an address to teachers in October 1896. He told them the agitation was inspired by Masonic and 'other sinister influences' and intended to deprive the priests of the managership of the schools. If such an event occurred, he declared, the bishops were prepared to spurn the entire system, 'fling it from them as a noxious thing,' no matter what sacrifices that course might involve. Those teachers would then be without schools or scholars, as the bishops would not allow young children to fall into the hands of a 'baneful secularism.' The National system was a bad system, he repeated, but by the careful vigilance of the clergy, the good could be extracted from it and the children safeguarded from its evil tendencies. 'If that guiding influence of the clergy were removed,' he concluded, 'then the system could no longer be tolerated.'[28] The speech shows that not only did MacEvilly and the bishops now see the system as denominational but as their own creation and even possession. Reaction, then, to any threat to ecclesiastical control was swift and angry.

At their June meeting in Maynooth in 1897, the bishops amended the 1984 resolution to protect teachers from summary dismissal, which had become a contentious issue. At the same time, the bishops were angry and delivered a warning: 'Efficiency in our schools comes before comfort for the teachers.'[29] The amended resolution was to be a final settlement of the question of tenure. The I.N.T.O. moved hastily to reassure the bishops, thanking them for the satisfactory settlement.[30]

The Parnell split, which had such a disastrous effect on Irish society, also served to increase tensions between priests and teachers.[31] In a public speech in October, MacEvilly stressed the importance of education, which, he said, could mean that the Irish would no longer be the 'hewers of wood and drawers of water' in other countries. He took the opportunity to launch another attack on 'agitators who claimed independence for the teachers from bishops and priests' and that he equated with claiming independence from God. What was strange to hear was MacEvilly paying public tribute to his 'great predecessor' John MacHale for condemning the National system. But MacEvilly continued that now that the National system had become practically denominational, thanks to the priests, he could support it. He would like to see the teachers get twice their present salary but they could not sever themselves from the guidance of the church.[32]

One of MacEvilly's very last public addresses was on education. Once more he made the same points and added that unfortunately even a good education did not assure a catholic a worthwhile post, as the top positions in the country were filled by protestants.[33]

In all such speeches, MacEvilly was simply acknowledging the fact that at primary level the catholic church had succeeded in winning a system which they could control. All that remained to make the victory complete was the formal recognition of the denominational principle.

SECONDARY EDUCATION

The story of intermediate education in nineteenth century Ireland is very much the story of the private school, and, as the major battles took place in the fields of primary and university education, intermediate education was left very much to fend for itself.

Following on the establishment of the National system in 1831, it was proposed that Model schools be set up.[34] The Model schools were so called because, in addition to training national teachers, they were to serve as examples for other schools in the area.[35] The first district Model school was opened in 1848 and eventually another twenty-four were added.[36] Unlike the National schools, the Model schools were to be built entirely at government expense and there was to be no local manager. The scheme was not opposed at first by the catholic hierarchy, but after Paul Cullen condemned a proposed new Model school at Drogheda in 1851,[37] his lead was followed by the rest of the bishops.

The Model school was well established in Galway when MacEvilly arrived in 1857 as bishop, and at that time had on its rolls over two hundred catholic students.[38] This challenge MacEvilly was prepared to meet. He enlisted the Brothers of St. Patrick to open a new school for boys and the Sisters of Mercy to open one for girls.[39] On 3 January 1863, MacEvilly had a statement read in all the churches informing the people of the start of these schools 'for the middle class of society,' and urging parents to withdraw their children from the Model school.

One year later, MacEvilly took his campaign against the Model school another step further by making attendance there a reserved sin.[40] His intention, of course, was to clear the school of the few remaining catholic pupils.

MacEvilly had indeed won the battle in Galway. The commissioners' report of 1867 concedes that 'the hostility of the Roman Catholic clergy to this school has in no way diminished: – that every means is employed to force the Roman Catholic pupils to withdraw from it, and that to this cause alone we are to ascribe the great reduction in the attendance which has taken place of late years.'[41]

The report of the Powis commission which appeared in June 1870 recognised that the Model schools were a failure and recommended that they be discontinued gradually. Established in their place were training schools for teachers, controlled by religious bodies and committees under certain conditions.[42] In this much at least, the bishop of Galway had registered a clear and decisive victory. His own attempt to establish a training school was a failure, however.

1878 was an important year in intermediate education. A new system was created by the Intermediate Education Act, to be administered by seven unpaid commissioners and endowed with the interest on one million pounds, which had been appropriated from the funds of the late established church. The commissioners, who did not at all have the same powers as their counterparts on the National Board, were confined to acting as an examining body and paying premiums to schools on the basis of examination results. The new system also gave funds to denominational schools, with a conscience clause to protect the religious beliefs of all pupils.[43] The catholics were quick to take advantage of the new provisions and the number of catholic schools rose remarkably from 24,693 in 1881 to 43,137 in 1911.[44]

The Act's greatest shortcoming was that it created a system which became increasingly competitive and examination-centred. MacEvilly referred to this in a speech at Westport in 1885: 'The whole system as regards examination tests is absurd. How unfair to subject young lads in their teens to such a trying, useless ordeal,' and he called on the examiners to put a stop to 'such pendantry.'[45]

While the catholic bishops again did not achieve all that they desired in the matter of intermediate education, they were successful in preventing the government from developing a state system. MacEvilly's intervention in Galway had been crucial in that it had proved a valuable pilot case for the bishops and shown that they held a trump card in their influence with the people. While some of MacEvilly's measures might be construed as spiritual blackmail, undoubtedly he felt that, in this case, the end justified the action.

THE UNIVERSITY QUESTION

For two centuries and a half, there was but one institution in Ireland providing university education and that was Trinity College. In its early years, the College had many catholic students and was supported by the catholic Anglo-Irish gentry. This was changed by the statutes of Charles I in 1637, obliging all students to attend divine service and receive communion according to the Anglican rite. Catholics, therefore, had a particular grievance in the matter of university education and the injustice was highlighted after Catholic Emancipation had been won in 1829. A more vocal and vigorous catholic representation in parliament focussed attention on the university question. A solution was attempted by Sir Robert Peel in 1845 with the establishment of the Queen's Colleges. The Colleges, which were sited at Belfast, Cork and Galway, were strictly non-denominational. They met with strong catholic opposition. They were condemned by the Holy See and that condemnation was reaffirmed by the Irish catholic hierarchy at the Synod of Thurles in 1850. No bishop was to co-operate in the administration of these 'godless colleges,' as they became known to catholics; the clergy were forbidden to take any office in them; and the laity were ordered to 'repudiate and shun' them because of the dangers to faith and morals.[46]

The catholic bishops were left with no alternative but to provide an institution of their own. To this end, the Catholic University project was launched, and, after some delay and despite the opposition of MacHale, the University finally opened in November 1854, with John Henry Newman as its first rector.[47] Newman's unhappy tenure of office lasted for three years[48] and a successor was not found until April 1861, when Dr Bartholomew Woodlock was appointed.[49]

From the beginning, however, the Catholic University was unable to compete fairly with the Queen's Colleges as it lacked the royal charter of incorporation.[50] The fight for the charter began in March 1859, when a deputation of Irish M.P.s visited Disraeli. He promised to raise the matter in cabinet; however, the government fell.[51]

In their August 1859 pastoral, as part of their overall statements on education, the bishops declared that more funds for the Catholic University would place it in a stronger position to demand a charter.[52] The pastoral address was issued following the bishops' meeting in October.[53] Early in 1860, MacEvilly wrote to Kirby to say that because of the many collections for religious institutions in the town, he was obliged to postpone the collection for the Catholic University.[54] When the collection did take place, it amounted only to a disappointing £70 for the entire diocese.[55]

In 1861, MacEvilly reported an 'immense increase' in the number of Catholics attending the Galway Queen's College. 'To be denouncing the Queen's College,' he declared, 'without some endeavour to procure a substitute is to my mind a mark of insincerity and real practical folly, only calculated to create resistance to authority.'[56] Part of the problem certainly was the lack of unanimity among the bishops themselves, caused largely by MacHale's refusal to co-operate – and this stemming from his antipathy to Cullen. Cullen complained that in Connacht only Dr Gillooly and Dr MacEvilly collected for the Catholic University.[57] So, the Catholic University could not give legally valid degrees, it was short of funds, opposed by MacHale and neglected by students.

At their meeting in Dublin in December 1865, the bishops decided to press again for the grant of a charter and endowment for the Catholic University. A memorial containing a petition was forwarded to Sir George Grey, along with the memorial on the National system of education.[58] Grey replied on 30 January 1866. The government were prepared to grant a charter to the Catholic University but not on the lines proposed by the bishops.[59]

MacEvilly suggested that perhaps the wisest course now for the bishops, considering the few M.P.s who were willing to support them, was to make the best terms possible under the circumstances, without compromising principle or giving up their claims – which might later be achieved; but MacEvilly assured Cullen that he would join in any measure his Grace would suggest.[60]

Cullen objected to the government proposals on two grounds: the manner of appointing the professors, and the exclusion of the bishops from all control over the Catholic University.[61]

In November 1866, MacEvilly had a communication from Michael Morris, M.P. for Galway city and a supporter of the Tory administration, on the subject of the university charter. Morris was of the opinion that the Conservative government would grant a distinct charter, insisting principally on the admission of catholic laymen to the senate of the university. MacEvilly replied that he would not speak for all the bishops but that if Morris could ascertain Cullen's views on the subject, he would then have the views of the Irish hierarchy.[62]

Morris wrote again, saying that he was anxious to know whether the bishops would prefer the supplemental charter by which a degree could be obtained from the Queen's Colleges university, or a 'power given the Catholic University itself to confer degrees.' Morris had gathered that Cullen was in favour of a distinct charter for the Catholic University. He believed there were legal difficulties in the granting of a supplemental charter against the will of the convention of the Queen's Colleges, but he was sure that unless the present government took it up, the question would not be settled for many years. Morris felt that he did not know Cullen sufficiently to approach him directly and asked MacEvilly 'as a matter entirely between ourselves' to find out Cullen's views before he began to press the government.[63]

Without doubt, a man of MacEvilly's shrewdness must have been asking himself what Morris was working at. His reply was framed in the finest MacEvilly caution. From all he could learn, he told Morris, the bishops would accept a charter for the Catholic University requiring among its conditions that one half of the governing body be laymen. This very condition, however, opened up such a wide field of discussion, MacEvilly pointed out, that probably an entire session would pass before anything could be done, 'leaving matters in a more unsatisfactory state than they are in at present.' He also made the point that a charter without endowment was useless. MacEvilly enclosed a document listing the requirements of the bishops.[64]

It was Morris's move. 'I think I collect from your letter,' he ventured, 'that the Bishops and Cardinal attach considerable importance to the supplemental charter.' He wished assurance in this, as the opposite view had been suggested to him.[65] MacEvilly asked Cullen what answer he should make to Morris 'in a general way.' MacEvilly thought that the 'rabid opposition' offered to the supplemental charter showed there was something good in it. 'I know the Queen's College people here are very nervous about it,' he remarked.[66]

In a postscript to a letter he wrote MacEvilly the following month, Cullen stated: 'I suppose all we have to do in regard to the supplemental charter is to let it take its chance until we see how it will work – but at the same time to call for Catholic education and a Catholic University.'[67] It was probably as far as the cardinal was prepared to commit himself on the subject at that time and in that manner.

MacEvilly then wrote to Morris saying that he considered the supplemental charter a step in the right direction, 'although very far remote from what we had a right to expect.' Indeed, MacEvilly did not expect anything from the Tories and only gave the information so that they could not plead ignorance later. 'I am afraid,' he concluded sadly, 'it is stones not bread, serpents and not fishes this truly paternal government have in store for us.'[68] The fate of the supplemental charter was finally decided in the courts. The charter was challenged by the Queen's Colleges and declared void on a legal technicality,[69] as Morris had said could happen.

When disestablishment had been successfully accomplished in 1871 and an attempt had been made at solving the land problem, Gladstone was ready to tackle the third of the three great questions, that of education, and university education in particular. In February 1873, he introduced a bill proposing that there be one university in Ireland, the University of Dublin, which would become an Irish national university with affiliated colleges, including the Catholic University in Dublin. There was also good news for MacEvilly as the Galway Queen's College was to be suppressed.[70]

The bishops opposed the bill on the grounds that no endowment was granted to any catholic institution and also that the new university would be secularist in character.[71] The bill was defeated by three votes and led to the fall of Gladstone's government.[72]

MacEvilly was angry with Sir Rowland Blennerhassett, member for Galway city, who had voted for the bill 'without any reference to his constituents.' MacEvilly observed as well that Lord St. Lawrence, former member for Galway, whose election was due in no small way to MacEvilly's favour, had presented a petition in favour of Galway Queen's College. 'There is no trusting politicians,' remarked MacEvilly. 'Some leading government Irish members are greatly blamed for this shocking university bill.' He concluded piously, 'I suppose almighty God wishes once more to try our people, and he knows what is best.'[73]

As the 1870s wore on and MacEvilly's disillusionment with the Liberal party grew, he began to look more and more to an independent Irish party to achieve reforms in education. Although he did not really trust Isaac Butt's Home Rule party, by 1877 certainly MacEvilly was convinced that any chance of a favourable education bill was through a combined Irish party. For that reason he felt it necessary to subsidise Butt, 'who in his public capacity seems to be the chief link to keep them together.' Some measure in education would have to be achieved soon, MacEvilly thought, as the people were 'passing fast away to other condemned institutions.' The Queen's Colleges, he reported, were becoming worse every day and hardly one out of a hundred left them 'without having his faith seriously undermined.'[74]

Butt did bring in a university bill in 1877, which proposed putting the Catholic University on equal footing with Trinity College within Dublin University. It was defeated by a large majority on the second reading.[75]

1878 saw the passing of the Intermediate Education Act, and also renewed activity regarding the university question. In a letter to a public meeting held in the Rotunda on 26 April, MacEvilly put forward what had become the favourite and perhaps strongest argument in favour of a system of denominational education, namely, that there was such a state endowed system in England, and to deny it to Ireland on religious grounds was simply persecution. Persecution was twofold, MacEvilly argued, 'positive in the infliction of unjust punishment and negative in the arbitrary denial of rights.'[76]

In February 1879, the Irish bishops met to protest the fact that the university question had been ignored in the measures announced in the coming session of parliament.[77] 'We have been treated scandalously by the government regarding the University education,' MacEvilly complained. 'Their organs held out every hope to the last moment and then dashed them to the ground. Did any country ever suffer so much for the faith and attachment to the See of Peter?'[78] MacEvilly returned to the topic again in his Lenten pastoral of that year, describing the university issue as the leading question. 'If we fail in carrying it,' he declared, 'the blame is to be laid at our doors.' He called on the Irish representatives to unite, and he ended by stating: 'The history of revolutions is but the record of the practical development of godless education in every age.'[79]

There was, however, a growing feeling that the government was anxious to find some solution to the university question. For this reason, a private member's bill was introduced by the O'Connor Don, M.P. for Roscommon. It was modelled on the Intermediate Act and proposed setting up a new university, St. Patrick's, with power to affiliate colleges, and endowed by the same device of results' fees.[80]

The O'Connor Don's bill, although meeting with strong opposition, was successful in that, on 25 June, the government announced the introduction of the new University Education (Ireland) Bill. This proposed the setting up of the Royal University of Ireland, as a purely examining body. It provided for twenty four fellowships, to be equally divided between catholics and protestants. These were to be examiners in the university and professors in teaching institutions, approved by the senate.[81]

The bishops and the government entered into negotiations which dragged on for two years. At the time the Senate of the Royal University finally was to vote on the distribution of the fellowships, on 12 April 1882, the archbishop of Dublin, Edward McCabe, had to travel to Rome to be raised to the cardinalate. The bishops' March meeting was being held despite the archbishop's absence. Before he left, McCabe announced that he would be satisfied with twelve fellowships as a fair catholic share. The meeting did not carry out his wishes, however, as, under the influence of Croke and Nulty, the bishops decided to ask for two-thirds of the fellowships, along with conditions.[82] McCabe and his educational adviser,

Most Rev. Dr MacEvilly

Monsignor Neville, rector of the Catholic University, were busy at Rome, and the result was a letter from Cardinal Simeoni, prefect of Propaganda, quashing the resolutions of the bishops.[83] This letter came at the most sensitive time. The Land War was raging in the country, the bishops were divided, and the people were highly suspicious of English activity at Rome.

Further disappointment followed. The Senate of the Royal University granted the Catholic Colleges only nine fellowships, while the Queen's Colleges were given twelve. As well as that, five of the nine catholic fellowships went to English and Scottish converts.[84]

In the following years, the university question was pushed well into the background by the land troubles and the Parnell crisis of 1890-91. There were occasional noises from the bishops, as in June 1889, when they pressed for a solution. They did not name a particular system, contenting themselves with a call for an end to inequality in education.[85] Again there was no response and the question lay dormant until 1895, and the Conservative return to power. In October 1895 and October 1896, the bishops repeated their 1889 demands, emphasising that they were not committed to any one principle of settlement. A petition was presented to Lord Salisbury, the prime minister, signed by influential catholic laymen and a dozen protestant Irish M.P.s.[86]

1897 brought renewed government interest in the university question. At their June meeting the bishops clarified their position. In general, they had no objection to the opening up of the degrees, honours and emoluments of the university to all comers, and they were not seeking a preponderance or even equality in the number of ecclesiastics on the governing board. This meant that the bishops were now willing to accept a university which would be *de facto* catholic.[87] MacEvilly, however, was complaining about the lack of interest on the part of the laity. 'Even those who ought to be most zealous seem indifferent.'[88]

In an effort to arouse popular support for a catholic university, a public meeting was held at Tuam on 28 August 1898. Emphasis was on lay participation, the meeting being called by laymen and the chair being taken by a layman, John Nolan. The meeting was addressed by MacEvilly, who first of all told his audience that he would speak at greater length were it not that it was a meeting to promote the interests of the catholic laity of the country. He then went on to speak at length, beginning with the 'clumsy calumny' that the catholic university agitation was the work of the bishops and that the laity were perfectly content with the existing state of things. What they as catholics wanted to have understood was that they had the right at least to have equality in all the higher educational advantages. If they had a catholic university, as catholic as Trinity was protestant, then MacEvilly would not say a word against Trinity, which had 'furnished the ablest men and patriots to Ireland.'[89]

The bishops returned to the question in 1900 once more and, from their meeting on 20 June, issued a statement calling on catholics to vote for those pledged to a catholic university in the coming election.[90] The Tories were returned, and MacEvilly for one was not expecting too much from them. 'In the present temper of England they only want an opportunity of showing their contempt for catholicity.'[91]

MacEvilly's last reference to the university question was in his Lenten pastoral of 1901, and the tone was very much that of a tired and rather disillusioned old man. The bishops had been pressing their case for half a century; the most reasonable and logical arguments had been put forward and yet 'such is the blind, unreasoning bigotry of certain influential parties, that out of sheer hatred of the catholic religion, which they understand not, our just claims are always unmeaningly opposed.' They were told every day that catholics were unfit for certain offices in the state for want of university training and yet that training was 'capriciously' withheld. Any catholic who would show indifference in this matter could hardly be regarded as a genuine catholic, MacEvilly asserted; 'His patriotism, however specious, is a mere sham.'[92] At John MacEvilly's death in 1902, the question was still unanswered.

In general, MacEvilly appeared much more at ease in the politics of education than in any other area. It was his utter conviction that education was the special province of the bishops. He saw it as their duty and obligation to strive for the achievement of catholic education for catholic people. As well, he had the security of knowing that, in this pursuit, he had the support of the entire catholic community and so could proceed without fears of causing divisions. While in his enunciation of doctrine MacEvilly was inflexible, in practice he was open to suggestion. Unlike MacHale, who obstinately refused to have anything to do with state education, MacEvilly was prepared to explore all avenues, to consider alternatives, to seek the best possible terms.

The question arises as to why MacEvilly did not impose spiritual sanctions on catholics attending the Queen's College as he did so readily in the case of the Model school. There was, of course, no alternative to the Queen's College and the catholics attended because they were determined to have higher education, episcopal condemnations notwithstanding. MacEvilly and the bishops were no doubt reluctant to impose ecclesiastical censures which might be challenged or ignored. Right here is evidence of an informed and independent catholic laity before the era of the Land League and Parnell, which, in present day writing, is generally regarded as the beginning of modernisation.

Chapter 6

Tenant Right and the Tenant League

JOHN MACEVILLY WAS of the farming class in west Mayo. His father was a tenant farmer, probably working a small holding of land. The land itself could have been of no better than fair quality. John MacEvilly, therefore, had first hand knowledge of the problems of the tenant farmer. He would have witnessed the hardships and poverty of such an existence – at all times a battle to survive. An early familiarity with the basic curse of tenantry, the lack of security and protection in law, would have impressed on MacEvilly's mind the absolute dependence of the tenant on the person of the landlord. He must also have seen the anxiety that each year's rent brought, and the frustration of the farmer whose hard work was rewarded often with an increase in rent. As might then be expected, MacEvilly later had much to say about tenant problems, and yet, as evidence of how little progress was being made, his speeches are almost monotonous in their repetition of these basic demands – a fair rent, security of tenure, compensation for improvements carried out on holdings, and, in later years, appeals for redistribution.

There was a growing demand for tenant right which, fed by the horrors of the Great Famine, saw a spawning of tenant protection societies throughout the country in the late 1840s and early 1850s.[1] On 9 June 1850, a meeting was held in the Town-house of Tuam for the purpose of forming a Tenant Protection Society and to make arrangements to co-operate with the forthcoming national conference, to be held on 6 August at the Royal Exchange, Dublin. The requisition notice for the meeting bore the signatures of John MacHale, archbishop of Tuam, and John MacEvilly, then a professor at St. Jarlath's College.[2] This tenant association and others like it were merged in the Tenant League resulting from the conference.[3] As well as seeking redress of tenant grievances – the famous three Fs : fair rent, fixity of tenure and free sale – the League also gave a new lease of life to the principle of independent opposition in parliament.

From the beginning, the League had the backing of MacHale and other members of the hierarchy who had formerly supported O'Connell's Repeal Association.[4] The triumph of the capture of forty-eight seats in the 1852 general election was short-lived, following the defection of Sadleir and Keogh who, contrary to the pledge they had taken, accepted positions in the new Whig administration. The movement was split and the bishops too were divided in their loyalties. MacHale immediately condemned the action of the 'pledge-breakers' as 'an undoubted breach of morality.'[5] Cullen chose to remain silent, but in the situation it was a most significant silence. MacEvilly, at this point still loyal to his archbishop and the cause of the Tenant League, was found among the ranks of the 'Carbonari curates,' as clerical supports of the League had been christened by Cullen.

Early in 1854, a Tenant League banquet was held in Tuam for the purpose of drumming up support for the ailing Independent party. The guests included G.H. Moore, Frederick Lucas, Dr Gray and MacHale. MacEvilly, now president of St. Jarlath's College, was one of the principal speakers. Although the main burden of his speech was concerned with clerical involvement in politics, MacEvilly also made reference to tenant rights, in terms which he was to repeat over and over again throughout his career. His plea was for a 'a fair and equitable tenant right measure, consulting alike for the true and permanent interests of landlord and tenant.' MacEvilly declared, 'People of Ireland, you are but half emancipated,' adding that if given the choice, he himself would opt for a tenant right bill before emancipation. 'Only give the people a security that they are not doomed to be outcasts in the land of their birth,' said MacEvilly, and they would not be forced to emigrate. In his favourite scriptural allusion relating to the land, he called for 'the redress of a crime crying to heaven for vengeance – the crime by which the labouring poor have been deprived of the just wages of the sweat of their brow.'[6] MacEvilly's speech, which was praised equally by Lucas and Gavan Duffy,[7] was his first major public statement on the land question. It was a topic to which he would return many times.

The Independent party sought to maintain support in the west by holding demonstrations and banquets. In February 1855, MacEvilly attended a demonstration of support for tenant rights at Castlebar[8] and, two years later, he attended a grand banquet in honour of G. H. Moore, the member for Mayo and prominent figure in the Independent party.[9] How genuine MacEvilly's support was at that stage is questionable, as he was by then on very friendly terms with Cullen and certainly would not have backed Moore, the friend of MacHale. Meetings such as those at Castlebar could not save the movement, which had never recovered from the disastrous split. The division which it had brought about in the ranks of its clerical supporters shows, as Oliver MacDonagh rightly points out, that politically the bishops were acting quite independently, with each dictating policy in his own territory.[10] It was a freedom that MacEvilly too was to enjoy when he went to Galway as bishop in 1857.

The passing of the Tenant League meant the temporary eclipse of the land question as a predominant political issue. Nevertheless, it still remained an essential ingredient of any programme seeking popular support; and was included in the three-point programme of the National Association launched by Cullen in 1864. In the list of episcopal priorities, however, it was a poor third behind disestablishment and education, for Cullen considered the land question a potentially divisive issue. Therefore, as regards land reform, the Association was specifically pledged to seek compensation for improvements, a safe demand as this was a reform long overdue and recognised by all.[11]

The aims of the National Association were given an airing at election times particularly. Thus, in 1865, MacEvilly devoted his Lenten pastoral to urging support for the Association. He pointed out that the first aim of the new movement was to achieve a legal security for the tenant, that to deprive the tenant of compensation for improvements in his holding was 'a gross violation of the laws of God and nature.' He deplored the fact that the civil law continued to protect 'such enormities.'[12] Again in his Lenten pastoral of 1867, MacEvilly returned to the tenant problems. Still, disestablishment was given top billing in the Liberal programme for the 1868 election.

The Liberals were victorious and disestablishment was duly accomplished. Solving the land question was altogether a different and much more thorny undertaking. Pressure was maintained from Ireland with the holding of mass meetings in favour of tenant right. In a letter to such a meeting at Gort, Co. Galway, MacEvilly declared the country would never know peace or prosperity until the just rights of the landlord and tenant were legally secured, and the basis of just legislation must be security of tenure and fair rents.[13] MacEvilly's reference to the rights of the landlords as well as the tenants was an ever present feature of his land speeches. Causes such as education and disestablishment were sure of universal support from catholics but the land could place class against class; hence MacEvilly's consistently cautious approach.

The clergy of Galway issued a series of resolutions, declaring their detestation of the confiscation of the landlords' proprietary rights, and their equal detestation of the confiscation by the landlords of the tenants' capital and the fruits of their labour.[14] So, as the *Freeman's Journal* pointed out, they denounced in the same breath 'the revolutionary who dreams of confiscation and the landlord who practices it daily under the protection of the law.'[15] These resolutions bore the stamp of MacEvilly's conservative attitude to the land question. Until the last years of his life, MacEvilly's condemnations remained double-edged.

The Land Act which Gladstone delivered in 1870 did at least grant official recognition to the problems of the land system and it did make a start towards a solution. That said, however, this woefully complicated piece of legislation did little to benefit the small farmers.[16] Tenants evicted for reasons other than the non-payment of rent were entitled to compensation. Since most evictions, and particularly those in the west of Ireland, occurred for the very reason of non-payment of rent, the Act made no difference to the great body of the tenants with whom John MacEvilly was concerned.

In the Galway by-election of 1872, the land question was very much to the fore. Captain Nolan, a catholic landlord, was cast in the role of tenants' champion against the landlords' candidate, Le Poer Trench.[17] In MacEvilly's eyes, therefore, Nolan was dividing the catholic community and only received MacEvilly's support when the landlords made the charge of priestly interference. Letters from MacEvilly, read at all the important meetings, dealt more with the disappointment he experienced from the action of the landlords than with the tenant grievances. All his life, he said, he had worked for harmony between tenant and landlord, and he warned the landlords of the consequences if the 'bonds of religious restraint should be loosed.'[18] He did voice the hope that the pressing question of tenant right would be finally and firmly settled by the incoming government.[19]

For the time being, however, the land question lost its urgency as the demand for home rule took the centre of the stage. It was not until changed times brought a new impetus that the land question came once more to the fore.

THE LAND LEAGUE

When the era of relative prosperity which Ireland had known came to an end in the 1870s, and when the late 1870s brought widespread distress, the land question took on a new urgency. This was particularly true in the west of Ireland where the disastrous harvests of 1877 and '79, combined with the slump in Britain, meant that famine was once more in prospect for the small farmers. The cause of the tenants could no longer be pursued in a leisurely fashion and in refined tones. Out of the crisis the Land League was born, an Irish agrarian movement which was urgent and strident, forceful and forthright in its demands, and a movement which had the mass support of the tenants.

This new Land League, with its aggressive attitudes and direct style, immediately presented bishops like MacEvilly with a problem. Despite his professed sympathy for the plight of the tenants, he set himself against the League from the start. How was it that MacEvilly should be found on the other side?

The answer is two-fold. Like his mentor Cullen, MacEvilly was much happier when calling for reforms in areas where he could count on widespread catholic support, landlord and tenant, rich and poor alike, and the League pledged itself to the cause of the tenants exclusively. Another reason for MacEvilly's hostility was the type of agitation chosen by the Land League. He was committed to achieving reforms by means which were strictly within the compass of the law. This attitude he had inherited again from Cullen, as he had Cullen's distaste for Fenianism. From the start, MacEvilly was acutely conscious of the Fenian connection. He allowed no distinction between the outrages practised by secret societies and the more legitimate forms of agitation encouraged by the Land League.

It must be remembered too that Paul Cullen had died in October 1878, and MacEvilly must have sorely missed the advice of his trusted counsellor. Cullen's successor, Edward McCabe, had been a classmate of MacEvilly at Maynooth and was a man obviously chosen to continue Cullen's policies in Ireland. McCabe, however, had not the will of Cullen and the bishops adopted varying attitudes toward the new movement, ranging from the warm support of Croke of Cashel to the outright hostility of others.

On 8 June 1879, Parnell took the Land League platform at Westport. Ten days after that meeting, the *Galway Vindicator* published a statement from MacEvilly and the clergy of Galway. The statement pointed out that because of the depression in trade, the succession of bad harvests, poor prices for stock and agricultural produce, the tenants were unable to pay rents fixed in more prosperous times. The landlords of the diocese were called on to follow the example of landlords in other parts of the United Kingdom by granting a reduction in rents. This, the clergy claimed, would 'prevent all illegal combinations against the rights of property, and foster the good relations which should exist between landlord and tenant.'[20] MacEvilly hoped by this appeal to 'the sense of justice' of the landlords to keep the land question in its old framework of moderate politics, but the Land League had changed the terms of reference irrevocably.

When a public meeting to highlight the distress in the county was being arranged for Galway in October, MacEvilly was invited to attend a preliminary meeting of the organising committee. He replied that the meeting would do 'positive mischief' unless it confined itself to two leading points. Firstly, MacEvilly proposed 'a respectful representation to landlords' for a reduction in rents. 'If landlords are menaced,' he declared, 'the worst possible way is adopted for gaining a request.' Secondly, there should be 'a clean, strong, respectful representation to government as to the necessity of saving the lives of our people now in peril . . . . This being a Galway meeting,' he continued, 'having solely in view local charitable objects, there are . . . plenty of eloquent men to propose and speak to resolutions – I would consider it an insult to Galway to introduce outsiders, among whom our parliamentary representatives could not, of course, be reckoned.'[21]

This reply was the nearest MacEvilly had yet come to a public statement of his opinions of the Land League and its leader. *The Nation* picked up MacEvilly's reference to 'outsiders,' regretting that any action ruling out Parnell should be contemplated in Galway, 'and especially that it should have been suggested by a prelate so distinguished and so highly respected as the Most Rev. Dr MacEvilly.'[22] Reporting later on the Galway meeting, *The Nation* was pleased to record the presence of 'the most notable outsider of them all, Mr Parnell.'[23] The clergy too were present, the chair being taken by the Rev. Peter Dooley.[24] The presence of the clergy is a clear illustration of the policy that MacEvilly had decided upon, namely, that priests should attend these meetings, even though he himself might not approve of them.

Aware that reports were being made to Rome and anxious to forestall any negative statement from there, MacEvilly wrote to Kirby to warn him of the consequences of any such pronouncement just then. His letter clearly articulates MacEvilly's dilemma – how to oppose the League and yet not be seen to be in opposition. But it also shows MacEvilly as the shrewd observer of the situation. He was fully aware of both the power of the League and the consequence of open clerical opposition. 'Whether the priests will it or no,' he wrote, 'the meetings will be held. The people will assemble under the pressure of threatened famine to expound their wrongs to landlords and government; if the priests keep aloof, these meetings will be scenes of disorder; if the priests attend they will keep the people attached to them.' He followed this with a warning for the authorities in Rome: 'It would render the Holy See very odious to seem to be influenced by the English against those who sacrificed everything for the Faith, and when the general evictions come, as come they will in some districts, it would ruin us, if the authorities could be quoted as against our people.' He concluded rather dramatically, 'Religion in this country would never get over it.'[25]

After Croke of Cashel, the most prominent supporter of the Land League among the bishops was Duggan, the gentle bishop of Clonfert. MacEvilly and Duggan had attended St. Jarlath's and Maynooth together and had been priests together in Tuam diocese.[26] No doubt because of their friendship, MacEvilly had been requested to speak to Duggan about his support for the League. MacEvilly, however, was reluctant to do so. He reported that Duggan was subject to depression and should be spoken to 'very cautiously.'[27]

Whether or not MacEvilly did speak to his friend, Duggan's diocese became a focal point of Land League activity, and the bishop's support remained unwavering. Early in 1880, the town of Loughrea hosted a tenant right meeting. A letter from MacEvilly was read in which he restated his familiar theme of tenant right which respected landlord right. 'I speak not of men but of a system,' declared the cautious MacEvilly, 'and the sooner the system is changed, the better for the peace and tranquility of the country.'[28]

MacEvilly was now treading the most delicate of paths. While personally hostile to the methods of the Land League and its leading personalities, he was not prepared to say so directly. He was anxious that priests be present at meetings and yet wished to restrain those whom he considered had overstepped the mark. To compound the issue, he had full control over the Galway clergy, but MacHale was taking all possible measures to prevent him exercising any power in Tuam. One can understand therefore that MacEvilly's reports to McCabe and to Rome of clerical excesses were confined exclusively to Tuam priests.

Of the more extreme cases reported by MacEvilly, one concerned John Flatly, a curate at Belclare, outside the town of Tuam. Flatly had publicly denounced a prominent local landlord, Robert Bodkin, who had been the target of several outrages and, a month later, denounced another landlord, John Kilkelly. According to Kilkelly, who was present at the mass, Flatly addressed the congregation in Irish, accusing Kilkelly of having written a letter to the *Freeman's Journal* in which, among other things, Flatly was accused of having called the landlord a 'dirty blackguard.' Some of the people turned on Kilkelly, while others came to his defence. Kilkelly himself stated that had he not drawn his revolver, he would not have escaped unhurt. The landlord went to see MacHale but was interviewed by the archbishop's nephew, Thomas MacHale, who told him they would send for Flatly.[29]

According to MacEvilly, Kilkelly had received no satisfaction and was threatening a lawsuit.[30] The affair, he wrote, was causing 'a terrible commotion' as the chapel had almost been the 'scene of murder and bloodshed during the mass.' Anxious to use the incident to embarrass MacHale, he asked McCabe to mention it to Rome.[31] The affair dragged on and at the end of May 1880, MacEvilly was complaining that the case was urgent but he would not interfere without a special mandate from Rome.[32] Obviously the mandate did come as, some weeks later, MacEvilly informed Kirby that the dispute had been settled. He had written out an apology for Flatly to send to Kilkelly, who had accepted it and so the affair was ended.[33]

MacEvilly's troubles with the Tuam priests continued throughout the year, however, particularly with the younger clergy. In November, he wrote that he was endeavouring to 'pull up some wild young curates relative to the present agitation.' These curates had promised moderation, he claimed, but they had not complied. He was also enforcing a rule forbidding priests from attending meetings in the parish of another unless they were invited.[34] Clearly this was done with a view to preventing League sympathisers from agitating in the parishes of priests who were neutral or opposed to the League.

At the end of the year MacEvilly wrote to McCabe telling him of his refusal to subscribe to the defence fund which had been set up following the prosecution of Parnell and other leaders. At the same time, he did not think that it would do any good for Rome to 'speak authoritatively against it' just then, as feelings were running high and 'no doubt, the landlords as a class have oppressed our Catholic people.' He ended with a statement which pointed to a softening of his attitude or, at the very least, to the beginnings of doubt: 'I have not interfered one way or the other,' he stated, 'as I can't see my way.'[35]

MacEvilly's remark about Rome speaking authoratively had particular point just then, as English influences in Rome were busy inducing the Holy See to denounce the Land League. It was a favourable time from the English point of view. The Italian government was threatening to take over the property of Propaganda in Rome and the Vatican was anxious to maintain good relations with the British government in order to prevent this. George Errington, an Irish catholic Whig and M.P. for Longford, had gone to Rome early in December 1880 and, while Gladstone might claim that he was there voluntarily and independently, the Irish were under no illusions about the purpose of Errington's visit.[36]

In 1881, Gladstone's government decided that the time had come to meet the challenge of the Land League head on. This they proposed to do with a two-fold policy of coercion and conciliation. But first the coercion. The chief secretary, W. B. Forster, received special powers to deal immediately and effectively with the land agitation. In February and March, two coercion bills passed through parliament and Forster proceeded to round up local leaders.[37]

Outrages however did not decrease, and in his Lenten pastoral MacEvilly made reference to them, while at the same time he felt that their number was greatly exaggerated 'for sinister motives.' Nevertheless, such outrages were the greatest obstacle to a just settlement to 'the great question of the hour.' He also declared that any line of action 'not thoroughly in accordance with the teaching of religion' would lead to ruin.[38] In the course of a Sunday sermon at St. Nicholas' church in Galway, MacEvilly warned the people against becoming 'entangled in secret societies,' as he was hoping that the land question would be settled by the government 'on equitable principles.'

MacEvilly went on to speak about the Ladies' Land League, an organisation which had been formed early in February and which had Parnell's sister, Anna, as president. Political agitation was the business of men, MacEvilly declared, 'but women – and the purity and modesty of Irishwomen is proverbial – should not be seen on public platforms, forfeiting the national character and bringing discredit on themselves.' In MacEvilly's view, the women should mind their homes and their families and leave agitation to 'the stronger sex whose special business it is.'[39] In a letter to McCabe, MacEvilly said that he had 'vigorously interdicted any priest' in his diocese 'from having anything to say either by word or act or encouragement to this abomination of female speech making gatherings,' and he was doing likewise in the deaneries of Tuam.[40]

The Ladies' Land League was also condemned by McCabe in a pastoral.[41] This condemnation stung the Archbishop of Cashel to reply and he wrote publicly to A.M. Sullivan, whose wife was one of the promoters of the Ladies' League.

Croke's letter, published in the *Freeman's Journal* of 17 March, defended the 'good Irish ladies' who had joined the League and challenged 'the monstrous imputations cast upon them by the Archbishop of Dublin.'[42] Such a public rebuke from one archbishop to another, as unusual as it was courageous, raised a storm. Writing to sympathise with McCabe, MacEvilly spoke of 'the heartfelt pain' he had felt on reading Croke's letter. However, he said, it was not just for McCabe's feelings that he was sorry but for 'the terrible injury such a letter is calculated to inflict on the best interests of our country and religion.' He ended, 'I don't wish to trust myself in saying more'; and piously added, 'I fervently pray that God may avert evil from our poor people.'[43] The aspect of the incident, then, most upsetting to MacEvilly was that the disagreement of two archbishops should be aired in public.

The end of the matter was that Croke was prevailed upon to write an apology to McCabe. This the archbishop of Cashel duly did, although his apology read more like a defence of his original action.[44] What the offending letter had done of course was to make public what must have been already well known in the country: that there was a pro-League faction among the bishops and an anti-League group behind McCabe. Croke's real offence was that he was not prepared to pretend that all was agreement and sweet harmony.

The Coercion Acts put the country in a very disturbed state. The arrest of the leaders of the agitation left vacancies which were sometimes filled by priests. The number of evictions also rose and in places ruthless landlords were denounced by the local clergy.

The second part of Gladstone's plan to smash the Land League was the conciliatory offering of the Land Act of 1881, which established the principle of joint ownership of landlord and tenant. The three Fs were effectively conceded with the setting up of the special Land Commission to settle fair rents. Tenants were promised protection and a fair price on the sale of holdings. Still, the Act was such a complicated piece of legislation that it was difficult to operate. Furthermore, tenants who owed arrears of rent were barred from its operation,[45] which again meant the exclusion of the bulk of the tenantry in the diocese of Tuam. Nevertheless, MacEvilly thought it 'a good bill, taken all in all' and worthy of 'a fair trial.'[46]

For Parnell this Land Act posed a dilemma, which he solved by abstaining from voting on it in parliament while making strong speeches in the country. He thus prevented the party from splitting, which had seemed probable. The speeches resulted in his arrest and, along with other leaders, he was lodged in Kilmainham Jail – and just then this was politically the best place for him.

From Kilmainham on 18 October came the No-rent Manifesto, calling on all tenants to withhold rents. The manifesto met with disapproval all round. It was denounced by the *Freeman's Journal* and *The Nation*.[47] Most significantly, it was condemned by Croke in a letter to the *Freeman*[48] and Croke's lead was followed by other bishops.

Preaching in Tuam cathedral on 30 October, MacEvilly condemned the 'no-rent' doctrine as contrary to 'every principle of religion, every dictate of morality.'[49] Privately, he saw it as bringing a 'world of good' in that it opened the eyes of 'all who are not willfully blind.'

McCabe's reaction was to call a meeting of the bishops.[50] He sounded MacEvilly, who was not in favour just then, as the bishops had met recently and he felt that their resolutions were still fresh in the minds of the people, especially the resolution calling on the people to test the Land Act. Also, MacEvilly felt that Croke's denunciation, at which he was delighted, was in itself sufficient. He assured McCabe, however, that he would attend if a meeting were called. He summed up his feelings with the remark, 'We have an Irish adage "often does not get honour."'[51]

On 9 November 1881, John MacHale died; and for MacEvilly the long wait to assume full authority in Tuam was ended. Reports to Rome concerning the disastrous state of Tuam diocese were not now so frequent and so detailed, and where they were made, MacEvilly was careful to point out that his problems were inherited.

Undoubtedly it was a difficult time in the country. Agrarian crime was on the increase since the imprisonment of the leaders. Illegal activity was particularly rampant in those areas, like the diocese of Tuam, where the majority of tenants had been excluded from the benefits of the Land Act. MacEvilly laid the blame on the government, commenting: 'If they attended to our recommendation in regard to Arrears, the inextricable and interminable compulsion now existing would be avoided. Arrears the people *won't* and can't pay.'[52]

The Land Act was being tested, and at such a rate that the courts were unable to cope. In some cases, landlords sought to prevent tenants from taking advantage of the Act. Such a case occurred in the area of Robeen, Hollymount, Co. Mayo. The landlord in question was Dennis Browne, a former M.P. for Mayo. The charges were made in a letter to the *Freeman's Journal* from the local curate – none other than the redoubtable John Flatly, landlord denouncer. In this instance, however, Flatly had MacEvilly in his corner. Flatly alleged that on the day before the sub-commissioners sat at Ballinrobe, Browne and his land agent, Hughes, announced that all tenants who went to court would be immediately sued for arrears. Remissions in rent were promised to all those who accepted Browne's terms outside the court. Some tenants agreed to the unfavourable terms offered from fear of court costs and inability to pay arrears. Others went to court and were punished as promised. Eviction procedures were served on those who owed less than £20 arrears, while those whose arrears exceeded the £20 limit for qualification for the Act were awaiting eviction notices. Flatly wished to have the entire circumstances of these eviction cases put before the county court judge so that, if possible, execution would be stayed and costs refunded. He was therefore appealing to the public for their support.[53]

In a backing letter published in the same edition of the *Freeman*, MacEvilly wrote: 'I hardly see my way in the shocking, almost incredible, case you speak of . . . . I see no other way but to solicit public aid and to invoke public opinion.' He then spoke of the duty of every clergyman to defend the oppressed and miserable. His conclusion was: 'Exposure of such criminal conduct as described by you in the Dublin court of law would do much to prevent repetition of such scenes and remove the great blot of the Land Act in regard to arrears. I should gladly subscribe to any fund got up to prosecute the case to the end.'[54]

In his Lenten pastoral of 1882, MacEvilly dealt with the growth of secret societies and the recent spate of outrages. In a strange departure, he claimed that the 'circumstances of peculiar atrocity, so utterly un-Irish' proved that the outrages were 'of foreign importation, the work of the enemies of our people.' He referred to the arrears question, observing that many of the people were still unprotected by law and 'victims of harassing threats of eviction,' which were 'so many sentences of death.' This state of things must be remedied by all fair and constitutional means, said the archbishop, before asking: How could 'the commission of crime, the violation of the law serve to remedy it?' He warned the people against having any communication with those who committed such crimes or with 'their wicked abettors.'[55] The editor of the *Connaught Telegraph*, James Daly, described it as a most important pastoral.[56] Daly articulated a disillusionment with the Land League which was being felt in the west and particularly in Mayo. The chief reason for such disenchantment was that, as the evictions continued, the people resented the fact that the Land League devoted only a small fraction of its income to help the evicted tenants.[57]

The stalemate that had arisen in the country was finally resolved in the so-called 'Kilmainham Treaty' of 1882. Parnell, anxious to be free, undertook to pacify the country in return for government concessions, including an end to coercion and the abolition of arrears. The latter measure must have pleased MacEvilly, since he had urged it all along as the means of placating those who had been excluded from the Land Act.

The 'Kilmainham Treaty' resulted in Forster's resignation as chief secretary. His replacement, Lord Frederick Cavendish, had just arrived in Ireland when he and the under secretary, T. H. Burke, were murdered in the Phoenix Park by members of the Invincibles. The murders sent shock waves through the country and there was almost universal condemnation. As letters to Kirby show, MacEvilly was clearly horrified.[58] He consoled himself by laying the blame on foreigners, 'some wicked English or American rowdies,' who were determined to wreck Gladstone's policy of conciliation. He was alarmed at the state of the country, describing it as 'worse then Fenianism – a kind of nihilism.'[59]

Publicly too, MacEvilly denounced the Phoenix Park murders. In a letter read at a special meeting of the Tuam town commissioners, the archbishop spoke of the shame and disgrace the killings brought, repeating his hope that they had not been committed by Irishmen. The motive for the crime was obvious, he thought. It was to frustrate the 'beneficent designs' of Gladstone's policy of conciliation 'by maddening our powerful neighbours.' The people of Tuam were entitled to express their feelings, he declared, as Mr Burke was himself a Tuam man, 'holding property in its immediate neighbourhood.' Burke, he said, had been 'a model landlord . . . kind, indulgent, attentive to the wants of his people.'[60]

MacEvilly then made a shrewd observation: 'The release of the suspects and the resignation of Forster will create a new departure in politics.'[61] What exactly that change would be he was not prepared to say, as for him there was 'nothing fixed or constant in the Land politics.' He even felt that 'the less one has to do with them the better.' But, ever the pragmatist, MacEvilly concluded, 'However, they must be used as a means of good.'[62]

When McCabe, now a cardinal, arrived home from Rome, he sought the opinions of the bishops about the holding of an episcopal meeting.[63] MacEvilly certainly was not enthusiastic. However, the cardinal prefect of Propaganda instructed McCabe to call a meeting immediately.[64] And this meeting was crucial. McCabe's elevation to the cardinalate was not without its significance, coming at the time it did. It was a definite indication from Rome as to which group of Irish bishops was then in favour. There was also the question as to how much the honour owed to English influence in Rome, and there were rumours in the country that McCabe had received extensive powers. The agenda for the meeting, which had come from the cardinal prefect of Propaganda in his letter, was based on suggestions made by MacEvilly and others to McCabe, and included a reference to the Ladies' Land League, which was obviously the suggestion of the new cardinal himself.[65]

The bishops met on 6 June and it seemed that there was general satisfaction and harmony. MacEvilly certainly was elated at the outcome. On 17 June, he made his report to Kirby:

> It gives me great pleasure to tell you, that having attended episcopal meetings for the last twenty-five years, I never attended a meeting that gave me such pleasure as this. I never saw such cordial unanimity . . . and all terminated with an unanimous address presented to the Cardinal by the Primate in an eloquent speech and seconded in still more eloquent speech by the Archbishop of Cashel.

Everybody had obviously been trying very hard, and MacEvilly had words of praise for Croke.

> The stand His Grace took at a certain period in this terrible agitation and crisis through which we are passing had a great effect in keeping the people

from passing away from the clergy as they were instigated to do by bad men. I wish His Grace's differences with (our) excellent Cardinal had never existed. This I need not say, I could never approve. But he is a thorough Irishman, a thorough defender of the rights of the Holy See under all circumstances. I write this because there is a rumour that His Grace is misrepresented in some quarters.[66]

This belated tribute from MacEvilly shows that, however he might differ from Croke in attitudes towards the Land agitation, he was fully aware of the importance of the stand Croke had taken, from the bishops' point of view.

This episcopal harmony seemed to vanish as surprisingly as it had appeared. The occasion of renewed disagreement was a report which appeared in the *United Ireland* of 8 July. It stated that at conferences of the clergy of at least two dioceses, Tuam and Ossory, a circular directed to the priests and signed by all the hierarchy was read. This consisted of a series of resolutions intended to regulate the conduct of the clergy in regard to any future development of the Land movement. The first resolution, the paper claimed, directed the priests not to support or encourage the Ladies' Land League; the second forbade any priest to attend a public meeting without the consent of the parish priest of the place where the meeting was to be held; the third forbade any curate to attend any meeting, even in his own parish, without the consent of his parish priest.[67]

Three days later, the *Freeman's Journal* reported that the Primate, Dr MacGettigan, had read a similar circular in Drogheda.[68] The next day there was a letter from Croke saying that this report was false in two respects. Firstly, the Ladies' Land League had not been condemned by the bishops, or the clergy instructed not to support it. Secondly, he disputed the wording of the third resolution as printed by the paper, which actually stated that in the case of a dispute between curate and parish priest concerning attendance at a meeting, the matter would be referred to the bishop. In such a case, Croke was convinced that the bishop would 'never interfere with the civil rights and liberty of his subject without ample and evident cause.'[69]

So for all MacEvilly's claims about the state of agreement existing among the hierarchy, it would appear that it was not quite certain what they were agreed upon; and it had taken just a mention of the land agitation to expose once more the two fundamentally opposed positions among the bishops. For Croke, it meant further trouble with Rome. To satisfy English complaints, Pope Leo XIII issued a rather general letter to McCabe again urging the use of constitutional methods.[70] Kirby suggested to MacEvilly that he might have a word with Croke. MacEvilly replied typically: 'If I get an opportunity, I shall not omit speaking to him, but it must be done cautiously.'[71]

Croke, however, was unmoved and the division remained; and would remain as long as the two opposing points of view were represented by two men of such differing attitudes as Croke and McCabe. Times however were changing. The question was changing and the people were changing. But John MacEvilly so far had changed very little. He had steered his careful course between outright disapproval and unwilling acceptance – the position of a pragmatist in politics. For the present, though, the land question had to give best to Parnell's priority, home rule.

AFTER THE LAND LEAGUE

The story of the years following the Land League is the story of the attempt by the Irish party to achieve home rule. In MacEvilly's case, it is the story of his changing relationship with the party and of his gradual conversion both to it and to home rule. The problems of the land, though still remaining, were not allowed to detract from the question of the hour, as Parnell and his party strove for a native parliament. The times, however, continued to be depressed and the recurring hardship meant that the land question still demanded attention. This was particularly true in an area like the diocese of Tuam, which included the poorer parts of Galway and Mayo. Indeed, a major factor in the conversion of MacEvilly to the Irish party was his disillusionment with the government, stemming from continued and unavailing appeals to help a people in distress.

In January 1883, a delegation of bishops from Connacht, led by MacEvilly, went to see the lord lieutenant to discuss the relief of distress in the west of the country. The manner in which the proposals of the bishops were dismissed, and the effects of that dismissal, will be discussed elsewhere.[72] While the bishops were concerned chiefly with obtaining relief for a starving people, they listed as a cause the unsatisfactory system of land tenure. The people were presented with the choice of starvation or emigration, and thousands were choosing the latter.

There was, of course, a third way which was chosen by some few. This was to take vengeance, and as the hardship increased, so too did the number of outrages and secret societies. MacEvilly referred to the growth of both in his Lenten pastoral of 1883. He condemned 'the shocking outrages on human life' which, he said, had made 'our country a by-word of reproach' and which had brought disgrace on religion and humanity. He warned young people particularly against 'the wicked men, who going about in the dark, themselves kept harmless, with the hollow hypocritical profession of love of country on their lips.' These men would say it was no sin to love one's country. This was so, MacEvilly agreed, but he would ask: Is it no sin to betray their country by 'secretly carrying out . . . decrees of blood, to compel our fellow-men to join, under penalty of death, in the perpetration of crimes at which every instinct of humanity shudders?' By associating with such societies, MacEvilly told the people that they would become sharers in their guilt.[73]

More than any other factor just then, the peace and quiet of the country was dependent on the success of the harvest. The harvest of 1883 was good and so the country was relatively quiet over the next year. At the end of 1884, the bishops passed their vote of confidence in the Irish party by entrusting them with the management of educational affairs. It was a victory for Parnell as now to oppose him was to oppose the people, and it was a victory for Croke, whose views had finally prevailed over those of the Rome-McCabe axis.

In the land question, gains were made, mainly as a result of the political bargaining between Parnell's Irish party and the two major English parties. It was the anxiety of the Conservatives to secure the support of the Irish party that led to the next major advance, the Ashbourne Land Purchase Act of 1885. Under the terms of this Act, the government provided five million pounds to enable tenants to borrow the full purchase price of their holdings, and which would then be repaid by 4% annuities over a period of forty-nine years. The initial grant was so quickly exhausted that it had to be doubled to ten million three years later. As a result of these government grants, over 25,000 tenants bought out their farms.[74]

Such grants still did not relieve the struggling tenants of the west. The winter of 1885 was a hard one. A slump in the British economy meant falling prices for livestock and agricultural produce. The harvest was bad and the potato crop failed. The situation was aggravated by the wet spring of 1886, which meant delayed sowing of crops. 'The times,' MacEvilly reported to Kirby, 'are dreadfully depressed, no price for anything, the people unable to pay rents.' He himself had charge of some charity property and had had to reduce the rents by fifty per cent. 'Many landlords are insisting on their pound of flesh and the people can't pay,' said MacEvilly.

In February 1886, the four archbishops met in Dublin and, in a subsequent letter to Gladstone, they called for home rule and also for a final settlement of the land question. They felt the government should purchase 'the landlord interest in the soil' and relet it to tenant farmers at a figure well below the present judicial rents. The archbishops stressed that they were not urging any form of confiscation but were seeking only 'fair play as between man and man.' In their view, every disturbance that had occurred in recent years had arisen from 'a sense of wrong entertained by a large majority of the occupiers of the soil, owing to the remorseless exactions of needy or extravagant landlords.' Pending final settlement of the land question, the bishops requested that the power of eviction be suspended in Ireland, and that in the poorer districts some form of remunerative employment be provided to support the starving poor.[75]

The persistent emphasis by MacEvilly that a solution to the land question was the key to peace is not difficult to understand. He lived and worked in an area which had been the scene of many bitterly fought campaigns in the Land War. The mass support which the Land League had attracted was ample testimony to the deep-seated desire of the people with whom MacEvilly had to deal. He had high hopes of Gladstone's Home Rule Bill of 1886 and, in May of that year, he wrote: 'Our poor suffering bleeding country has long been robbed of her rights, and our poor people cruelly oppressed by landlords because they were catholics and devoted to the see of Peter.' He was sure that great peace would prevail if Gladstone's measure were passed but he stated that he 'would tremble for the consequences' should it fail.[76]

The Home Rule Bill did fail and MacEvilly's fears were justified. The country was deep in agricultural depression. Tenants were again unable to pay their rents and evictions followed. The situation was aggravated by the refusal of the government to accept Parnell's Tenants' Relief Bill in the autumn.

Out of this crisis came the Plan of Campaign, Timothy Harrington's scheme to combat evictions and obtain reductions in rent. If the landlord refused to lower the rent when requested, then the tenants of his estate would combine to offer him reduced rents. If he refused to accept this offer, the tenants would withhold payment and, instead, put the money in an 'estate fund,' which would be used for the upkeep of evicted tenants. And the boycott was to be applied to any who took the land of an evicted tenant.[77] The Plan received widespread support in the more depressed areas of the west and south. It met with Parnell's disapproval, however, as he was not favourable to any project which might detract from home rule, and also he feared that the Plan might endanger the Liberal alliance.[78]

Coercion, which might achieve a temporary peace, was no solution to the pressing problems of the western tenants. At the beginning of 1887, a meeting to support the Irish party was held at Tuam and a letter from the archbishop was read. MacEvilly returned to his old theme of 'an equitable settlement, on a fair and just basis, of the land question.' 'If this vital question of the land were once equitably settled,' he declared, 'we would have a people so far contented and advanced in intelligence so as to be able and willing to carry out fully into practical effect the long denied blessing of home rule.' He then dealt with what he called the 'specious objection' regarding the binding force of contracts between landlord and tenant. Of course contracts must be kept, the archbishop asserted, but only 'if there be question of just or valid contracts.' And were the contracts, 'or rather arrangements,' between the majority of landlords and tenants in this country valid? 'I unhesitatingly assert that they were not,' MacEvilly declared, for they did not meet the very first requirement that a contract be free in order to be valid. 'In truth, there was but one party to such arrangements, viz. the landlord, who dictated to his tenants whatever terms he pleased.' Of course there were kind and humane landlords, MacEvilly averred, but these were exceptions.[79]

This letter contained MacEvilly's most outspoken pronouncement to date on the land question. Previously his emphasis had been on the necessity of satisfying both landlord and tenant. Now he was calling for an end to tenant wrong, and carefully explaining the injustice involved. This new-found assertiveness is for the most part explained by MacEvilly's adoption of the cause of the Irish party. But more than that, in the changed situation in Irish politics, the archbishop was freed of his dependence on the goodwill of the landlord to achieve reform. The people, informed by their new leaders, were now calling the tune and MacEvilly, sensitive as always to changes in the popular mood, was not going to oppose them. In a sense, too, MacEvilly was now very much his own man. Freed of the necessity to bend to Cullen's will and the need to oppose MacHale, there can now be seen in the mature MacEvilly a blend of the pragmatism learned so well with Cullen and a reawakening of his early nationalist leanings encouraged by MacHale. In this new expression of nationalist sentiment, MacEvilly was at one with most of the catholic bishops who were just then being so ably led by Walsh of Dublin.

1887 saw the arrival in Ireland of a new chief secretary, Arthur Balfour, who let it be known that he would take a hard line on all forms of agitation. The Plan of Campaign he met head on with the introduction of a Crimes Act which gave the lord lieutenant added powers of suppressing certain organisations and of proclaiming areas where disturbances were taking place. Again by way of conciliation, a Land Act followed which allowed judicial rents to be revised after three years and which brought 10,000 leaseholders within the scope of the 1881 Act.[80] Both the Crimes Act and the Land Act were condemned by the clergy of the diocese of Tuam at a meeting on 19 April, presided over by MacEvilly. The resolution dealing with the Land Act declared that it was 'chiefly a landlord bill, eminently designed to pauperise the tenant and lead to the wholesale extermination of the bone and sinew of the nation.'[81]

The Plan of Campaign was scarcely the type of action that the earlier MacEvilly would have defended. But he was adapting well to his new role, and while he did not declare himself directly in favour of the Plan, he did attack unjust landlords.[82]

On other fronts too, the government was carrying its fight against the Plan. The work of English agents in Rome and the continuous reports of agitation from Ireland, led to the visit of Monsignor Persico in 1887, sent by Leo XIII to investigate at first hand the situation in the country.[83] The papal delegate toured the country, calling on the bishops. In August, he visited MacEvilly at Tuam. Commenting to Walsh on the visit, MacEvilly regretted that he had forgotten to draw Persico's attention to 'this fact, that whatever may be said of the Plan of Campaign, be it right or wrong, it was practised for centuries by the landlord class in putting any rents they pleased on their tenants. This might not be a good argument,' MacEvilly conceded, adding the wry comment, 'but it is a good *argumentum ad hominem*.'[84]

Whether he was requested by Persico to do so, or whether on his own initiative,

Walsh wrote to MacEvilly requesting details regarding the performance of catholic landlords in his diocese. MacEvilly replied that he would have the administrator in Tuam prepare a detailed account; but he felt humbled to have to state his belief 'that in general catholic landlords have been more grinding than protestants.' Then he remarked: 'It may be said to be universally true that the rents on the estates of all catholic landlords were considerably reduced either in the courts or by extrajudicial arrangements. Bear also in mind that most of the property of the country is in the hands of protestants and with very few exceptions considerable reductions have been made either judicially or extrajudicially in all. This wholesale reduction of rent,' he continued, 'shows that our people have been robbed and this judicially proved.' So, MacEvilly concluded, who could complain 'if priests, the fathers of their people, raise their voices in any way even in the most constitutional form of agitation, to save their people from injustice, the workhouse or exile . . .'[85]

Later, MacEvilly forwarded Walsh details of the reductions made by catholic landlords. He also observed that the Tories seemed to be 'utterly ruthless, without regard to law or justice, outcromwelling Cromwell.'[86] In this of course MacEvilly was echoing Arthur Balfour's famous dictum that he would be 'as relentless as Cromwell' in enforcing the law.[87]

The results of Persico's visit and of English activity in Rome became known in April 1888 with the publication of the papal rescript condemning boycotting and the Plan of Campaign.[88] MacEvilly was less than enthusiastic about implementing the decree, and he publicly denounced what he called 'the cruel use made of the just act of the Pope.' He told Kirby that the cruel evictions were maddening the people and the clergy, remarking that in Tuam some of the evictors were 'pious catholics.' He stressed that poor people had been turned out for not being able to pay impossible rents. 'The clergy prevailed on them not to resist,' he stated, 'but vengeance was deep down in their hearts.'[89]

By 1889, the Plan of Campaign was near to total failure, unable to bear the burden of caring for the victims of the agitation. Parnell, still hostile to this new agrarian agitation, reluctantly agreed to the formation by William O'Brien of an association to collect funds. He would not, however, place himself at its head or take any part in its proceedings. The new organisation, the Tenants' Defence Association, was also a counter to the syndicate of Irish landlords which had been formed in the south of the country. This syndicate, which had the backing of Balfour and wealthy English financiers, subsidised the landlord to undertake the eviction of all tenants on the Ponsonby estate at Youghal, where the Plan of Campaign had been in operation. The tenants on the estates of Arthur Smith-Barry, the head of the landlord syndicate, stopped paying rent in sympathy with the Ponsonby tenants and were consequently evicted. The tenants then opened up a shanty-town to which they gave the name of New Tipperary, the maintenance of which was proving a big drain on Plan funds.[90]

The Tenants' Defence Association received MacEvilly's backing. In a letter to the County Galway convention on 10 December, he said that it would be strange if the tenants did not combine in the face of 'a landlord syndicate, professedly organised to perpetuate the old state of injustice and abject serfdom.' He referred to the landlords' association as 'a powerful and opulent confederacy, threatening what may be regarded as nothing short of a war of extermination to be carried on, not simultaneously, but piecemeal, against the bravest and most determined, in the first instance, as a deterrent to their weaker and more dependent brothers elsewhere.'[91]

Privately too, MacEvilly was full of praise and encouragement for the newly-formed association. He told Kirby he regarded it his solemn duty 'as a Catholic bishop and in view of future judgment' to give the association 'every encouragement and support *intra limites juris.*'[92]

Why did MacEvilly give the new movement such enthusiastic backing? It was not just that he was now a supporter of the Irish party, as there were many party supporters who did not encourage O'Brien and his association. Certainly a prime motive was that, despite all the gains made in successive land acts, the problems of the small landholders of the west had not been solved. This had resulted in mass emigration and, in this respect, MacEvilly's diocese was harder hit than most areas. In MacEvilly's view, the basic solution to the problem of emigration was the satisfactory settlement of the land question.

Even with the efforts of the new association, however, the problems of the evicted tenants still remained. At the Galway convention in November 1890, MacEvilly was asked to lend his support to the plea for the relief of evicted tenants. In his reply, MacEvilly expressed the hope that the government might see its way to restoring them 'to the homes they had created by the sweat of brows, and hardly less dear to them than life itself.'[93]

A month later, the Irish party was in disarray and the problems of the land and of the evicted tenants faded into the background as the storm over Parnell's leadership raged in the country. The question of relief for evicted tenants remained on the agenda for county conventions and resolutions of support were passed, but this was only a distraction from the main battle.

1891 was the year of the Balfour Land Act. The Conservatives argued that if the landlords could be persuaded to sell on terms which were reasonable for both landlords and tenants, then a fundamental cause of discontent would be removed – a point insisted upon by MacEvilly since he had first interested himself in the land question. This Act provided £33,000,000 for the purchase of land, but the process of buying was legally so complicated that many tenants were discouraged. What was more significant was an attempt to deal with the special problems of the less developed areas of the country. To this end, a Congested Districts Board was set up, composed of two land commissioners, five experts appointed by the government and the chief secretary. The principal function of the Board was to aid the development of agriculture and fishing. Among its other functions was the encouragement of local industry and the establishment of other suitable industries. It was also hoped to increase the size of farms by purchasing and redistributing unused land.[94]

The situation as regards the extent of land available for increasing the area of small holdings was quite different in counties Galway, Mayo and Roscommon than in the rest of the country. With the decline in population in the west, much of the land that was previously cultivated had been converted to large grazing tracts, while tenants still struggled on their small, uneconomic holdings. As long as land reform was concentrated on revising landlord-tenant relationships on existing holdings, it was not possible to create an economically viable society in these western areas.[95] MacEvilly pointed to this basic deficiency in a letter to the Mayo county convention at the end of 1892. In his view, unless there were some statutory enactment 'rooting the people in the soil,' and respecting the rights of all classes, any legislation would be as 'comparatively useless as patch work.' In an agricultural country like Ireland, the archbishop argued, only laws which made the tenant owner of the land could 'form an effectual and permanent antidote against the ever recurring cry of distress.' The convention passed a resolution asking for the division of lands and the Congested Districts Board was condemned for its inaction in the matter.[96]

The continued delay by the Board made it the object of attack by MacEvilly and others over the following years. The Board, however, was hampered by the lack of compulsory purchase powers and so could not act in the matter as quickly as it might wish. Gradually the powers of the Board were enlarged so that it was enabled to buy large tracts of land and divide them into suitable holdings.[97] One of the first of such projects was the purchase of Clare Island off the Mayo coast. At first, the Board hesitated because of the notorious difficulty experienced by landlords in collecting rent from the islanders, who struggled against evictions and rack-rents.[98] The project was completed only on the assurance given by MacEvilly and William O'Brien, the former stalwart of the Land League and Parnell's party and founder of the Tenant's Defence Association, who was then residing outside the town of Westport. The archbishop and O'Brien gave a formal undertaking that they would, within certain limits, guarantee the amount of the new owners' instalments of purchase money for the first seven years.[99] O'Brien later stated that 'to the islanders' immortal credit,' it never cost MacEvilly or himself 'a farthing.'[100] Since the Congested Districts Board could not sell to tenants through the Land Commission, a scheme was adopted under which the tenants purchased their holdings for annuities at 3¼% payable to the Board for 68½ years. The resale of Clare Island on these terms was of special interest because Wyndham in his Land Bill of 1903 generally adopted the same terms.[101]

By his action, MacEvilly gave clear notice of his support for the policy of redistribution. He also made evident that he would countenance only the use of constitutional means in the pursuit of that goal. When some priests to the north of Westport organised a local demonstration during 1895-96 to force tenants of several large grazing farms to give up their land for redistribution among neighbouring small farms, MacEvilly condemned the boycotting and outrage connected with the agitation, and he transferred one of the priests involved to another parish.[102]

The issue of redistribution was taken up by William O'Brien, who was struck by the difference between the wretched lives of the small farmers and their more prosperous neighbours on the 'ranches.' O'Brien returned to national politics with the launching of a new land movement on 16 January 1898 at a public meeting in Westport.[103] This United Irish League, so called because it originated in the centenary year of the United Irishmen, was in many ways a throwback to the earlier Land League. The new League had as object the breaking up of the large grass farms by compelling the graziers to surrender their lands to the Congested Districts Board for redistribution.[104]

From the beginning, the United Irish League had the firm backing of MacEvilly and the clergy of Tuam – an indication of just how far MacEvilly had moved since the days of the earlier Land League. The new land movement was recommended to their congregations by the priests,[105] and MacEvilly devoted a large part of his Lenten pastoral to the topic. The archbishop recommended, 'as the only effectual remedy' against recurring distress, the 'parcelling out to our people in fair proportions . . . the large, comparatively unproductive tracts of land which, from foreign competition and other causes, are likely to become more unproductive still in the near future.' He was careful to stress that this change must be brought about 'under legal sanction' and 'without trenching on the just or equitable rights of any class in the community.'[106]

The clergy in the Westport-Newport area promoted the League enthusiastically. One parish priest, Fr Coen of Islandeady, instigated a boycott of some local graziers. A police official who called on MacEvilly in March left with the impression that Coen would be disciplined, although MacEvilly had made clear his own sympathy with the aims of the League. The police noted little change in Coen's behaviour; in September, they learned that MacEvilly had instructed some priests who had opposed the League to drop their opposition. The archbishop argued that the people had taken up the matter so warmly as to have gone beyond the control of the clergy, and that clerical opposition would only lead to friction between clergy and people.[107] It was indeed an interesting variation on MacEvilly's old theme of preserving the relationship between priests and people. In the days of the Land League, MacEvilly had urged clerical participation, although he was himself hostile to the movement.

As the organisation spread beyond parish level, a South Mayo convention was held on 16 November. Ten of the delegates were priests and the meeting was presided over by Archdeacon Kilkenny of Claremorris, who had formerly opposed the League. The League now met with clerical opposition only in places where the agitation entered the specifically religious sphere. This happened in Ballinrobe, where the local parish priest was blamed by the people for a government proclamation of a proposed League meeting. Ballinrobe had invented the boycott, and the weapon was now used against the local clergy when they went to say mass in outlying villages. For this, the locality was placed under interdict.[108]

MacEvilly, by urging the claims of the League and denouncing any excesses attaching to it, set a guideline which was followed by his priests throughout the diocese. The result was considerable clerical control over League affairs. The civil authorities decided not to proclaim a proposed meeting near Claremorris when they learned that there had been a conference between Michael Davitt, who was to address the meeting, and the local clergy. In announcing the meeting to his Sunday congregation, the parish priest stated that he had not sought the meeting but, as it was being held, he would attend. He stressed that the meeting would be constitutional, as otherwise he would take no part.[109]

In the beginning, William O'Brien had not visualised his movement as anything more than an association to achieve a better deal for the local tenantry. As with the Land League, however, the movement spread quickly. By October 1898, the League could claim a total of 53 branches, most of them in Mayo, and it had established footholds in six other counties. In January of the new year, O'Brien claimed that there were over 180 branches of the League in Connacht with 35,000 members, and it continued to grow.[110] It was obvious that O'Brien had struck a chord with the people, who were disillusioned with the feuding politicians. The politicians too saw the popularity of the League and realised that they could not afford to ignore it.

So it was that, when the United Irish League called a provincial convention at Claremorris in January 1899, the politicians and the clergy were well represented. The chair was taken by Archdeacon Kilkenny, and on the platform with O'Brien were other leading politicians, such as John Dillon, J. J. O'Kelly and David Sheehy. In a letter read at the meeting, MacEvilly said that his views on the necessity of enlarging the peoples' holdings were already well known. 'Coercion, violence or terrorism would only throw us back,' he stated. The object of the League was to secure the land for the people and, in MacEvilly's opinion, it was 'the most important object' they could engage in.[111]

Later in the year, a letter from the bishops of the province of Connacht was sent from the provincial synod at Tuam to Gerald Balfour, the chief secretary, and chairman of the Congested Districts Board. The first resolution praised the

Board's efforts to promote peasant ownership with enlarged holdings in the west of Ireland. The bishops believed that the 'sense of permanent ownership' would prove a strong incentive to thrift and industry. Secondly, the bishops hoped that the Board would continue with its policy of purchasing the large uncultivated grazing farms of the west and dividing them among the poorer tenants. Otherwise, many of these tenants had to migrate at the busiest season of the year to find the means of paying their rent. The third resolution encouraged the Board to seek extended powers from parliament to implement this policy throughout the province of Connacht. In this way, 'desolate tracts' might be made productive by the hard work and skills of the peasant owners. Finally, the bishops expressed their conviction that this policy could be carried out 'without causing wrong or injury to any man,' and they pledged that they would support only methods of action which were just and legitimate.[112] Balfour's reply simply acknowledged the letter and thanked the bishops for their interest.[113] It was the kind of cold courtesy to which MacEvilly must, by then, have become accustomed.

The United Irish League continued to grow and by 1901 had a membership of about 63,000.[114] This rapid growth and popularity were undoubtedly factors in influencing the reunion of the Irish parliamentary party under the leadership of John Redmond in 1900.[115] In his Lenten pastoral of 1901, MacEvilly, now in his eighty-fifth year, was still hammering out the message.[116] MacEvilly's final speech on the land question was made four months before his death in 1902.[117] If one is to measure the progress in land reform over half a century by this speech, then one must conclude that very little progress had been recorded, for the content is remarkably similar to his first public contribution. On the other hand, it could be argued that considerable progress had been made in land reform as evidenced by the various land acts that had been won from successive administrations. MacEvilly could answer that such reforms were not sufficient for the area with which he was concerned, and he could point to the fact that the people were fleeing a country which did not offer them security. The problem of the west of Ireland was a singular one and solutions which had proved successful elsewhere were likely to fail there. Arthur Balfour had realised this, and the establishment of the Congested Districts Board was at least a recognition that something special was required. Unfortunately the board was not bold enough in tackling the massive problems that faced it. It suffered too from a severe limitation of its powers. With the failure of the Board, emigration became the road to survival for an increasing number of people from the western counties.

Chapter 7

Famine and Emigration

JOHN MACEVILLY MINISTERED all his life in the west of Ireland, in dioceses which included the largest part of the counties Galway and Mayo and also part of Clare. He was, then, much involved with the related problems of famine and emigration. He had of course lived through the Great Famine and, as a priest in Tuam, he had witnessed the ravages wrought by hunger and disease. There is a tendency in Irish history to associate all hunger and suffering with those years 1846-8. The Great Famine brought death and suffering on so widespread a scale, and it was an occurrence of such consequence in the history of this country, that it was etched indelibly on the consciousness of succeeding generations of Irish people. Because the Great Famine looms so large, it is often forgotten that there were parts of the country where the hunger was as real, and disease as menacing, right through the nineteenth century and even into the twentieth. Famine was an ever-present threat for the poorer people, and the battle to prevent a recurrence of the earlier disaster was one with which John MacEvilly was to become all too familiar in the course of his episcopal career.

There were several factors contributing to recurring distress in areas within the Tuam diocese. Holdings in the 1-5 acre category, in which the diocese abounded, had fallen dramatically in the decade 1841-1851. The situation had stabilised after the Famine. Much of this land was of poor quality but tenants in the west were prepared to work or reclaim land which tenants in other parts with higher expectations might have ignored.[1] Another factor was the survival in the west of a pre-Famine economy, with a peasantry relying almost entirely on the potato for existence. The potato economy lasted longer in parts of Mayo, Galway and Donegal than anywhere else. As late as the 1890s, consumption per capita on the small holdings in areas such as Claremorris in Mayo still reached one ton per annum.[2] This heavy reliance on the potato made existence precarious. Along with the small tenant farmers, the landless labourers and the unemployed poor of the town were always at risk in times of crisis. In particular, they were at the mercy of an uncertain climate. For them, winter always brought hardship but, in a bad season, many were threatened with hunger, disease and even death. Furthermore, as is clear from MacEvilly's appeals, if the season was very wet, it resulted in a two-fold crisis, because as well as shortage of food there was a 'fuel famine.'

Government structures appointed to deal with these crises were not altogether satisfactory. Under the Poor Law Act of 1838, the country had been divided into 130 unions. Each of these unions was responsible for building and maintaining its own workhouse, and for providing for its own poor by means of a local 'poor rate' which was levied on all the property owners within the union. The body which had the task of administering this system was the Board of Guardians, elected by the ratepayers of the union. The Poor Law commissioners were unfortunate in that, just when the system was operational, it was confronted by such a large-scale disaster as the Great Famine of 1846-8. The system had been geared to meet the normal needs of Irish poverty and was not at all equipped to deal with a major catastrophe.[3] Originally only those within the workhouse would receive relief. During the Great Famine the workhouses were so overcrowded, despite the people's loathing for them, that outdoor relief was granted only on a small scale. The refusal to extend this remained a bone of contention during the nineteenth century. In 1851, the Medical Charities Act divided the unions into dispensary districts and a dispensary doctor was appointed to each district. The doctor provided free treatment and medicine to those who were adjudged by the Guardians to be in need of it. In addition, fever hospitals had to be maintained in each county.[4]

From the beginning, the workhouses were unpopular.[5] Before they could enter, the poor had to undergo a humiliating examination of their circumstances. Also the workhouses were often places of extreme discomfort and sometimes dangerously unhealthy. In the catholic mind, there was the suspicion that they were not free of proselytising activities, a suspicion that MacEvilly often expressed as a fact. For these reasons, therefore, many poor people preferred starvation and even death to what represented for them degradation and humiliation.

The conventional wisdom of the educated classes disapproved of poverty and of methods of direct relief, which, it was felt, encouraged idleness. In times of distress, calls were made to the government to provide public works rather than grant direct relief. Money for this was administered through the Board of Works, established in 1831, which was also responsible for drainage, canals, waterways and public buildings. It could also lend money to landlords for drainage and farm improvement and later the building of railways and piers, particularly in the west.[6] Because of the failure of the government to provide adequate structures, however, the relief of distress depended for a great part on the activities of voluntary organisations and local *ad hoc* committees. The biggest and best known of these was the Mansion House Committee, an interdenominational body which met in times of crises.

Because of his position, MacEvilly as bishop would have been expected to take part in the efforts of these local committees to relieve distress. For convenience, I have charted MacEvilly's involvement in two sections: his efforts as bishop of Galway and his efforts as archbishop of Tuam; while dealing separately with the question of emigration.

DISTRESS IN GALWAY

Prolonged bad weather was the usual forerunner of times of distress. The agricultural depression which affected Ireland during the years 1859-64 was unusual in that the initial cause was not excessive rain or cold but a severe drought in the late spring and summer of 1859. When the rains did come, there was a deluge, and the years 1860-2 were almost certainly the wettest three consecutive years in the entire nineteenth century.[7]

The greatest casualty of this bad weather was the potato crop and this led to severe distress in the west and north-west of the country. In December 1861, MacEvilly was writing to thank Paul Cullen for a donation towards relief, thanks which was to be repeated many times in these years.[8] Efforts were being made publicly too, and MacEvilly wrote to the Mansion House Committee thanking them for their donation of £50. In this letter, he pointed to the dual nature of the famine, reporting that the fuel famine was over but that the food famine would become more intense. He told how country people were pawning clothes to get food, trying in every way to avoid the dreaded workhouse. He stressed that but for the efforts of relief organisations, thousands would have died. 'People think that not only is the government neglecting them', he wrote, but they 'regard with disfavour every effort to save them.' He ended on a bitter note: 'No doubt, we enjoy very great liberty in this country. Where is there in any other country on the face of the globe such liberty to starve?'[9]

A month later, MacEvilly addressed a letter to Paul Cullen in his capacity as chairman of the Mansion House Committee. Again he attacked the government for its neglect. The distress in Galway was extensive, he reported. 'The failure of the potato crop and the difficulties of meeting the demands for rent which, in general, are rigidly exacted from the country district, leaves but very little business to be done in the town.' He then gave details of particular areas. The local committee was administering relief to 1300 families but funds were low and unless timely aid were supplied, 'God only does know what may be the consequences.' This number did not include one hundred families of Claddagh fishermen who could not put to sea. Miss Fanny Grattan, who owned the Claddagh, had spent more money in their relief in one year than she had received from them over many years. The Sisters of Mercy at Oughterard had told him how pitiable it was to see the number of able-bodied men who were applying for relief to support themselves and their families. In the district of Barna, nearly two hundred families were destitute. There were no seed potatoes or oats. In the Oranmore district many of the children at the school run by the Presentation Sisters were suffering from hunger. He next launched an attack on the poor conditions of the workhouses. He wrote:

> I need not inform your Grace, that the amount of relief given in the workhouse is no test of distress. The people are determined to die sooner than enter these charnel houses. For my own part, until the whole poor law system is totally changed, I will never advise them to enter institutions where the life of the old and the morals of the young are not safe.[10]

In his efforts to rouse the government, MacEvilly wrote to J. F. Maguire, M.P., who read the bishop's letter to the House of Commons in the course of a speech on Irish distress. MacEvilly had outlined the efforts of the local committee, quoting again the figures given to the Mansion House Committee. He stressed that were it not for 'this timely ministration of relief, hundreds of those for whom accommodation could not be provided, even if it were desirable, within the walls of the workhouse, would have perished . . . during the unusually inclement and severe winter through which we have passed.' It was deemed expedient, he went on, before applying for government aid, 'that the committee should wait upon the Board of Guardians, with a view of obtaining temporary outdoor relief.'[11]

Three years of rain were followed by an unusually dry spring in 1863.[12] The suffering of the poorer classes was intense. On 3 January, MacEvilly told Cullen, 'There is no starvation, no want of food or fuel, but the small landholders are quite unable to meet the demands accruing from past years. It is the conviction of the clergy here that were the American war to end, every one that could, would emigrate to America.'[13] Later in the month, he wrote about a preliminary meeting to prepare for a great general meeting to be called by the Sheriff of the county. All denominations were represented and all were agreed that 'the only proper way of dispensing charity, as far as it goes, would be in labour of some kind or other.' They were agreed too that 'the hordes of strolling ragged beggars with which the streets are filled should go to the workhouse and then the guardians should give outdoor relief to the starving artisans and householders.' The beggars, he added, were 'tempted' and they intercepted whatever relief might reach 'the starving householders.'[14]

The general meeting was held in January and the following resolution was put by MacEvilly:

> That owing to the defective harvests for three consecutive seasons, the complete paralysis of trade and the total want of employment experienced by the artisans and working classes, there is at present existing in this city

and neighbourhood deep distress, the people suffering privations greater than those in the famine years.[15]

The Galway relief committee was also renewed with MacEvilly in the chair, and at their meetings over the next three months, they discussed reports of widespread distress being experienced by trading classes, shopkeepers and farmers.[16]

MacEvilly was moved particularly by the sight of starving children, who were 'in every way so much exposed.' He told Cullen that the distress in the town had been greatly relieved because of 'the spring labours' and the employment given by the local relief committee. He reported that the tradespeople were still suffering a great deal. Times were worse for the small farmers, 'owing to the total want of means and the accumulated debts for food, together with rents and arrears of rent, which they cannot possibly meet.' He reported that Fr Peter Daly had received £20 from Sir Robert Peel, although MacEvilly was sure that it was meant more as an expression of approval for Daly's support for the Model school, which MacEvilly was just then attacking.[17] According to MacEvilly 'the Protestant party' was so furious at his attack that they had refused to attend the meetings of the relief committee. However, the bishop remarked, the meetings had 'gone on remarkably well without them.'[18]

By June, the distress was still widespread. The Galway relief committee had provided works, which had, MacEvilly claimed, 'as far as possible done away with the demoralising practice of granting purely gratuitous relief.' He also complained bitterly about the continued failure of the government to do anything. Some idea of the misery prevailing could be gathered from the fact that the clergy had requested MacEvilly to postpone episcopal visitations and confirmations because only a few people could attend 'for want of the necessary clothing, their clothing being pawned.'[19]

The bishop and clergy of Galway decided to make public their feelings and, in a series of resolutions published on 6 June, they spoke of the 'alarming state of destitution which prevails in this diocese especially.' They called on the government to come to the aid of the people there and then. In the longer term, they stated that before the evils of this country could be remedied, 'an equitable adjustment of the land laws must take place.'[20] Towards the end of the month, MacEvilly was able to report that matters were improving, as the prospects for the coming harvest were 'most encouraging.' Still, he informed Cullen, the people would be badly off for a long time.[21] Later, he confirmed that the worst was over, due to a very fine season. He had himself returned from a visit to the most distant part of the diocese, 'the wildest part even of Connemara,' and he was consoled to see 'the poor mountaineers' coming in crowds to receive the papal blessing. In Rosmuck alone, he reported with satisfaction, he had administered communion to 'upwards of 2,000 people.'[22]

The winter of 1863 was relatively mild and, as a result, food and fuel were much more plentiful. Nevertheless, because of accumulated debts there was continuing hardship for the country people, leaving them defenceless in any future crisis.[23]

For the poor people of those years, it must have seemed as if there was to be no end to their suffering. The exceptionally mild weather of 1863-4 was followed by an intense drought during the summer of 1864.[24] Once again the dread spectres of hunger and disease appeared, and once again Galway prepared for a public meeting to present its sad case to the world. At this meeting, which was held on 23 January 1865, MacEvilly took the chair. He described the meeting as important both for the city of Galway and the people themselves. Private subscriptions, he said, would be totally inadequate to meet the present crisis – 'it would be like one drop of water in the ocean.' As regards appealing to the government to provide some kind of remunerative works, he stated that the lord lieutenant would of course receive a deputation, but after hearing their claims, 'he would politely bow himself off and perhaps say – "God helps those who help themselves." ' A third measure would be to apply to the ratepayers of Galway and have a resolution adopted to the effect that application be made to the Poor Law Commissioners to sanction the giving of outdoor relief. He praised the people for remaining peaceful 'in their trying hardships' and he stated that it was work alone they wanted – 'They simply wanted to gain their living with their own stalwart arms and by the sweat of their brow.'[25]

Elsewhere in the county matters were as bad. The bishop of Clonfert described Loughrea as being in a 'miserable state' and he cried, 'What will become of our poor people?'[26] The Galway relief committee was forced to renew its activities under the chairmanship of MacEvilly. In an attempt to provide some remunerative work themselves, it was resolved to put one hundred men to work under the supervision of Fr Peter Daly to improve the sewerage of the town, and a further fifty men to work at Grattan Road.[27] The situation in the town was aggravated by the influx of those who had no work in the country plus those who had been evicted from their homes. The distress, which was now painfully evident, strengthened MacEvilly in his conviction that the only real solution was a satisfactory land measure.

There was no letup for the hard-pressed relief committees during the following winter. Coal was distributed to the 'really destitute,' but so extensive was the suffering that they decided they would have to try and provide food as well. The *Galway Vindicator* stated that never was there greater distress in the town, and meal was distributed in an effort to keep the poor alive.[28] Catholic and protestant clergy and magistrates had combined in the effort to save the people. Sadly however, the bishop announced, all their efforts were not sufficient and he called again for government aid. A circular was issued, asking for help for over one thousand Galway families in distress. If Galway had been treated as it should have been by a 'paternal government,' the circular declared, then it would have been one of the most flourishing centres of trade in the United Kingdom.[29]

By the end of January 1867, the situation was still critical. The relief committee met and although upwards of £50 had been subscribed, it was not at all sufficient to buy food as well as fuel.[30] MacEvilly in his pastoral offered little consolation by telling people to take up their cross and asking: 'How often does not a jealous God visit with temporal and spiritual misfortunes unfortunate children in punishment of the infidelities of their parents?' One feels too that it was more in hope than in confidence that he prayed that 'the almighty, who holds in his hands the hearts of men, would inspire our rulers with a spirit of justice to redress the trying wrongs of our misgoverned country, and by just legislation dry up the sources of the dissatisfaction and discontent.'[31]

Despite the bad harvests and weather, famine had been averted and there were no serious outbreaks of disease. This had not been due to the efforts of a government which continued to provide assistance only in a limited way by its application of the rigid poor law. While there were notable efforts by the Mansion House Committee, the Society of Friends and local relief committees, the fact that famine did not occur again was due to other circumstances. The population of Connacht had been greatly reduced since the Great Famine. The government was much more sensitive to the threat of death by starvation, and landlords no longer carried out large-scale evictions. Perhaps, most important of all, when the potato crop did fail, cheap alternative supplies of food could be distributed quickly and on a wide scale through the recently improved network of wholesaling, retailing and credit. Indian meal, which took the place of the potato, was a lifesaver for many of the poor in the years of crisis.[32]

Not until 1872 was there cause again for real concern. It had rained all through the summer. Once more a public meeting was held in Galway to raise funds for fuel for the poor.[33] It was a most severe winter and, in January 1873, MacEvilly reported that the country was under water. 'Such weather was never witnessed by any one living,' he wrote.[34]

As bishop of Galway, MacEvilly had striven to call attention to, and relieve the plight of the poorer sections of the community. In doing this he adhered to the conventional methods of his time. He had repeatedly called for government aid and had organised public meetings and voluntary bodies to try and cope with the overwhelming demands. He had criticised the government for its failure to save the people and he had many times pointed to a real and lasting solution. The disastrous harvests of 1878 and 1879 gave rise to a movement which set itself to achieve this lasting solution. The Land League would no longer be content with the temporary relief provided by private subscription and public charity, but looked for reforms of the land laws which, it was hoped, would remove the underlying causes of distress and provide permanent security for the long-suffering tenant farmers of the west.

DISTRESS IN TUAM

When MacEvilly came to the diocese of Tuam as coadjutor towards the end of 1879, he was coming to a diocese which had the kind of problems he already knew too well. Within Tuam's boundaries were some of the most neglected areas in the whole country. Here many people lived at subsistence level for most of their lives. The people of Achill and areas of Connemara were always at risk. For them one bad harvest was sufficient to bring ruin, and whether they lived through these winters might well be a matter of chance. The diocese of Tuam also included a number of islands, such as Inisboffin, Clare Island, and the Aran Islands. The islanders were even more at the mercy of the elements and certainly they experienced more than their share of hardships and suffering during the latter half of the nineteenth century.

The season of MacEvilly's arrival in Tuam was reckoned to be the worst since the tragic one of 1848.[35] It was particularly bad in Galway and Mayo, where over £61,000 was spent on relief in the years 1879-80.[36] MacEvilly was having a difficult time trying to establish himself as coadjutor in Tuam. The refusal by MacHale to grant him any recognition certainly hindered MacEvilly from taking as active a part in the organisation and working of relief committees as he had done previously. The hard-pressed people of Mayo looked to the Land League to save them and the movement was quickly and firmly established in the diocese of Tuam. As we have seen elsewhere, MacEvilly withheld his support, being concerned mainly with the involvement of the Tuam clergy in the agitation.[37]

Certainly the country was in a dreadful state. As a result of the complete failure of the harvest of 1879, there were over 105,000 cases of pauperism and evictions numbered more than 2,000 families. There was also a sharp increase in agrarian crime.[38] In a public acknowledgement of a donation, MacEvilly stated that within a month those in want would number thousands. The terrible misfortune was no fault of the people, he declared, but was due 'in a great measure . . . to the visitation of Providence.' And again he placed all responsibility on the government.[39] He reported the same prospect of a 'very severe famine' to Kirby, acknowledging a sum of £142 from Pope Leo XIII for relief of distress in Connacht.[40]

Undoubtedly one of the factors leading to MacEvilly's conversion to Parnell's Irish Party was the unsatisfactory response which he and the other western bishops received from the government early in 1883. On 9 January, the bishops went in deputation to the lord lieutenant in Dublin and presented a long memorial which outlined the problems of their dioceses and offered some possible remedies. The document described the extent of the suffering affecting one third to one half of the population in the country areas and still more in the towns.[41] The bishops then commented on the various relief measures proposed. Firstly, relief within the workhouse would be so revolting to the people that they would rather starve than accept such aid. Secondly, on the question of outdoor relief to householders and small landholders, the bishops deplored its many evil effects on both recipients and ratepayers. Thirdly, employment on public works would also be demoralising, as well as totally inadequate. It could not be made promptly and generally available so as to afford immediate relief when and where required. Fourthly, there was the employment of destitute landholders on their own holdings, with advance of government loans in consideration of, and in proportion to, improvements made thereon. This method of relief met with the bishops' entire approval and they urgently recommended that it be adopted. They also made detailed suggestions regarding this system of relief.[42]

Finally, the bishops summed up the situation. Great and widespread distress was fast approaching; government relief was necessary; such relief should be prompt and general; it should be such as the destitute would accept and such as would prevent the necessity of future public relief; it should also be in the interests of social peace and prosperity. The bishops were confident that the system of loans that they advocated and the consequent agricultural improvements would fulfill all of these conditions as no other measure of relief would. They also recommended that loans to small tenants be continued and liberally extended when the distress was over. They urged the government to undertake the purchase, reclamation and division of waste lands and to provide public works on a large scale. The document ended: 'These and like Government measures will be taken by the people as evidence of good will and sympathy; and they are, in our opinion, indispensable helps in remedying the chronic discontent and destitution from which all classes in the country are suffering.' The memorial was signed by MacEvilly and the bishops of Elphin, Clonfert, Killala and Achonry.[43]

The statement of the bishops was obviously one which had taken time, thought and trouble. It was comprehensive and, as social, economic and political comment, it was a reasoned and reasonable statement, well worthy of the most careful consideration by the administration. When, however, the response did come, it amounted to a studied insult; and was signed by a civil servant, R.G.C. Hamilton. He informed the bishops that the lord lieutenant had laid their statement before the Treasury.[44]

The bishops were extremely displeased, and after MacEvilly had acknowledged the reply,[45] they met to consider the situation. A series of resolutions was passed and these, together with the entire correspondence to date, were published in the *Freeman's Journal*.[46] The first resolution deplored the refusal of the government to aid destitute people by granting loans for the improvement of their holdings. Secondly, in default of the remunerative employment which these loans would have provided, the bishops called on the government to grant adequate outdoor relief to all destitute landholders and householders. Thirdly, to refuse relief to the destitute until they became inmates of a workhouse was 'an outrage on humanity and a violation of one of the first duties of a government.' The bishops were advising their people to cling to their homes and should they die therein from hunger, then the government must take the full guilt and responsibility for these deaths. The fourth resolution condemned measures of parliament aimed at emigrating the labourers and the small tenant class. In its social consequences, the bishops declared that this policy would soon be seen as 'a grievous political mistake.' The next two resolutions dealt with the need to reclaim and divide large tracts of waste land. There were in the province about two million acres of rich pasturage, most of which was used to feed flocks and herds for the English market. This land was formerly tilled by Irish tenants who, in the famine years and after, had been driven from their holdings to the towns and workhouses, or to the bogs and mountains which the government now said were overcrowded. The bishops ended with an appeal 'to our brethren at home and abroad to supply us with the means of saving our people from the temporal evils, and what is infinitely more important, from the great spiritual dangers with which they are now threatened.'[47]

The accuracy of the bishops' prediction that government policy would soon be seen as a grievous political mistake is discussed elsewhere.[48] Certainly MacEvilly was gradually alienated over the next two years and when the next crisis arose, in 1885, he was a supporter of the Irish party.

In such times of distress, the situation of the islands always gave cause for serious concern. So grave were matters in the 1885-6 season, that an appeal had to be made to the public by the parish priest, Fr O'Donohue. In supporting it, MacEvilly stated that he had similar reports from Achill and Boffin. The failure of the potato crop, the archbishop pointed out, left the people 'hardly any available resource for prolonging a miserable existence.' Because of the sea journey even the dreaded workhouse was impossible for the islanders. An application had been made to the authorities but to no avail. Nothing then remained but to appeal to the public.[49]

That same year brought hardship everywhere. The harvest of 1885 had been poor while agricultural prices remained depressed.[50] The wet spring meant delayed planting and this aggravated an already serious situation.[51] Again an appeal had to be made to the public.[52]

This pattern of temporary relief and recurring crisis was repeated over the following years. When, in October 1887, it was proposed by Propaganda to hold a collection for the contemplated national church of St. Patrick in Rome, MacEvilly protested that it was the most inopportune time for the diocese of Tuam. The bishops had already decided that there would be no collection that year as the people were 'on the point of bankruptcy and suffering from the greatest depression ever remembered.' Such a collection now would certainly fail, and, he added, 'failure . . . would be most humiliating.'[53]

The crisis, which brought the greatest hardship and gave rise to the Plan of Campaign,[54] also brought renewed suffering on the Aran Islands. The potato crop had failed and, since the previous November, almost the entire population of the three islands had been in want. In October 1887, the Local Government Board was sent a report on the situation by the parish priest, Fr Michael O'Donohue. In reply the Board stated that there were no enactments in force which would allow relief works to be opened or exceptional relief to be provided. The destitute people on these islands would have to rely on the operation of the ordinary Poor Law Act. The guardians of the Galway Union, at a meeting on 22 February 1888, passed a resolution refusing to carry out the instructions of the Local Government Board or to sign a cheque for provisional relief. As the parish priest stated starkly, people were dying while government bodies squabbled and so he had decided to appeal to the public. He informed the Irish executive of the situation and was told by the lord lieutenant that the necessary steps had already been taken by the guardians for coping with any destitution that might arise. The lord lieutenant also told him that there were no funds for seed potatoes, and wished him well in his appeal.

Again MacEvilly wrote to support the appeal.[55] He told of a visit to Aran the previous summer when 'on the greater portion of the island the crops were badly burned up – hardly a sound stalk to be seen.' The fine weather which had been welcomed everywhere else had had disastrous results on the limestone surface of Aran. 'How often did I see with grief and sorrow,' the archbishop recorded movingly, 'these hard-working industrious islanders carry the sea sand, mixed with sea weed, on their backs, and spread it on the barren limestone rocks? Dearly were they forced to pay in the shape of rack rents for the land watered by the sweat of their brow.' He expressed his surprise at the 'blunt refusal' of the government to come to the aid of a starving people. Millions had been spent for 'at best doubtful military projects on the banks of the Nile' but now a few thousand pounds would not be spent on works which could save these people. 'To propose to these poor people, young and old, the alternative of starving or crossing Galway Bay – a distance of over thirty miles – at this inclement or indeed at any season to enter the cold walls of a workhouse, looks like cruel, heartless mockery of the unhappy conditions to which they are reduced through no fault of their own . . . ,' MacEvilly wrote, and then asked whether the starving poor in any part of England were so treated. There was no choice but to appeal to the generosity of the public. In conclusion, MacEvilly still echoed the popular sentiment of the time when he asked that 'not a farthing should be given in gratuitous relief save where absolutely necessary as it would be sure to end in utter demoralisation.'[56]

Some of the more enlightened attempts at a solution to the recurring problems of the west sprung from Arthur Balfour's policy of conciliation. In 1890 the chief secretary made a tour of the distressed areas. He concluded that the only permanent solution to the problems there was a combination of emigration and land purchase.[57] In the meantime, there were pressing demands to be met and a programme of relief works was launched by the government at the end of the year.[58] Relief works, however, were but a temporary measure to avert disaster. As an attempt at a more permanent solution, the Congested Districts Board was set up under the Land Purchase Act of 1891.[59] In general, the Board was to promote native industries, to effect the amalgamation and improvement of holdings through purchase, to resettle tenants on holdings made viable by the Board's intervention and to give instruction in modern farming techniques.[60] Committees were organised and a series of schemes initiated in the districts designated 'congested.'

Balfour himself is said to have considered the Congested Districts Board as one of his crowning achievements in Ireland, and it was praised by Davitt and John Dillon.[61] W. L. Micks, an official of the Board and its historian, was not as enthusiastic. He praised the Board as a novel attempt to provide a solution but he criticised it as too limited in powers to achieve its aims. In his view, the chief value of the legislation of 1891 was the recognition it gave to the principle of the duty of the state to intervene in a situation where there was 'widespread poverty, lapsing periodically into absolute destitution.'[62]

To observers 'on the ground', like John MacEvilly, the Board did not appear significantly successful in solving the problems of the 'congested' areas, as throughout the 1890s the problem of feeding the hungry remained and the people continued to flee the land. In 1895, for instance, it was necessary to form a relief committee in the town of Tuam and start to aid the poor.[63] In his Lenten pastoral, MacEvilly called on those who were 'blessed with the goods of this world' to contribute towards the relief of the 'exceptional distress,' which was threatening to become worse, especially in mountainous areas and along the coast. The only way to remedy this, said MacEvilly, was to appeal to the government 'to save the people by the construction of useful convenient public works.'[64]

By the late 1890s, Irish emigrants in the United States were helping greatly by their contributions to families and friends at home. MacEvilly wrote to publicly acknowledge this help. In a letter published in the *New York World* in September 1897, he expressed his thanks and outlined the grim situation in Tuam. 'It is most humiliating,' he wrote, 'to be eternally sending round the hat, but what can be done? Hunger pierces stone walls . . . . On the whole, I look on the coming time as boding misery.' The archbishop ended, 'I give you a gloomy picture, but I am sorry to say a true one.'[65]

MacEvilly's gloomy forebodings were all too accurate, as 1898 proved to be a year of want and hardship, affecting many people in Tuam diocese. The archbishop, in his Lenten pastoral, warned that unless the poor people were relieved in time, their condition would soon become 'intolerable.'[66]

Later in the year, MacEvilly wrote to the editor of the *Boston Pilot* to thank readers for their contribution of three hundred dollars. He denied reports circulated by 'some men in office on this side of the Atlantic' that there was no distress. In fact, MacEvilly stated emphatically, 'the deepest distress' existed all along the coast, in Connemara, Achill and the island of Boffin. This covered an area of about sixty miles and it was, as MacEvilly was careful to point out, an area where the people were entirely dependent on the potato and where there were no factories. The letter ended with a strong statement of what, in MacEvilly's view, was the only satisfactory and lasting solution.

> Our people, after having been unjustly banished from the rich lands fertilised by the sweat of their brow, in gross violation of the laws of God and nature, are relegated to the bogs, on small patches of worthless land. To this in a great measure may be traced, even in the most prosperous years, the ever-recurring distress. We must patiently await the restoration to them of the lands, by peaceful legislation, of which they have been robbed.[67]

The archbishop also wrote a letter of thanks to the *Irish World,* the editor of which was the influential Patrick Ford, a man whose strong nationalist views would hardly have endeared him to the MacEvilly of earlier years. The continuing refusals of various administrations to heed the repeated pleas of the archbishop can account for the tone of angry frustration, and even bitterness, evident in this long letter, wherein he reiterated all his views.[68]

By November MacEvilly could report that the crisis had passed. 'But,' he added, 'I fancy the bishops may make use of the amount forwarded in looking to the coming year and making some provision against famine, especially in seeing that spraying be properly attended to.'[69] And indeed it was the spraying of the potato crop that was an important factor in putting an end to the recurring nightmare of a people who were over-dependent on this food. If, by the end of the nineteenth century, the tale of woes from life in the west was not so horrific, the credit was due as much to the external circumstances as it was to any enlightened policy on the part of the government. Apart from the intervention of an effective counter to the blight, the situation was eased by the fact that there was more money contributed on appeal. This money came in great part from those who, no longer content to risk their lives to the clemency of the weather, had chosen the way out – emigration.

EMIGRATION

As with hunger and distress, emigration was a feature of life with which MacEvilly was to become sadly well acquainted. The flight from the depressed areas of counties Galway and Mayo that began with the Great Famine continued throughout the second half of the nineteenth century, increasing sharply from the 1870s on. For many people it was a clear choice – emigrate or stay and risk starvation, disease and death.

Official figures for those years, as shown in the two charts, are suspect in some respects but they are sufficient to indicate the enormity of the problem.

POPULATION[70]

	1851	1861	1871	1881	1891	1901
Co. Galway	321,684	271,478	248,458	242,005	214,712	192,549
Galway City	20,055	16,448	15,597	15,471	13,800	13,426
Co. Mayo	274,499	254,796	246,030	245,212	219,034	199,166
Tuam Town	4,929	4,563	4,223	3,567	3,012	2,896

EMIGRATION[70]

	1851-61	1861-71	1871-81	1881-91	1891-1901	TOTAL
Co. Galway	50,838	38,758	23,665	51,121	36,820	201,202
Co. Mayo	29,317	27,496	24,705	42,368	40,703	164,589

While a study of John MacEvilly's correspondence does not provide evidence that is in any way conclusive, certainly the impression is conveyed of mass emigration. In the year 1863 particularly, MacEvilly seemed to have been very concerned about the flight from Galway. It was a year of great hardship in the west and on 3 January MacEvilly told Cullen that the clergy of Galway diocese were convinced that if the American civil war were at an end, 'every one that could, would emigrate to America.'[71] In March MacEvilly stated simply, 'Indeed the settled resolve on the part of the people seems to be to emigrate as soon as possible.'[72] In December he reported that the country people were 'totally bereft of means' and that they were preparing, with the coming of spring, 'to fly the county in crowds, as many of them as can.'[73]

In March 1865, MacEvilly wrote to Kirby that the people were 'emigrating in shoals.'[74] In 1867, in his Lenten pastoral, the bishop referred to those who were evicted. The only consolation offered them, said the bishop, was 'the cold assurances of heartless economists that the country needed depletion and that they should be offered up as victims for the supposed general good of society.'[75]

As the nineteenth century wore on, there was growing support for that school of economists which favoured emigration as a solution to Ireland's problems. State-sponsored schemes of emigration had actually been put into effect as early as 1823 and 1825.[76] Again after the Great Famine, various schemes were proposed for emigration as a mode of relief.[77] The idea was viewed with alarm and resentment by those who saw emigration as symptomatic of the government's failure to produce any policies which would enable people to earn their living in their own country.[78] It was an area of great sensitivity, where governments had to tread warily. The opposition, which included the Irish bishops, was always on the alert for any measure which hinted at government aid and encouragement for impending emigrants. The debate, then, was between those who viewed emigration as the primary indication of decline and those for whom emigration was a sign of economic recovery and progress.

MacEvilly entered this debate in October 1883, when the *Freeman's Journal*, in a major scoop, published a sixteen-page document marked 'confidential' and entitled 'Suggestions by the Emigration Committee relating to the manner of conducting state-aided emigration, submitted by them to the Local Government Board.' The 'confidential circular,' as it came to be called, was signed by C. T. Redington, W. P. Gaskell and John Ross of Bladenburg. The circular proposed the establishment of a Bureau of Emigration, with a chief inspector, a staff of clerks and all the machinery of a department under the Local Government Board. It was recommended that a certain sum of money be assigned for the payment of union officers who managed the 'business of emigration.' Suggested rates of pay would range from £25 for 100 emigrants up to £140 for 1,500 emigrants. Not only was it proposed that every clerk of a union be a paid emigration agent but there was to be 'an army of touters' for emigrants in every county in Ireland. There was also to be a contract, for which shipping companies would be invited to tender, 'for the wholesale deportation of the people.'[79]

Immediately, the scheme was denounced by the archbishop and clergy of Tuam, who pledged themselves to resist in every legal manner any such scheme, and they called on the parliamentary representative to oppose the plan, which they described as 'at once anti-national and impolitic.'[80] This brought a response from the chief secretary. In his letter to MacEvilly, which was subsequently published in the press, the chief secretary stated that he was disregarding the *Freeman's Journal*, which had printed the contents of 'a confidential document surreptitiously communicated,' but he felt it his duty to set the archbishop's fears at rest. The Tramways Act had placed £50,000 at the disposal of the government for the purpose of assisting poor persons who wished to emigrate from certain areas of Ireland. This sum would be administered on much the same lines as the £100,000 assigned by the Arrears Act of 1882, with this modification: that the lord lieutenant was now empowered to give a grant up to £8 a head, instead of £5 as fixed by the Act. The government had no power whatever to spend any money for emigration except under these two Acts. There followed an attempt to explain away the circular as 'merely a confidential list of suggestions made by three of the gentlemen employed in emigration work' the previous year. 'These suggestions,' the letter ended, 'which were printed for office convenience, had not even been read by any person in authority at the time when, through a breach of confidence, they were communicated to a newspaper.'[81]

The archbishop's immediate reply to this feeble explanation put three pertinent queries. Firstly, why did the document, if it had no reality, remain unchallenged for days by the gentlemen who drew it up? Secondly, why should those men, whose names were given, draw up such a document except at the behest of the government? 'However estimable they may be in their private capacity,' MacEvilly remarked, 'apart from government support they could naturally exercise but very little power in the matter.' Thirdly, what was more natural than that the archbishop and clergy of Tuam should denounce a scheme by which poor people were to be induced 'by largesses and blandishments to abandon under pressure of dire want the land of their affections, to perish amidst the snows of Canada?' As to whether the *Freeman's Journal* or the government had the truth of the matter, MacEvilly summed up his opinion of the circular by saying, 'although confidential it seems to be nevertheless a reality.'[82]

The *Freeman's Journal* of 14 November carried a letter from one of the signatories of the circular, C. T. Redington of Kilcornan, Oranmore, Co. Galway. According to Redington, the suggestions were intended simply for the guidance of the government in administering funds already voted by parliament to aid the voluntary emigration of poor people from certain strictly defined districts in the country. There were not, therefore, said Redington, any grounds for the assertion that these suggestions formed part of a 'gigantic scheme for the wholesale deportation of the Irish people.'[83]

The clergy of Tuam were not impressed. On this issue, certainly, the clergy were as one, denouncing in the strongest terms the proposed scheme and expressing appreciation for the prompt action of the *Freeman's Journal* and their archbishop.[84]

The furore died away but the fears it had aroused remained. MacEvilly's opposition to the circular was an indication of his new direction, and indeed the government attitude was a factor in MacEvilly's declaration of support for the Irish party.[85] It was now clear to him that the government was not going to provide remedies for the problems of emigration and that solutions would have to be sought elsewhere. It was this which led him to encourage the notion of migration as opposed to emigration, and to give his backing to schemes for the movement of people from one area of the country to another.

The Irish Land Purchase and Settlement Company Limited was formed in 1884 with the aim of making migration possible. The chairman was C. S. Parnell and board members included Jacob Bright, M.P.; Colonel Nolan, M.P., for Galway county; Edmund Dwyer Gray, M.P.; and William Henry O'Shea, M.P. and husband of Katherine. Managing Director was Thomas Baldwin, assistant land commissioner. The company proposed to purchase suitable estates, where the lands were not too thickly populated, and to sell to tenants willing to buy their holdings. Where the lands were congested, it was proposed to remove the surplus population to such other company lands as were available.[86]

MacEvilly gave the grand scheme his blessing from the beginning. At a meeting of the clergy in the deanery of Tuam, the archbishop and priests declared that having opposed successfully 'the insidious project of emigrating our people,' they should now back the effort to provide comfortable homes and farms for the people from overcrowded districts. The assembled clergy took 530 shares, MacEvilly himself heading the list with the acquisition of 200 shares.[87]

MacEvilly informed McCabe in Dublin that he was doing his best for 'the Migration Company,' as he believed it 'the only plank – since we cannot have manufactures – to save the country from shipwreck.' Two further meetings were held in Tuam in May. A first meeting of clergy and laity at the presbytery was addressed by MacEvilly and Baldwin; a committee was appointed and shares sold.[88]

The second May meeting was a much bigger affair. This was held on Sunday, 25 May in the cathedral grounds in Tuam. MacEvilly again presided and he told the crowds that they were assembled to promote 'one of the most patriotic projects that was ever put forward in the memory of living men for advancing the interests of our country.' The Migration Company, he said, had 'for object to root the people in the soil without injuring the rights of any man living.' This meeting would be followed by more throughout the diocese, and he urged his listeners to take shares in the company, arguing that a hundred shares were worth two hundred speeches.[89]

On the Thursday following this meeting, the company made its first venture into the market. The Bodkin estate at Kilclooney near Tuam was purchased for £43,300, which was made up of £1,000 of the company's own money and a loan of £42,300 from the Irish Land Commission.[90] But for all MacEvilly's enthusiasm and the backing of national figures, the project never really succeeded. In 1886, the Irish Land Commission appointed a receiver over the Bodkin estate, having from the beginning collected all the rents and profits. Part of the estate was later sold to the tenants and the purchase money was retained by the Land Commission.[91]

1894 was also the year when the plight of migrant workers was highlighted in the most tragic way. Achill Island had built up a tradition of migrancy and every year tenants left their farms for Scotland to subsidise their meagre incomes. In June 1894, twenty-three of one hundred migrant workers were drowned in Clew Bay when the hooker taking them from Daly's Point to Westport capsized. The workers were mostly in their teens and for many of them it was their first trip to Scotland for the harvest. It seems that in their excitement at seeing the Glasgow steamer, they stood up and caused the boat to overturn. Many more would have been lost but for the prompt action of the steamer's crew.[92]

The disaster focussed attention on the migrants' situation and provoked a flurry of activity aimed at improving the workers' lot. MacEvilly was approached by the Lord Mayor of Dublin, V. B. Dillon, asking his support for a committee to administer an Achill improvement fund.[93] MacEvilly himself had already broached the formation of a committee of priests and laymen of all denominations before there was any talk of a Mansion House Committee.[94] He gave his 'most cordial approval' to the Lord Mayor's project in a reply which was published in the press. He suggested some names, including William O'Brien and Michael Davitt. He also recommended the inclusion of 'some charitable and respectable Protestant gentlemen' who had shown 'benevolence and charity' in this case. He thought that the committee should be composed of men of every religious persuasion and political viewpoint.

'Too long,' he wrote in a rare burst of ecumenism, 'have these accursed religious and political differences kept the children of the same soil asunder. It is time they should cease.' MacEvilly's idea was that once the immediate needs had been catered for, the remainder of the fund which had been subscribed should be invested and the interest 'rejudiciously distributed' and carefully supervised. To dispose of the total amount contributed all at once would, he felt, 'only raise false and demoralising hopes each successive year, and lead to apathy and want of self-respect and self-reliance.'[95] He then reflected on the sad state of things that compelled poor boys and girls, such as the victims of the Clew Bay catastrophe, 'to fly to another country at such risks to gain the means of prolonging existence at home.' This was made even worse, he declared, by the fact that 'in the very sight of Achill, along the southern and western coasts of Clew Bay,' there was plenty of land, which, 'if judiciously parcelled out,' would 'easily clear Achill of its congestion' as well as benefitting the owners materially.[96]

By the end of the century, MacEvilly, tired and embittered as a result of many useless pleas to governments, was turning his attention more and more to the fate of those who were leaving. In 1900, he wrote to a priest who had opened a hostel for Irish immigrant girls in New York. In his letter, which was published in the influential Irish-American paper, the *Irish World,* MacEvilly thanked those who were protecting immigrants 'against the dangers they are exposed to in a foreign land; the desolate children of decent, respectable, once comfortable parents.' He ended with a prayer for that 'great country' which had 'hospitably opened wide her arms to rescue them.'[97]

In one of his last public statements, MacEvilly also issued a warning to all intending emigrants. 'Little did the poor boys and girls know of what was before them' in America. He implored them to think twice before they left, for unfortunately there were accounts now that in various cities, hundreds of poor Irish boys and girls were going about with nothing to do, although they were willing to work.[98]

In his addresses on education too in his latter years, MacEvilly seems to have accepted the inevitability of emigration and he urged the people to ensure that their children receive a good education so that they might be better prepared to emigrate. In an address in 1898, he said that Irish catholics educated their children in the christian doctrine but that secular education was sometimes neglected. The Irish were the hewers of wood and drawers of water in other countries and if they were better educated, the archbishop thought that they might make 'five or ten times as much of their time.'[99] MacEvilly does not seem to have made much use of what might be termed the 'missionary' argument, in which emigrants from Ireland were often praised as bearers of the Christian message to foreign lands. All his speeches on the subject were marked by regret. Certainly their going represented a serious diminution of his catholic flock, but there was also concern that those who left were ill-equipped for their new life.

In 1902, the year of MacEvilly's death, the Irish bishops discussed the question of emigration at their annual meeting. They pointed out that in ten years the population of Ireland had fallen by a quarter of a million and almost four millions in the half century. They warned people against going to America, saying that it was reckless in the present state of the American labour market. They commended the work of the Congested Districts Board in having large grazing tracts divided and they called for the establishment of suitable industries and factories.[100]

How much the bishops thought their call would influence government policy is difficult to say. Certainly MacEvilly had not too much confidence at that stage of his career – a career that had seen the counties Galway and Mayo lose at least 365,791 people to emigration.[101]

Chapter 8

The Irish Party

WE HAVE SEEN how John MacEvilly was opposed to the Land League from the beginning. Equally he was opposed to the parliamentary arm, and to Parnell himself. Like Butt before him, Parnell was not a catholic and therefore more independent of clerical control and episcopal influence. This fact in itself would have, in MacEvilly's opinion, rendered him unsuitable to be the leader of a catholic people. As regards the party, its connections with the Land League meant for MacEvilly the danger of a movement which again might be independent of the priests and wield more influence over the people. Since to oppose the movement outright would certainly have met with popular resistance, for the most part MacEvilly's hostility showed itself in a negative fashion, such as refusing to allow the clergy to take an active part in the organisation of the party.

The results of the 1880 election in Mayo displeased MacEvilly greatly. Parnell, who had stood for the constituency and been duly elected, opted to sit for Cork, and his Mayo seat went to Rev. Isaac Nelson, a Presbyterian minister from Belfast.[1] Politically it was not a move likely to win the support of MacEvilly. 'Think of catholic Mayo,' he reacted, 'returning a presbyterian minister to represent it at the bidding of Mr Parnell who wields such power.'[2] Nor was Mayo's other elected representative any more pleasing to the coadjutor bishop of Tuam, who saw the return of O'Connor Power as the fruit of Fenianism.[3] But if the result of the Mayo election was painful for him,[4] MacEvilly was able to report that Galway had been 'saved,' and wrote that if any of the 'faction' had attempted anything there, he himself would have canvassed personally.[5] And when MacEvilly succeeded MacHale in Tuam, he quickly let it be known that new attitudes would prevail. So effective was the new archbishop's campaign that there was no representative from the diocese of Tuam present at the inaugural meeting of the National League in October 1882.[6]

If, however, MacEvilly thought that in seeking to redress grievances, more could be achieved by dealing directly with the government than through the Irish party, he was to be disappointed. The beginning of disillusionment came in January 1883, when he led a deputation of the bishops of Connacht to the lord lieutenant, Earl Spencer, at Dublin Castle to present him with a long memorial.[7] After a month had elapsed without a reply, MacEvilly expressed his annoyance that the lord lieutenant had not seen fit to answer what had been an urgent request for help.[8] In March, a reply did come, but one which amounted to nothing more than an acknowledgement and stated that there were 'insuperable difficulties.'[9] A further set of resolutions followed, with as little result.[10]

This snub, however much it may have hurt him, was not in itself sufficient to drive MacEvilly to support the Irish party. His hostility to, and suspicion of, Parnell remained. Yet, he became increasingly conscious of the leader's popularity in the country. This clash of sentiments is well illustrated in his reaction to the condemnation by Rome of the Parnell Testimonial Fund in May 1883, forbidding the clergy to take any part in it. MacEvilly's cautious attitude to the condemnation was clear enough – 'Rome has spoken, our duty is simple hearty obedience.'[11] He knew however that the matter was not so simple, being well aware of the popular view that the condemnation had been achieved by English influence in Rome, and also the conviction of the people that Parnell had rescued them from 'the direst tyranny ever endured by a people from the landlord class.' Once more, his main fear was that the people would be alienated from the clergy.[12]

Episcopal appointments constituted a highly sensitive area at the time, and MacEvilly's opinion was sought with regard to the appointment of a coadjutor bishop to Cardinal McCabe of Dublin. This was an appointment of crucial importance and all were well aware of the political significance. William Walsh, president of Maynooth College, a man of known nationalist sympathies and the choice both of priests and people, was opposed by the English government and its supporters in Ireland. MacEvilly was therefore at his most cautious and prudent. He believed that the ablest man was Dr Walsh, who had no equal in 'learning, zeal, industry, indefatigable vigilance.' He was not sure, however, how the appointment would please McCabe,[13] which almost certainly means that he was sure that McCabe, opponent of the Land League and Parnell, would strongly resent the appointment. So once more, MacEvilly was trapped between two stools: loyalty to McCabe and his policy and the increasingly aggressive mood of Irish nationalism.

As if to drive MacEvilly more firmly behind the Irish party, on 29 October, the *Freeman's Journal* published a sixteen-page document marked 'confidential' and headed 'Suggestions by the Emigration Committee relating to the manner of conducting state-aided emigration, submitted by them to the Local Government Board.' It proposed setting up a Bureau of Emigration under the Local Government

Board and paying the union officers who managed the business of emigration, this payment to be determined according to the number of emigrants who left. As we have seen, the scheme was denounced by the archbishop with all the clergy behind him.[14] Indeed, MacEvilly found himself the recipient of praise from such unlikely sources as erstwhile opponents, Canon Ulick Bourke of Claremorris and Father Patrick Lavelle of Cong.[15]

In March 1884, a branch of the National League was founded in Tuam.[16] MacEvilly, however, was not yet prepared, or sufficiently convinced, to declare his support publicly. Parnell visited Tuam in connection with the purchase of an estate near the town for his Irish Land Purchase and Settlement Company. He was given a public welcome, but again the clergy were significantly absent. In his reply to the address of welcome from the town commissioners, Parnell was most politic, and perhaps even poked a little fun. 'I am glad to find,' he stated, 'that the great John of Tuam has such a worthy successor which must be to you a source of great pride and satisfaction and consolation. I regret it was not in my power to find the Archbishop of Tuam at home to-night, but I trust at some future time when I come again amongst you to have the pleasure of seeing him.'[17]

Yet all the while MacEvilly's losing battle with the government was continuing and his frustration was becoming more apparent. When, in this same year, the property of the Propaganda in Rome was threatened by the Italian government, Kirby wrote to MacEvilly from Rome suggesting that the Irish bishops should forward a request to the English government or the queen, asking them to intervene.

The bishops decided in favour of a joint appeal, which was drawn up at their Maynooth meeting early in July and presented to Gladstone.[18] After the prime minister's non-committal reply had been received, MacEvilly reacted to Kirby in a letter: 'We all knew what it would be, but as Propaganda authorities wished it, we of course applied to the government. But rely on it, they will never give catholics or Ireland anything they can refuse.' And he ended with the very significant remark, 'I am not, as you are aware, a violent politician. But I feel very strongly the injustice practised towards us.'[19] MacEvilly's indignation was further fed by the refusal of the chief secretary, G.O. Trevelyan, in July to provide funds to build an industrial school in Connemara, and he complained bitterly to Kirby.[20]

It was as if MacEvilly was being pushed more and more to the support of the Irish party. The final straw, and that which killed whatever little faith MacEvilly had left in an insensitive administration, was the Maamtrasna affair. This extraordinary and bizarre sequence of events began on the night of 17 August 1882 in the remote area of Maamtrasna in the Partry mountains, when John Joyce, his wife, his mother and a young daughter were murdered in their little cottage. Joyce's two sons were so badly injured that one died the following day and the other's life was in jeopardy for some time. The police arrested ten men, who were duly returned for trial. Two of the accused, Anthony Philbin and Thomas Casey, became approvers and prosecution witnesses. Three men were sentenced to death, while the others were persuaded to plead guilty on the promise of escaping capital punishment. One of those condemned to death, a man named Myles Joyce, continued to protest his innocence to the end. Even as he stood on the scaffold with the rope round his neck, he shouted his innocence.[21]

Two years later, when MacEvilly was administering confirmation in Partry parish, Thomas Casey, one of the prosecution witnesses, confessed publicly before the archbishop, clergy and large congregation that he had sworn falsely against Myles Joyce. The following Sunday, the archbishop said that the government must take its share of the blame for what had occurred, and called on them to release those in prison and compensate both the imprisoned and the family of Myles Joyce.[22] MacEvilly then wrote to Spencer, the lord lieutenant, with the details of Casey's confession, as well as his allegations that George Bolton, solicitor for the crown, had promised him his freedom and a large sum of money to give evidence against the others. MacEvilly added that Casey's sworn statement had been fully corroborated by Anthony Philbin, who was also prepared to make a similar public declaration. He concluded by asking the lord lieutenant to direct a sworn inquiry into the case.[23]

By way of reply, MacEvilly had a letter from R.G.C. Hamilton which enclosed a memorandum that stated:

> Having satisfied himself after the fullest inquiry that the verdicts in the several cases were right and that the statements of Casey and Philbin now made are wholly unreliable, his Excellency has come to the conclusion that no grounds exist for interfering with the course of the law in respect of the prisoners now undergoing penal servitude.[24]

MacEvilly again wrote to Spencer, pointing out that, since the circumstances of the case had so changed since the trial, nothing short of a public inquiry would satisfy a 'discerning and expectant public.' He testified once more to Casey's sincerity, as a man who was now prepared to undergo death if necessary in atonement for his guilt. As regards Bolton, MacEvilly stated that he had been a witness in his own case to the lord lieutenant's inquiry and for this reason, too, a public inquiry would be more satisfactory.[25] To this courteous statement of his position, MacEvilly received a curt reply from an under secretary, W. S. B. Kaye, stating that the lord lieutenant was unable to alter his decision and that 'his Excellency must decline to reopen the question.'[26]

All in all, it was an incredibly impolitic performance from the Castle. Indeed had they set out with the sole purpose of alienating the archbishop, they could not have been more successful. MacEvilly must, on the other hand, have been impressed at the persistence and zeal with which the Irish party, and Timothy

Harrington in particular, pursued the affair in the House of Commons.[27] They continued the attempt to obtain a public inquiry and in this they had the support of a number of Conservatives, notably Randolph Churchhill,[28] who seized the opportunity of embarrassing Gladstone. Harrington's amendment calling for a public inquiry was put to the vote and defeated decisively on October 29th.[29] As a footnote, it should perhaps be added that in late October 1902, and a week before MacEvilly died, three of the Joyces were released from prison.[30]

Before the debate on the Maamtrasna affair had been terminated in parliament, a meeting of the Irish hierarchy was held in Dublin on 1 October. Here, the momentous decision was taken to entrust the Irish party with the task of furthering the demand for all branches of catholic education. It is hardly surprising that the motion to do so should have been proposed by Croke of Cashel, nor, in the light of what had occurred, is it surprising that the seconder was MacEvilly of Tuam.[31]

The capture of MacEvilly's support was a coup for the Irish party. He had held out doggedly for a long time, but when his capitulation did come, it was all the more important in that it had been so hard earned. MacEvilly later stated his own position perfectly when he wrote:

> Some parties affect to be scandalised at the Irish bishops at the Synod placing the education question in the hands of the Irish party. But the fact is, many of the bishops who, like myself, never joined the Irish party, feel that there is no other possible way of gaining our rights from a government that will give catholics nothing from love.[32]

Thus, for the moment, did the archbishop concede victory to the all-conquering Parnell.

The bishops' declaration of support could hardly have come at a more propitious time. A general election was looming and the support of the catholic bishops strengthened what was already a strong hand, as both major English parties made their bids for the support of the Irish party. The Reform Act of 1884, which had extended the franchise, had given a new importance to the Irish vote. Also, the Crimes Act of 1882 was due to expire and any attempt to renew it was bound to be obstructed by the Irish party. Since this would mean the sacrifice of all other legislation, the Liberal party would be obviously reluctant to go to the country with only a new crimes act on the books.[33] Parnell then was ready to receive all offers.

Late in 1884 MacEvilly began to prepare for the journey of the Irish bishops to Rome. In November he had written to Bishop Gillooly of Elphin, speculating about possible topics that might be raised. He remarked on what must have been obvious to all: 'I somehow have a presentiment that our relations with the government will have a prominent place.' He really had no doubt but that the bishops were being called upon to defend their new position in relation to the Irish party, and he was not relishing the task. The new convert, steeling himself for the confrontation, stated: 'Upon our unanimity and respectful firmness a great deal will depend.'[34] Writing again to Gillooly in January 1885 about the coming bishops' meeting, he remarked: 'I consider the religioso-political questions, if brought forward, the most important both in regard to our present relations with our people – with whose feelings and just aspirations, we should be, as far as allowable, in accord – and prospective results.'[35]

In April MacEvilly set out for Rome, where the immediate concern of the bishops was the pending appointment to the vacant see of Dublin. Croke of Cashel certainly had no doubt as to the reasons for their presence in Rome. 'We were not brought out here,' he wrote, 'for these conferences, but as I always thought for a lecture on politics from the Pope.' He added that the Pope had taken the archbishop of Tuam and the bishop of Elphin into his confidence and that, at his request, a statement representing the political requirements of the people and the views of the bishops was to be prepared by Gillooly and read at their parting audience.[36] MacEvilly used the occasion to press strongly for the appointment of William Walsh to Dublin, pointing out that the refusal to do so would be seen by the people as Rome showing greater deference to the English government than to the wishes of the Irish clergy.[37] Dr Walsh was indeed appointed and the Irish bishops prepared to return home to the most enthusiastic welcomes. In a letter of MacEvilly to Manning, he declared that the appointment had made the Pope the most popular man in Ireland.[38]

By nature, John MacEvilly was a man who shunned public displays.[39] On this occasion, however, he embarked on a round of public welcomes in the towns of his diocese. He had a new gospel to preach – faith in the Irish parliamentary party – and he preached it with all the verve and enthusiasm of a recent convert. The round began at the seat of the archdiocese, the town of Tuam, where MacEvilly was presented with an address of welcome by the town commissioners. The archbishop began his reply on popular ground, referring to the man of the moment, the new archbishop of Dublin, and saying that he had no doubt from beginning to end but that Walsh would be appointed. He then launched on a theme which was for him a new departure. Agitation, he told his audience, conducted within the limits of right and justice 'is the only legitimate means we have of making known to legislators the wants and reasonable wishes of the people.' But as always, he was careful to add his usual rider that such agitation must be free of outrage or crime.[40]

At Castlebar, the archbishop dwelt on his familiar theme of the identification of clergy with people, emphasising that the priests were sprung from the people.[41] At Westport he told the people that they would no longer suffer from misrepresentation, that they were free now to choose trustworthy men who would act in concert with the Irish party, 'through whom alone we can expect the restoration of our long-denied rights.' He referred to the action of the Irish bishops in entrusting the care of educational matters to the Irish party. Some people had professed to be horrified at this, he said, but for years the bishops had gone 'cap-in-hand' to parliament and all they received was 'a very polite reply – we were bowed out from the council chamber and no more.' Finally, he added that 'following the example of the old man and the naughty apple-stealing boy, when flinging polite words and flinging tufts of grass had failed, we tried what virtue there was in stones.'[42]

MacEvilly was now laying great stress on the constitutionalism of the Irish party, as undoubtedly he saw it as a way of checking what he himself called 'the extreme men.'[43] Reporting to Kirby later in the year, he wrote that the Irish party was 'extremely constitutional.' But, he warned, 'Behind them are a wild lot of extremists.' Such men would only be thwarted by clinging to the Irish party, he declared, and thus would 'the insane efforts of the extremists and disguised Fenians be rendered null and void.' Later again, he wrote that he saw the Irish party as the salvation of the country – 'I was hitherto afraid of them, but now I am not.' He did fear, however, the 'wild revolutionists' from whom the Irish party, if well supported, would save the country. It was indeed a new day when MacEvilly was able to make the distinction, which had so long escaped him, between the Irish party and its Fenian support.

MacEvilly now turned his attentions to the organisation of the party in the diocese, something which up to the archbishop's conversion had been lacking. At a meeting of the clergy and representatives of the laity which was held at St. Jarlath's palace, Tuam, it was resolved to form a branch of the Irish National League immediately, and to arrange a public meeting at which Parnell and other members of the Irish party were to be invited. His Grace expressed his entire approbation of the movement.[44]

The public meeting was held in Tuam on Sunday, 25 October. Parnell did not attend but the chair was taken by John Dillon. In a long letter read to the meeting, MacEvilly reaffirmed his support for the party and called for the setting up of an Irish parliament. No other body, he stated, could legislate properly for the Irish people. He still hoped that both countries would be united by 'the golden link of the crown,' as in his view a native parliament did not at all mean separation from or dismemberment of the Empire. Indeed, he declared somewhat dramatically, that throughout Ireland there was not to be found 'a man who would not be a fit subject for a lunatic asylum' who would seriously urge separation. If Ireland had her own parliament, the archbishop argued, fisheries and land 'would not be left undeveloped or the country left without railways.' Emigration too would be halted, he thought. He had a word of advice for the government. 'Remove by salutary legislation,' he told them, 'the cause of their misery and you make our people abidingly loyal. Every man would then become the courageous defender against dastardly outrages, so vigorously denounced by the Irish Parliamentary Party, of his own and his neighbour's possessions.'[45]

On the day following the Tuam meeting, the county Galway convention was held at Athenry to select candidates to represent the party in the forthcoming election. Large numbers of diocesan clergy were present, testifying to the wonders a change of episcopal heart could bring.[46]

When the election was over, MacEvilly reported to Kirby. In county Galway three of the Irish party candidates were returned unopposed, while in the borough 'an Englishman (protestant) who was trifling with the catholic people got 100 votes against 2,000 for the catholic party.' This latter he attributed to Dr Carr, bishop of Galway, who, said MacEvilly, 'did his business well.' MacEvilly himself had held conferences in the different parts of Mayo in his diocese a fortnight before the convention. In that constituency, he was happy to report, there were 'two walks over,' and the day before he wrote, he had received a telegram saying, 'an Orangeman who stood for the west division of Mayo got the large number of 130 votes – the Catholic 4,900.' Commenting on Dublin, he wrote: 'The bigots I see are completely beaten in Dublin. Dr Walsh flung himself into it like a man.' He sounded most pleased with the outcome. 'We are living in very eventful times,' he went on, 'the clergy in full accord with people.' Some landlords, he noted, 'calling themselves Catholic (orange catholic) Castle-hunters,' were the greatest enemies of the people, and 'would oppose the Holy See tomorrow and insult it, if their Masters so willed it.' Our reliance, he stressed, 'must be on our poor persecuted people, who will stand by us and religion in all circumstances, as they have always done.'[47]

1886 was, of course, test year for home rule aspirations. In the spring of that year, Gladstone laid the first of his home rule bills before the British parliament. 'Great peace prevails at present,' MacEvilly remarked to Kirby, 'and will surely [continue] if Mr Gladstone's measure passes. If not, I could not say, I would tremble for consequences. God grant it may all turn out for the best.'[48] Here MacEvilly was simply reiterating what was now his constant theme – that peace and security in the country were the responsibility of the government, and that any refusal on their part to grant reforms would have disastrous consequences.

Due mainly to the revolt by sections of Gladstone's own party, the home rule bill was defeated and Gladstone was forced to resign. Immediately, MacEvilly and the clergy of the deanery of Tuam convened and adopted a resolution tendering their grateful acknowledgements to Gladstone for 'his intrepid courage and able advocacy of Irish rights in the British House of Commons,' and saying that while they considered he had achieved a great moral victory even in his present defeat, they pledged themselves to give their 'strenuous support to him and to the Irish party in their future efforts for the regeneration of the Irish people.'[49]

Some days later, the *Irish Times* published what it claimed was a telegram referring to the Tuam statement. According to the *Times*, '. . . the Vatican has intimated to the Irish bishops its wish that they should abstain from political party strife.'[50] Reports like this simply added to the rumours sweeping the country that Rome was critical of the alignment of the Irish hierarchy with a political party. MacEvilly, anxious as always to clear his name at Rome, immediately wrote to Kirby to put an end to what he called 'a bogus business.' Apart from defending himself, MacEvilly's letter displays the fear of the Irish bishops that Rome might be contemplating just such a censure. It was his way of warning Rome against doing so, as his emphatic conclusion shows: 'It is monstrous to suppose the Vatican would sanction such a thing, especially after the numerous proofs of Paternal good will and deep interest of our Great Pontiff towards his Irish and devoted children.'[51] Archbishop Walsh of Dublin had written to Kirby in a similar vein.[52] The double appeal by Walsh and MacEvilly underlines the sensitivity of the bishops to anything of a contrary nature coming from Rome at a time when the people were so suspicious of the activity of English agents there.

Early in 1887, a great public meeting of the National League was held at Tuam, with Sir Thomas Esmonde M.P. presiding. A long letter from MacEvilly was read in which he dealt with the Irish question in its two-fold character – as a national claim to be satisfied by the concession of home rule, and as an economic problem to be solved by ending unjust land laws. Home rule he described as 'the great object, to which every other political object must be subordinate.' He dismissed the objection of those who feared that separation from the United Kingdom would follow, asserting that it would in fact have the contrary effect of 'breaking down the middle wall of partition,' so creating peace and good will between the two peoples, who, 'owing to injustice and national hate on the one hand, and a natural feeling of resentment on the other, are in feeling and sentiment as wide asunder as the poles.'[53]

That, however, was certainly not the view of the new chief secretary, Arthur Balfour, who had arrived in Ireland determined to 'be as relentless as Cromwell in enforcing obedience to the law.'[54] In his efforts to defeat the Plan of Campaign,[55] Balfour introduced a coercion bill which provoked a series of protests from the deaneries of Tuam. The resolutions of the clergy condemned the new bill which they felt would, by destroying all legitimate agitation, increase crime in the country; they declared that the proposed land bill, which was to accompany the coercion bill, was 'a landlord bill'; and they passed a vote of gratitude to Gladstone and his followers 'for their giant exertions in defending the cause of the Irish people in and out of the House of Commons.'[56] MacEvilly was also worried that the bill might provoke the people to outrage and 'thus provide a pretext for shooting them down'; and that the bill might drive the people 'into the arms of the secret societies.'[57]

Government action against the Plan and the nationalist episcopal alliance was not confined to Ireland, as efforts were being made to effect a condemnation of the agitation from Rome itself. Pope Leo XIII decided to have the situation viewed independently of both the English government and the Irish bishops and to this end sent to Ireland Monsignor Perisco as papal envoy.[57] Perisco embarked on a tour of the Irish hierarchy and on 22 August 1887 arrived at Tuam where he remained two days, before leaving for Galway.[58]

Meanwhile, Balfour's coercion act was being rigorously enforced. The treatment meted out to William O'Brien, particularly, led to protest meetings. At a great meeting in Dublin, a letter from MacEvilly was read in which he condemned strongly O'Brien's punishment in prison, and called for O'Brien's immediate release. Again he harped on his charge of an irresponsible government creating unrest and discontent as a result of their unjust laws.[59]

As the year 1887 wore on, it became apparent that the new departure of the bishops had not the undivided support of the hierarchy. While Perisco was still in the country, and perhaps indeed as a consequence of his visit, Bishop O'Dwyer of Limerick launched a strong attack on the members of the Irish Party, saying that the old struggle for truth and justice in the Penal times was preferable to independence in the 'hands of men who could not or would not use it for the ends for which all power is given to men on earth.' He also attacked the campaign for home rule, claiming that to grant home rule just then would assure the country remaining poor for a long time.[60]

A month later, the *Pall Mall Gazette* published a report that the British government had secured the services of Perisco and some Irish bishops in carrying out its policy of suppressing the nationalist movement. The report mentioned O'Dwyer and Healy, coadjutor bishop of Clonfert, in particular, and claimed that Perisco intended to 'put the screw on priests through their bishops' and that the papal envoy had been used by the Castle as a 'coercionist catspaw.'[61] The report brought an immediate reply from O'Dwyer in which he sharply denied the charges made against him. He was not, he said, a 'landlord bishop' or a unionist. The country was entitled to self-government, he felt, but not under a 'system of terrorism.' He condemned boycotting as irreligious and sinful and the Plan of Campaign as unjust. 'The guidance of the agitation,' he wrote, 'is not only politically stupid but morally wrong.'[62]

O'Dwyer's public disavowal of support was a sore blow for the Irish bishops already on their way to Rome to be present at the jubilee of Leo XIII. To add to their troubles, a leading article in the *Tablet*, the English catholic paper, claimed that letters had been received from Irish priests condemning the agitation, and that a number of priests had been forced to leave Ireland. The article also made reference to the struggle within the G.A.A. saying that the physical force men had forced the priests to retreat. There was support for the bishop of Limerick in his denunciation of 'methods that savour of communism and the revolution,' and the paper claimed that his utterance had been applauded by the catholic world.[63] The *Tablet* was owned by the catholic bishop of Salford, Dr Herbert Vaughan, an intimate friend of the Duke of Norfolk and bitterly opposed to the Irish movement for home rule. The editor of the *Tablet* after 1884 was a cousin of Vaughan, J. R. Snead-Cox, and under his editorship, the paper became decidedly anti-Irish. Several personal attacks were launched on Archbishop Walsh of Dublin.[64]

In Rome, the Irish bishops were received in audience by Pope Leo on 7 January 1888. The Pope then arranged for another special conference on Irish affairs with Walsh of Dublin and O'Callaghan of Cork.[65] So perturbed were the bishops about the growing influence of the British government in Rome that they drew up a joint statement to be presented to the Pope. In this document, of which MacEvilly was one of the five signatories, two reports in particular were mentioned – firstly, that of the *Times* correspondent who claimed that two English bishops had sent the bishop of Limerick's letter to the *Freeman* to Rome. The bishops called for an end to such interference in Irish affairs. Secondly, the bishops condemned the article of the *Tablet* justifying O'Dwyer's stand and they strongly denied the report that priests had been forced to leave Ireland. The document then continued, ' . . . as long as this paper, directed as it is by an English bishop, is permitted to follow its scarcely friendly course towards our country, the relations between English and Irish catholics, including the clergy, will become necessarily more tense every day, and that as long as this paper is allowed to keep even the appearance of being approved by the Holy See.'[66] On 21 January the Pope received the five signatories in audience and shortly after this interview MacEvilly left for home,[67] this time choosing to arrive quietly at Tuam.[68]

In April a papal rescript was published, condemning the Plan of Campaign and the practice of boycotting. The Plan was condemned on the grounds that a rent fixed by mutual consent could not be reduced at the arbitrary will of the tenant alone, thus ignoring the position of the landlord; while boycotting was declared contrary to the principles of natural justice and Christian charity.[69] The rescript was a serious set-back for the bishops who had constantly argued against the publication of just such a negative statement. It was condemned by the politicians in varying degrees of directness. The hierarchy, when they did choose to speak, drew the careful and just then convenient distinction between morals and politics, declaring that the document was concerned only with the former.[70]

The papal rescript was particularly embarrassing to a man like MacEvilly who, all his life, had been such a staunch and loyal upholder of Rome's authority and who earlier had expressed confidence that Monsignor Perisco's report would 'amply justify' the bishops.[71] Dismayed and even betrayed he must have felt, but his loyalty to Rome proved stronger and his public silence in the matter is in itself eloquent.

For close observers of the situation, however, there was evidence enough to show what MacEvilly really thought of the rescript and its condemnations. For instance, in July, the administrator and clergy of Tuam parish were present at evictions which took place on Cloondarone estate outside the town and addressed a meeting of sympathy with those evicted.[72] Duggan of Clonfert, a staunch supporter of the land agitation, sent the report of the evictions to Walsh of Dublin, asking the archbishop to note the presence of the administrator at the evictions, 'the decree notwithstanding.'[73] In August, MacEvilly subscribed twenty pounds to the National Indemnity Fund which had been established by the *Freeman's Journal* in favour of Parnell. In his accompanying letter, he declared that it was not simply the cause of Parnell that was on trial but the cause of the Irish people and of legitimate agitation. 'Take away agitation,' he wrote, 'and are not our legislators left in ignorance of the wants and aspirations of our people?' Parnell he described as 'the great liberator of our people' who had 'by word and act adhered to the golden motto which he in season and out of season proclaimed from the house-tops, "The man who commits a crime gives strength to the enemy." '[74]

Later in the year, MacEvilly was very upset by a 'terrible letter' which he had from Cardinal Rampolla of Propaganda, referring to a meeting which had been held in Ballyhaunis three months before. The purpose had been to obtain a reduction of rents from Lord Dillon and it was chaired by Canon Geraghty, the parish priest. A report in the *Freeman's Journal* stated that the meeting resolved to resort to the Plan, something which, said MacEvilly, was 'completely untrue.'[75] He had instructed Canon Geraghty to send a written contradiction to the *Freeman* and this had been done. He complained to Kirby that the Cardinal should have heard the other side of the story before acting.[76] Thus was MacEvilly suffering, and not liking, the type of misrepresentation his colleagues like Croke had earlier discovered was part of the price to be paid for supporting the Irish party.

MacEvilly, then, was quite unwavering in his support of the party and in 1889 gave his wholehearted backing to William O'Brien's Tenants' Defence Association, stating that he regarded the support of such an organisation as a sacred and solemn duty for a catholic bishop as it was 'a matter of absolute necessity for preserving our catholic people, whom the landlords are manifestly determined to exterminate.'

On August 25, 1890, MacEvilly wrote to his friend, Bishop Gillooly of Elphin, expressing his fear that there was some crisis at hand in regard to the authority of the bishops.[77]

When the news of the O'Shea divorce proceedings broke, MacEvilly, like the other bishops, remained silent. His correspondence with Walsh of Dublin shows, however, that he was none too happy about the position. On 20 November he reported to Walsh about the party convention being held that day in Galway, saying it was stipulated that no allusion would be made to the Plan or to boycotting, or 'to a very late important concern.' He did not know whether this would be adhered to, as the feelings of the priests and people there were very strong and 'no amount of attempted white-washing' would do. 'English pagan opinion may idolize great villians,' he declared; 'not so the sensitive instincts of catholic Ireland.'[78]

The appearance of the Parnell manifesto some days later was the occasion of another gloomy epistle from MacEvilly. He was plainly anxious about the effects of the silence of the hierarchy, stating that he felt humiliated in that protestant Englishmen were publicly 'standing up for the cause of morality' while Irish representatives made light of the affair. MacEvilly also expressed disappointment with the manifesto itself, asking pertinently, 'why not a word of defence?'[79]

In this letter, there surfaces as well the fear of MacEvilly that the church was losing ground to the party. He gives voice to a feeling of persecution, by writing: 'Home rule with such men, what would it be but the crippling of the Irish church and relegating the clergy to sacristies as long as they would be allowed even there.' This theme he was to return to and enlarge upon as the struggle unfolded. Finally, referring to the crucial vote about to be taken by the party, he predicted glumly, though accurately, that great harm would come of the party's breaking up but which he regarded as inevitable, 'be the result of Monday what it may.'[80]

The archbishop of Dublin prevailed upon his colleagues to hold their silence until the Irish party had made their decision, and when the majority of the party renounced Parnell's leadership, the hierarchy followed with their own statement condemning Parnell and calling for his resignation.[81] The resolutions of the deanery of Tuam itself were strongly worded, condemning Parnell and his supporters as 'traitors to the national cause' and 'sowers of bitter dissention and discord.'[82] Preaching in the cathedral, MacEvilly argued that Parnell's continued leadership would endanger morals, faith and fatherland.[83] This sermon set the tone for the clergy and Parnell was roundly condemned from the pulpits of the diocese. Reverend J. Loftus, administrator of Tuam, talked of Parnell living riotously on the thousands of pounds sent him by the half-starved people of Ireland, while an after-mass meeting at Cortoon in the parish of Tuam condemned 'the convicted adulterer Parnell.'[84]

MacEvilly himself was more restrained in his public statements, but in private correspondence he reveals his true feelings. He had never been enamoured of Parnell, and the support which he had eventually given was more to the party and its potential than to the leader. Now the two main targets of his attack were Parnell and the *Freeman's Journal*, which at this stage was backing Parnell. In a letter to Kirby, at the end of 1890, he wrote of the need for a catholic paper and reported: 'As recommended to us at Rome in 1885, such a paper is in the course of being established.' He himself had already taken twenty shares for £100.[85] The

National Press was founded to present the anti-Parnellite case.[86] The driving force behind it was Tim Healy, who used it as a vehicle for his vicious and slanderous attacks on all opponents.

In February 1891, the archbishop was writing that a 'crisis unexampled' had arisen. This time he referred to Parnell as 'an unmitigated villain' and described the *Freeman* as 'most treacherous.' He thanked God that Parnell had been detected before he had a regular government in Ireland because, argued MacEvilly, 'if vested with power, he would be a detestable persecutor of the church.'[87] He wrote in the same vein to Gillooly of Elphin.[88]

In his Lenten pastoral of 1891, MacEvilly made public his views on the *Freeman's Journal*. In a general warning against the reading of bad books, he singled out the *Freeman* as 'bad, dangerous reading, instilling . . . a subtle poison into the minds of our people.' He accused the paper of 'lessening due respect for authority' and condemned its attitude towards Dr Walsh. Finally, he wrote:

> By making light of it, nay, ostentatiously parading, as a matter of comparative indifference, a revolting public scandal, which should not be so much as named among Christians, the journal in question blunts the moral sense of the public in regard to the shocking crime of adultery, for the unblushing and shameless perpetrator of which it claims public honour from a people ever distinguished for their social and domestic virtues.[89]

MacEvilly's position was made more delicate by the fact of his residence at Tuam, a town which was already deeply and bitterly divided. It was the heart of the constituency of Colonel Nolan who had declared for Parnell and who had a loyal following in the town itself. At the approach of the crisis, the town commissioners had quickly voted confidence in Parnell.[90] The *Tuam News,* originally founded by MacHale, had, however, taken the anti-Parnellite and clerical line and called for the leader's resignation.[91] Then, following the declaration of the hierarchy, the Tuam branch of the National League voted to support Parnell and Colonel Nolan.[92] There followed blow and counter-blow as the two sides fixed colours firmly to their masts. In March 1891, the local branch of the National League invited Parnell to Tuam[93] and almost immediately a public meeting was held to declare support for the anti-Parnellite wing of the Irish party. This meeting was chaired by the administrator, Fr Loftus.[94]

On 10 March the anti-Parnellite delegates met at the Antient Concert Hall in Dublin and launched the National Federation. There were letters of support from the four catholic archbishops.[95] MacEvilly claimed that country people and traders were being terrorised in an attempt 'to stifle the honest individual and collective expression of the horror which our virtuous people ever entertain for public scandal and deeds of hideous immorality, so unblushingly paraded before the gaze of all, old and young.' He warned the new federation against giving too much power to individuals – 'measures, and not men, will, no doubt, be your motto,' he called, reviving for the occasion his old war cry of the 1860s.[96]

The more heated the struggle became, the more convinced MacEvilly was of the evil Parnell represented. Writing to Kirby on what he now saw as 'the sad condition of war,' he called Parnell a 'second Lucifer, who would fain drag the whole Irish race down to perdition, and trample on the clergy and catholic people.' He reported that matters were well in the diocese, except for the town of Tuam, 'where the friends of the *Freeman* are influential and zealous.' He was confident, however, that Parnell would be ultimately humbled, although 'only after a hard struggle'; and predicted victory for the anti-Parnellites in the coming Sligo by-election. He was full of praise for Walsh of Dublin, who, he said, 'has been day and night, as sleeplessly as Parnell and co. on the other side, battling for our country and Christianity.'[97] Later, amazingly, he thanked God that he himself had never praised Parnell 'by word or writing.'[98]

In June the catholic hierarchy met at Maynooth and, under the chairmanship of Cardinal Logue, declared that Parnell had 'utterly disqualified himself to be the political leader of the Irish catholic people.' Bishops and superiors were instructed to enforce the resolution immediately.[99] This was, in effect, a declaration of war by the bishops on Parnell and his supporters.

The death of Parnell on 6 October removed the central figure but, far from lessening the conflict, added considerably to the passionate intensity and bitterness of the struggle now raging in the country. 'The mysterious death of Parnell,' wrote MacEvilly, 'has given for the present breathing time. His ghost however is not dead. How fortunate home rule was not obtained under him. Hard to say how he would oppress the church.'[100]

Both sides now began to organise and work towards what they knew would be the first crucial test, the general election of 1892. Early in that year, MacEvilly informed Walsh of the 'efforts being made by the Harringtons to cause confusion and disruption.' In a reference drawn from one of Parnell's later speeches, he said that 'these hillside men and Sunday hurlers are their chief instruments and very dangerous they are.'[101]

When the *Freeman's Journal* switched loyalties and joined the anti-Parnellite camp, there was really no further use for the *National Press*. Healy was unwilling to abandon the paper altogether; eventually he and his fellow directors agreed to amalgamate with the *Freeman*.[102]

Hearing rumours of the proposed amalgamation, MacEvilly, who was one of two episcopal shareholders, wrote to Kirby that, although he did not understand it, he presumed the amalgamation was necessary.[103] 'Politics are a very crooked concern,' was his conclusion.[104] There was a dispute about the governing board of the *Freeman* which split the party in two. Ultimately, the issue was left to Walsh for arbitration. He attempted to set up a board which would be representative of both sides, but in fact neither side was satisfied. It is doubtful if a satisfactory solution could have been achieved, as the issue was not control of the newspaper but the control of the party.[105]

However crooked he felt politics to be, the archbishop was not at all deterred from entering fully into the election campaign. The issue for him, however it might be disguised, was clear-cut – whether or not Parnell's supporter, Colonel Nolan, would retain his seat in North Galway. In a letter to the convention in Galway to select candidates, MacEvilly outlined the reasons why he thought Nolan should not be supported. Nolan was a pledgebreaker who had sown dissention, had weakened the Irish party, and disregarded the feelings of his constituents. Furthermore, since Nolan was a landlord, he should be rejected by 'the tenantry of Ireland.'[106] In a letter to the Mayo convention, MacEvilly appealed for support of anti-Parnellites on the grounds of national unity. Anything less would 'amount to a political blunder.'[107]

'We have rather troubled times now on account of the general election,' MacEvilly told Kirby in June.[108] And indeed the campaign in Galway county was particularly bitter and there was violence. At a meeting in Tuam on 29 June, fighting broke out between supporters of Nolan and those of the anti-Parnellite candidate, Dr Charles Tanner. Some of the clergy were attacked and one priest, Fr Henry, had his teeth knocked out. The Riot Act was read and the police had to charge the crowd with batons drawn.[109] MacEvilly reacted to this in the most dramatic fashion. In a pastoral read in all churches of the diocese, he condemned in the strongest manner the events that had taken place, referring to 'a most determined effort to murder a clergyman,' and he proclaimed that all who had taken part in such outrages were under excommunication.[110]

MacEvilly then reported to Walsh of the action he had taken, saying that it might be strong, but that it was 'impudently called for.' He was angry about the lack of support from the party, complaining that there was no one to help Tanner, 'who poor fellow is fighting very bravely.' The party had looked on the contest as 'a doubtful affair,' the angry MacEvilly alleged, and so they had sent only J.F.X. O'Brien. John Dillon had been 'telegraphed to' but he had gone instead to Roscommon, avoiding 'the most important fight with Nolan, Parnell's grand vizier.' The party had not supported Tanner 'until the last moment,' MacEvilly complained bitterly.[111]

It would seem that not all of the outrages were confined to one side. There is a report of Colonel Nolan being attacked by the parish priest while canvassing in Headford, Co. Galway.[112] Later, in court proceedings arising from the disturbances at Tuam, members of both camps were charged, including a curate at Belclare.[113] The stormy election campaign ended in a victory for Nolan, who received 2,040 votes to Tanner's 1,651.[114]

'When this is over, I will make a vow never again to mind these things,' MacEvilly had told Walsh in July.[115] If he did take the vow, he certainly did not hold to it. MacEvilly would not retire from politics until Nolan had been unseated. The next opportunity to achieve this presented itself in 1895, and so determined was MacEvilly that he was named as proposer in the principal nomination paper of Denis Kilbride, Nolan's opponent.[116] Parish priests and curates took an active part in the canvass in the town of Tuam and the clergy of the diocese generally gave Kilbride their full support.[117] This time they succeeded, Kilbride winning by a margin of five hundred votes.[118]

Albeit not concerned with any major issues, the campaign of 1895 was the occasion of public feuding between the two principal groupings within the party, the group centered on Tim Healy and that led by John Dillon. As a result, the party declined in popularity and prestige, and the machinery which had so successfully controlled the constituencies in Parnell's time was now rendered useless. The framework of the county conventions was retained; but the power to summon them, the nomination of the chairman, and the authority to intervene in the selection of the candidates was no longer entrusted to the party.[119]

The victory of 1895, then, was somewhat hollow and MacEvilly, like so many others, was soon calling for party unity. Obviously he had been consulted by Walsh about the latter's proposals for reunion. MacEvilly commented that the majority rule could not be set aside in any circumstances. 'It is the indispensable rule,' he wrote, 'without which religion and social order would be reduced to a state of chaos.' As regards uncontrolled selection of members, MacEvilly had his doubts and asked the pointed question – 'uncontrolled by whom?' He felt that suggestions and recommendations regarding candidates should continue to be made. He agreed with extra-parliamentary control of national funds and would concur too with the principle of parliamentary independence. And MacEvilly declared that he was prepared to give his 'full adhesion to the project.'[120]

This project of Walsh for party reunion did not succeed. As a result, MacEvilly declared that he did not know where to turn and was resolved on 'utter abstention' for the moment. He felt that a new leader must be found, that this was the only hope. He did not think John Dillon would be generally followed and regretted that. 'It is so hard,' he concluded, 'to get a proper and efficient man, acceptable to all.'[121]

Three years after MacEvilly had written these words, the Irish party was reunited under the leadership of John Redmond. In Galway, it meant the reconciliation of Colonel Nolan and the archbishop; and in the election of 1900, Nolan regained his old seat in the constituency of North Galway, with full clerical backing.[122]

This reunion of the party was prompted to a large extent by the popularity and success of O'Brien's United Irish League.[123] The support given to the League by MacEvilly and his clergy has been treated of in a previous chapter.[124] It was certainly a changed MacEvilly who would not only countenance but actually lend his enthusiastic backing to a movement so akin to the Land League of the early 1880s. No doubt the charge of opportunism could be laid at the archbishop's door and, given his history, it is not a simple charge to refute. As always, MacEvilly read the signs of the times and gauged the popular mood. His later public statements were louder in their complaints, more bitter in their tone, more harshly critical of government inadequacies, especially as regards the failure to find satisfactory solutions to the problems peculiar to the west of Ireland. That MacEvilly had made his peace with the growing nationalism is clear from the fact that a movement as abrasive as the young Gaelic League should list among its earliest clerical supporters the archbishop of Tuam.[125]

Lying in State of the Late Most Rev. Dr. MacEvilly, Archbishop of Tuam.

Chapter Nine

Last Years

A MAN OF STRONG physique and robust health, John MacEvilly suffered very few illnesses in his long life, and certainly none that were serious. In his later years, he did develop those ailments commonly associated with old age, and suffered a good deal from rheumatism and sciatica. In August 1888, he went, on doctor's orders, to Buxton in England where he hoped to find relief from 'crippling rheumatism.'[1] At times, he was so badly afflicted that he found it 'most painful' to write,[2] and in his last years his movements were sometimes hampered considerably. The effects of rheumatism were evident too in the deterioration of his handwriting, and some of his later letters were penned by an assistant.

MacEvilly's vacations were generally spent at Lisdoonvarna, which, apart from being a traditional holiday resort for the clergy, had spa waters with famed curative powers. In 1896, he suffered an acute attack of lumbago and sciatica. He was recommended by his doctor to try the spa waters of Bath – a journey that was interrupted by a last visit to his old friend, Patrick Duggan of Clonfert, who was then dying.[3]

Mentally, MacEvilly did not flag, remaining alert to the end of his days. Evidence of this is the fact that he was able to complete the last of his scriptural commentaries at the age of seventy-eight. 'God has given me strength to finish the commentary on all the New Testament,' he wrote to Kirby in 1894, 'except Apocalypse, which I must hand over to some other madman.'[4] The archbishop's temper does not appear to have sweetened with age. According to D'Alton, he became peevish and querulous and was often offensive to his priests, sometimes humiliating them in public.[5] 'Nor was it unusual,' D'Alton writes, 'to have some priest express surprise that so many old men, like Bismark and Gladstone, had passed away, but that their example had not been followed in the Archdiocese of

Tuam. It was not, they avowed, that they wished the Archbishop's death, but they were anxious to see the Archbishop promoted to heaven.'[6]

On Wednesday, 5 November 1902, MacEvilly completed a visitation of several deaneries of the diocese and returned to Tuam. On Friday, 14 November, he suffered a sharp attack of sciatica.[7] His condition deteriorated quickly and on Wednesday evening, 26 November, John MacEvilly died.[8] The immediate cause of death was given as 'gangrene, supervening on an acute attack of sciatica.'[9] On the following Sunday, after a funeral procession through the streets of Tuam, his remains were brought to the cathedral, where they lay until the burial on Tuesday. Then came the final irony: John MacEvilly was laid to rest beside John MacHale.[10]

So ended a life that had lasted eighty-six years, a priestly career that had begun in 1842, and an episcopal career that spanned a remarkable forty-five years. He had seen and heard the great O'Connell, he had witnessed the devastation of the Famine years, and he had seen the failure of Repeal and the Independent Irish party. He had aided Gladstone's mission to bring justice to Ireland, he had battled through fifty years to achieve denominational education, he had watched as the struggle for the land was gradually won; and he had lived through the glorious years of Parnell, as well as observed the chief's final humiliation and downfall.

In all of these phases of the evolution of the Irish state, MacEvilly had played a part. The degree of his involvement had varied according to the event, his interest in it and his position at the time. In MacEvilly's episcopal career can be seen, in microcosm, the contribution of the nineteenth century Irish catholic hierarchy, under the direction of Paul Cullen and William Walsh, towards the state we live in now.

Only in our day has the question of the role of the catholic bishops been so discussed and analysed. Whether or not the influence of these bishops was paramount in the formation of the twenty-six county free state is a question which has been asked repeatedly, and not always by historians.[11] Some would hold that the state that did emerge was precisely that which the bishops had wished for, a catholic state for a catholic people.[12] Again there are those who would argue that the role of the bishops has been exaggerated, and that they merely reflected the opinions and attitudes of a conservative people.[13] Immediately, then, the question arises as to what extent those opinions and attitudes were the products of episcopal influence.

Did the bishops lead or follow? It is a vexed question and one that does not admit of facile answers. It is my contention that an examination of the type of power wielded by John MacEvilly, stemming directly from his position as bishop, can help towards an informed judgment. Perhaps the most outstanding example of his power and influence is shown in the 1868 election. We have seen how he set out deliberately to oust George Morris. Morris was the sitting M.P.;

he was a catholic; he was, by MacEvilly's own admission, a humane landlord; and he was popular in Galway. Yet, MacEvilly succeeded in deposing Morris, and succeeded so emphatically as to end all arguments of whether or not he possessed real power in secular affairs.

From where did such power come? MacEvilly was the disciple of Paul Cullen, and he was of the school which believed that religion was the dominant influence in a man's life. He believed that religion must permeate all of man's activities and, conversely, that all human activities must be subordinated to religion. It was only a question of how this might be best achieved, and here MacEvilly had the example and advice of Paul Cullen. Tight control was exercised over the clergy in the manner of the centralised, disciplined Roman church of Cullen. MacEvilly set himself to accomplish in Galway and Tuam what Cullen wished to accomplish nationally, and, let it be said, Cullen needed loyal and devoted servants like MacEvilly to achieve his end. Galway and Tuam were dioceses where discipline was looser and where priests had remained largely independent and autonomous in the parishes. MacEvilly challenged this 'old' church where he found it and, in such cases as that of Peter Daly, he showed his utter determination to dominate it. He won the victory precisely because he was doing the work of Cullen and Rome and therefore had their complete support. The rule established by MacEvilly called for, and got, the total obedience of the clergy. It did not allow for differences of opinion on the important issues; indeed, it scarcely made allowances for human frailty and eccentricity. The bishop's rule was law and that is very evident from a study of clerical involvement in a movement like the Land League. Where the bishops were favourable towards the League, as in Cashel and Clonfert, many priests took a leading part. Where the bishop was hostile, as in the case of MacEvilly, the clergy, whatever their sympathies, did not become involved.

The question of MacEvilly's relations with the people, however, is much more complex, and here finer distinctions must be drawn. For a start, we must distinguish between people. Certainly, the mass of the people held their bishop in awe. There was respect for his office and, depending on the bishop's particular personality and character, that respect was increased through fear or love. But there were people who refused to be overawed and who would cling to their opinions and beliefs even at the risk of excommunication. Secondly, a distinction must be made between issues. There were issues where the people were content to be led by their bishops and there were issues where they followed their own counsels, whatever the bishop's view might be.

In education, for instance, the mass of the people was content to follow the lead of the bishop. We have seen the emphasis placed by MacEvilly on this question. He was determined that control of education should remain with the church authorities. It was not a matter that was disputed by the people, who were interested primarily in obtaining the education for their children that they themselves had been denied. After that, they accepted that this education should be catholic and so were content to follow the lead of their bishop and to cede negotiation rights to him. Here it is not a useless exercise to speculate on the possible consequences of the bishops' refusing to compromise and failing to provide adequate services. The one area where this did happen was in university education. In Galway, certainly, there were catholics who were determined that their children should benefit by the university services that were available, regardless of whether that education had been declared 'godless' or not. There was some truth in English criticisms that it was really only the bishops that were interested in the question of denominational education.

If education was the special province of the bishops, the land was a different question altogether, and it was in the politics of the land that the Irish people were forced to learn the distinction between religion and politics and apply this in their lives. True, the Fenians had been articulating the distinction years before, but the Fenians did not have the broad-based popular support of the Land League and they did not have Parnell. What they did have was a formidable opponent in Paul Cullen. The Land League was opposed in similar fashion by Edward McCabe, whose denunciations were received more in sorrow and anger than acceptance by the people. Here MacEvilly showed himself the superior tactician and also more sensitive to the feelings of the people. Although just as opposed to the new popular land movement, he was quick to see that in the prevailing mood of the country, denunciations could prove harmful to the influence of the priests with the people. MacEvilly the pragmatist was therefore prepared to allow his priests to take part in the movement as the lesser of two evils. In this way, he reasoned, the position of the priests with the people could be sustained, and the danger of secular leaders usurping the role of the clergy could be averted.

Certainly the people were glad of clerical participation in popular movements of the day. They were much more comfortable when the clergy were working with them rather than in an opposing role. In dioceses like Tuam, where the people were aware of their archbishop's opposition, even though unspoken, Parnell's Irish party was spectacularly strengthened after MacEvilly's conversion. The participation and leadership of the clergy greatly increased the confidence of local branches. Nevertheless, the clergy were there only after it became clear that the party would survive without them.

We have referred many times to John MacEvilly's unswerving loyalty to Rome, a loyalty that had at times caused problems for him. Given this allegiance and his concern for the survival of the catholic church in Ireland, all other claims on MacEvilly's loyalties must be seen in the light of these priorities. One can accept, for instance, John MacEvilly's sincerity when he speaks of the tragedy of emigration. He was certainly aware of the trauma and suffering of the exiles, he was aware of the hardships facing them abroad and the state of unpreparedness in which they left. But one senses too that it was a tragedy for MacEvilly because his church was being depleted in numbers and consequently weakened. He could respond also to the nationalism of the late nineteenth century but he included in that the love of the catholic religion and indeed, in some of his speeches, he stated quite explicitly that the true patriot was the one who was devoted to country *and* religion. If, then, one might adjust Pearse's concept, MacEvilly was speaking of an Ireland which was not free merely but catholic as well.

In the final analysis, what emerges from this examination of the life and career of John MacEvilly is his pragmatism; his ability and the ability of his church to adapt to changing circumstances. As bishop, he enunciated catholic doctrinal principles in the most uncompromising terms, but when faced with the business of negotiation, he was ever ready to assess and, if necessary, accept, the best possible offer. Above all, what concerned him was that the offer be the best possible. That the catholic church survived so well the upheaval of the traumatic years 1912-22, and came to play a major role in the development of the new Irish state, was not simply the result of the stand taken at crucial times and on crucial issues by bishops like Croke of Cashel. The fact that the church retained so much of its power was due in no small measure to the adaptability and pragmatic sense of bishops like John MacEvilly.

MAYNOOTH COLLEGE CENTENARY CELEBRATIONS, JUNE 1895.
Archbishop MacEvilly is seated in the second row, fourth from left.

Notes

Introduction

1. 'Ireland and Anglo-Papal Relations, 1880-85', C. J. Woods, *Irish Historical Studies, XVIII,* No. 69 (March 1972). 'The Politics of Cardinal McCabe, Archbishop of Dublin, 1879-85', C. J. Woods. *Dublin Historical Record XXVI,* No. 3 (June 1973).
2. This information was given to me by Rev. Thomas Shannon, secretary to the archbishop of Tuam, in reply to my formal request.

Chapter 1

1. MacEvilly's date of birth is variously given as 1816, 1817, 1818. 1816 is the correct date. All sources are agreed that he was 86 years of age when he died in November 1902. Also, he himself gives his age as 75 in a letter of 1 January 1892 and 76 years in a letter of 29 December 1892. MacEvilly to Kirby, 1 January 1892; MacEvilly to Kirby, 29 December 1892. Irish College archives, Rome.
2. *Freeman's Journal,* 27 November 1902; Monsignor D'Alton, *History of The Archdiocese of Tuam* (Dublin 1928), Vol. II., p 101.
3. *Freeman's Journal,* 5 January 1894.
4. *Tuam News,* 29 November 1901.
5. *Galway Vindicator,* 27 March 1872.
6. MacEvilly to McCabe, 9 December 1881, DDA.
7. William O'Brien, *Recollections* (London 1905), p 225.
8. *Tuam News,* 12 March 1886; *Connaught Telegraph,* 13 March 1886.
9. Thomas Brett, *Life of Dr Duggan, Bishop of Clonfert* (Dublin 1921), pp 8-9.
10. John Healy, *Maynooth College 1795-1895* (Dublin 1895), p 367.
11. Brett, op. cit., p 11; D'Alton, op. cit., p 102.
12. Healy, op. cit., pp 295-305.
13. *Tuam News,* 28 November 1902.
14. Court of the Queen's Bench, *O'Keeffe v Cullen* (London 1874), p 518; Cf. Chapter Two, Elections and Fenianism, p 14.
15. Healy, op. cit., p 622.
16. D'Alton, op. cit., p 102; Healy, op. cit., p 353.
17. MacEvilly to Cullen, 30 August 1878, DDA; *Tuam Herald,* 3 September 1842.
18. *The Nation,* 28 January 1854.
19. Cf. *"The Politicization of the Irish Catholic Bishops 1800-1850"*; Oliver MacDonagh, *The Historical Journal,* March 1975.
20. Lawrence J. McCaffrey, *Daniel O'Connell and the Repeal Year* (Kentucky 1966), p 39.
21. *Tuam Herald,* 6 May 1843.
22. McCaffrey, op. cit., pp 56 ff.
23. *Tuam Herald,* 24 June 1843; 29 July 1843.

24. *Tuam Herald,* 25 October 1845.

25. *Tuam Herald,* 9 May 1846.

26. See for instance, *Tuam Herald,* 8, 29 August 1846; 17 October 1846; 2 January 1847.

27. *Tuam Herald,* 27 February 1847.

28. *Tuam Herald,* 22 May 1847.

29. *Tuam Herald,* 29 January 1848.

30. *Tuam Herald,* 8 July 1848.

31. *Tuam Herald,* 19 August 1848.

32. *Tuam Herald,* 1 June 1850.

33. Cf. Chapter Six, Tenant Right and the Tenant League, p 96.

34. *Tuam Herald,* 24 August 1850; 29 November 1902.

35. 'Political Problems 1850-1860,' John H. Whyte, *A History of Irish Catholicism,* edited by P. J. Corish, Vol. 5., pp 7-10.

36. Ibid., pp 10-11.

37. *Tuam Herald,* 22 February 1851.

38. *Tuam Herald,* 26 April 1851.

39. Whyte, 'Political Problems', p 11.

40. *Tuam Herald,* 3 April 1852.

41. *Tuam Herald,* 7 August 1852; D'Alton, op. cit., p 104. D'Alton states that MacEvilly was disappointed that he had not been appointed president of St. Jarlath's when the post was filled in 1849 and that this was the beginning of the friction between MacHale and MacEvilly. I have not been able to substantiate this.

42. *First Report of the Commissioners appointed to enquire into the Municipal Corporations in Ireland 1835,* pp 432-3.

43. Ibid., pp 436-7.

44. *Irish Municipal Reform,* Isaac Butt (pamphlet, Dublin 1840), pp 20 ff; Irish Corporation Bill, Isaac Butt (speech), p 50.

45. *The Nation,* 28 January 1854; *Tuam Herald,* 28 January 1854; Cf. Chapter Two, Elections and Fenianism, p 14.

46. *Tuam Herald,* 2 February 1856.

47. *Freeman's Journal,* 22 November 1902; Healy, op. cit., p 622.

48. D'Alton, op. cit., p 353.

49. Cullen to Kirby, 13 December 1856, 'Kirby Papers 1836-1861,' edited P. J. Corish, *Archivium Hibernicum,* Vol. XXXI, 1973, p 70.

50. *Freeman's Journal,* 18 February 1857.

51. *Tuam Herald,* 28 March 1857; *Freeman's Journal,* 24 March 1857.

52. *Tuam Herald,* 4 April 1857.

53. MacEvilly to Kirby, 23 March 1867, Archives of Irish College, Rome.

Chapter Two

1. *Freeman's Journal,* 27 November 1902 – obituary notice; *Tuam News,* 28 November 1902 – obituary notice.

2. Edward Lucas, *The Life of Frederick Lucas M.P.* (London and New York 1886), II, p 59.

3. *The Nation,* 28 January 1854.

4. Cf. Chapter Six, Tenant Right and the Tenant League, p 96.

5. *Tuam News,* 9 February 1883.

6. *The Nation,* 28 January 1854.

7. Cf. MacDonagh, art. op. cit., p 51.

8. Whyte, 'Political Problems,' pp 25-6; see also 'Cardinal Cullen and Irish Nationality,' E.D. Steele, *I.H.S.,* XIX, No. 75, March 1975.

9. Whyte, 'Political Problems,' p 34.

10. *Freeman's Journal,* 27 March 1857.

11. *Sir William Gregory, K.C.M.G.* An Autobiography, edited by Lady Gregory (London 1894), p 162.

12. J. H. Whyte, *The Independent Irish Party 1850-9* (Oxford 1958), p 122.

13. MacEvilly to Cullen, 12 July 1857, DDA.

14. 'Tories, Catholics and the General Election of 1859,' K. Theodore Hoppen, *The Historical Journal,* Vol. XIII, 1970, p 63.

15. Whyte, *Irish Party,* p 167; *Galway Mercury,* 7 May 1859.

16. *Freeman's Journal,* 5, 12 February 1859.

17. Hoppen, op. cit., p 53.

18. MacEvilly to Cullen, 30 June 1865, DDA.

19. *Galway Vindicator,* 19 July 1865.

20. *Galway Vindicator,* 24 February 1866.

21. MacEvilly to Cullen, 6 February 1871, DDA.

22. *Parliamentary Papers, 1872,* Vol. 48, Copy of the shorthand written notes on the judgment of Mr. Justice Keogh at the Trial of the Galway Co. Election Petition, pp 18-51; *Freeman's Journal,* 29 May 1872.

23. *Freeman's Journal,* 28 May 1872.

24. MacEvilly to Cullen, 29 May 1872, DDA.

25. MacEvilly to Kirby, 4 August 1872, *Arch. Hib.,* XXX, 1972, p 67.

26. MacEvilly to Kirby, 6 September 1872, Irish College Archives, Rome.

27. MacEvilly to Cullen, 30 January 1874, DDA.

28. MacEvilly to Cullen, 20 April 1874, DDA.

29. *Galway Vindicator,* 13 May 1874.

30. *Galway Vindicator,* 6 May 1874.

31. *Galway Vindicator,* 16 May 1874.

32. *Parliamentary Papers 1874,* Vol. 53, Minutes of Evidence at Galway Borough Election Petition Trial, p 19.

33. MacEvilly to Cullen, 21 May 1874, DDA.

34. *Parliamentary Papers 1874,* Minutes, p 62.

35. *Freeman's Journal,* 23 May 1874; *Parliamentary Papers 1874,* Minutes, pp 150-160.

36. *Freeman's Journal,* 3 June 1874.

37. *Parliamentary Papers 1874,* Minutes, p 160.

38. MacEvilly to Cullen, 1 January 1868, DDA.

39. MacEvilly to Cullen, 4 January 1868, DDA.

40. MacEvilly to Cullen, 1 April 1869, DDA.

41. Norman, op. cit., pp 126-7.
42. Corish, 'Political Problems,' pp 37-8.
43. Norman, op. cit., p 127.
44. MacEvilly to Cullen, 20 March 1869, DDA.
45. Corish, 'Political Problems,' p 38.
46. MacEvilly to Kirby, 11 January 1871, *Arch Hib.*, XXX, 1972, p 65.

Chapter 3

1. *Tuam Herald*, 24 August 1850.
2. *The Nation*, 28 January 1854.
3. Bernard O'Reilly, *John MacHale, His Life, Times and Correspondence* (New York and Cincinnati), II, p 369.
4. Cullen to Kirby, 13 December 1856, *Arch. Hib.*, XXXI, 1973, p 91.
5. Cullen to Canon Smithwick, P.P. Howth, 8 May 1866, from Peadar MacSuibhne, *Paul Cullen and His Contemporaries* (Naas, 1974), IV, p 196.
6. MacEvilly to Cullen, 10 September 1864, DDA.
7. Cf. Chapter Four, Administrative Problems, p 60.
8. Norman, op. cit., pp 412-3.
9. Norman, op cit., p 414.
10. Corish, 'Political Problems.' pp 6-7.
11. Ibid., p 7.
12. 'The Patriot Priest of Partry Patrick Lavelle: 1825-1886.' Tomas O Fiaich, *Journal of the Galway Archaeological and Historical Society,* Vol. 35, 1976, p 140.
13. Corish, *Political Problems,* p 10
14. Ibid., p 12-13.
15. MacEvilly to Cullen, 9 October 1863, DDA.
16. Corish, *Political Problems,* pp 13-14.
17. MacEvilly to Cullen, 5 December 1863, DDA.
18. MacEvilly to Kirby, 14 June 1864, quoted in Norman, op. cit., p 102.
19. Corish, *Political Problems,* p 14.
20. MacEvilly to Cullen, 10 January 1864, DDA.
21. Corish, *Political Problems,* p 14.
22. MacEvilly to Cullen, 7 February 1864, DDA.
23. MacEvilly to Kirby, 26 February 1864, *Arch. Hib.*, XXX, 1972, p 39.
24. Corish, *Political Problems,* p 15.
25. MacEvilly to Cullen, 7 March 1864, DDA.
26. MacEvilly to Cullen, 6 May 1864, DDA.
27. MacEvilly to Cullen, 29 April 1864, DDA.
28. O Fiaich, art. op. cit., p 142.
29. *Freeman's Journal,* 3 September 1864.
30. MacEvilly to Cullen, 23 September 1864, DDA.
31. MacEvilly to Cullen, 10 October 1864, DDA.
32. MacEvilly to Cullen, 11 November 1864, DDA.
33. MacEvilly to Cullen, 11 December 1864, DDA; Corish, 'Political Problems', pp 20-21.
34. O Fiaich, art, op. cit., p 142.

35. MacEvilly to Cullen, 4 January 1868, DDA.

36. *Parliamentary Papers 1872,* p 48, Judgment of Keogh on the Trial of the Galway County Election Petition; Cf. Chapter Two, Elections and Fenianism, p 14.

37. O Fiaich, art. op. cit., p 147.

38 MacEvilly to Cullen, 31 March 1874, DDA.

39. MacEvilly to Cullen, 20 May 1878, DDA.

40. MacEvilly to Kirby, 18 December 1879, Irish College Archives, Rome.

41. MacEvilly to Kirby, 13 May 1882, *Arch. Hib.,* XXX, 1972, p 110.

42. *Connaught Telegraph,* 27 November 1886.

43. MacEvilly to Cullen, 4 August 1863, DDA.

44. MacEvilly to Cullen, 10 September 1864, DDA.

45. Draft letter of *Relatio Status* to Cardinal Prefect of Propaganda, June 1862, GDA.

46. MacEvilly to Cullen, 10 January 1864, DDA.

47. MacEvilly to Cullen, 15 December 1864, DDA.

48. MacEvilly to Cullen, 30 January 1865, DDA.

49. Kirby to MacEvilly, 9 August 1866, GDA.

50. Mortimer Brennan, C.C. to MacEvilly, 7 September 1866. Enclosed is a copy of the protest of the clergy of Kilmacduagh, GDA.

51. MacEvilly to Cullen, 8 September 1866, DDA.

52. Cullen to Kirby, 10 September 1866, Irish College Archives, Rome.

53. MacEvilly to Cullen, 17 September 1866, DDA.

54. Kirby to MacEvilly, 23 September 1866, GDA.

55. MacEvilly to Cullen, 26 September 1866, DDA.

56. Cullen to MacEvilly, 28 September 1866, GDA.

57. J. Fahy, D.D., V.G., *The History and Antiquities of the Diocese of Kilmacduagh* (Dublin 1893), p 438.

58. Fahy, op. cit., pp 439-440.

59. D'Alton, op. cit., II, p 88.

60. O'Reilly, op. cit., II, p 598.

61. O'Reilly, op cit., II, p 602.

62. O'Reilly, op cit., II, p 600.

63. D'Alton, op cit., II, p 88.

64. MacEvilly to Cullen, 25 December 1875, DDA.

65. D'Alton, op cit., II, p 88.

66. MacEvilly to Cullen, 26 May 1876, DDA.

67. D'Alton, op. cit., II p 88.

68. *Freeman's Journal,* 17 August 1876.

69. *Freeman's Journal,* 17 August 1876.

70. Cf. D'Alton, op. cit., pp 98-99; MacEvilly mentions this many times in his letters to Cullen.

71. Cullen to Kirby, 17 August 1876, *Arch. Hib.,* XXXII, 1974, p 59.

72. *Freeman's Journal,* 18 August 1876.

73. Cullen to Kirby, 18 August 1876, *Arch. Hib.,* XXXII, 1974, p 59.

74. Cullen to Kirby, 21 August 1876, *Arch. Hib.,* XXXII, 1974, p 59.

75. MacHale to Cullen, 22 August 1876, quoted in O'Reilly, op. cit., pp 603-4.

76. MacHale to Cullen, 25 August 1876, quoted in O'Reilly, op. cit., pp 603-4.

77. Cullen to MacHale, 26 August 1876, quoted in O'Reilly, op. cit., II, pp 603-4.

78. MacHale to Cullen, undated, quoted in O'Reilly, *op. cit.,* II p 605.
79. O'Reilly, op. cit., II, p 609.
80. O'Reilly, op cit., II, p 609-10.
81. Cullen to Kirby, 12 November 1876, *Arch. Hib.,* XXXII, 1974, p 59.
82. Gillooly to Franchi, 7 September 1876, Irish College Archives, Rome.
83. O'Reilly, op. cit., II, pp 601-2.
84. O'Reilly, op. cit., II, p 612.
85. Cullen to Kirby, 29 December 1876, *Arch Hib.,* XXXII, 1974, p 60.
86. Cullen to Kirby, 14 March 1877, *Arch Hib.,* XXXII, 1974, p 60.
87. O'Reilly, op. cit., II, p 612.
88. D'Alton, op. cit., II, p 91.
89. MacEvilly to Kirby, 22 October 1877, *Arch. Hib.,* 1972, p 81.
90. O'Reilly, op. cit., II, pp 613-4.
91. O'Reilly, op. cit., II, p 617.
92. O'Reilly, op. cit., II, p 617.
93. MacEvilly to Cullen, 12 January 1878, DDA.
94. MacEvilly to Kirby, 14 January 1878, *Arch Hib.,* XXX, 1972, pp 81-2.
95. MacEvilly to Cullen, 18 January 1878, DDA.
96. MacEvilly to Cullen, 10 February 1878, DDA.
97. MacEvilly to Cullen, Easter Monday, 1878, DDA.
98. MacEvilly to Cullen, Ascension Thursday, 1878, DDA.
99. O'Reilly, op.cit., II, p 618.
100. MacEvilly to Cullen, 20 May 1878, DDA.
101. O'Reilly, op. cit., II, pp 618-9.
102. Cullen to Gillooly, 8 June 1878, quoted in Emmett Larkin, *The Roman Catholic Church and the Creation of the Modern Irish State 1878-86* (Dublin 1975), p 12.
103. Cullen to Kirby, 13 August 1878, *Arch. Hib.,* XXXII, 1974, p 60.
104. MacEvilly to Cullen, 30 August 1878, DDA.
105. MacGettigan to MacHale, 31 August 1878, quoted in O'Reilly, op. cit., II, pp 621-3.
106. MacGettigan to Croke, 10 September 1878, *Collectanea Hibernica,* 1970, p 116.
107. O'Reilly, op. cit., II, p 620.
108. Simeoni to MacGettigan, 26 January 1879, quoted in O'Reilly, op. cit., II, p 620.
109. O'Reilly, op. cit., II, pp 624-5 (from Latin copy among MacHale mss).
110. MacEvilly to Kirby, 2 April 1879, quoted in Larkin, op. cit., p 13.
111. MacGettigan to a priest of Tuam, quoted in O'Reilly, op. cit., II. pp 622-3.
112. Richard MacHale, the archbishop's nephew, had been appointed parish priest of Claremorris in 1876, although there were many priests senior to him. Another nephew, John, was a professor in St. Jarlath's College, Tuam, and of course, Thomas MacHale was vicar general of the diocese. D'Alton, op. cit., II, p 221; MacEvilly to McCabe, 8 October 1879, DDA.
113. *Irish Catholic Directory,* 1883, p 196.
114. MacEvilly to McCabe, 22 August 1879, 6 March 1881, DDA; D'Alton, op. cit., p.91.
115. MacEvilly to Cullen, 17 March 1879, Irish College Archives, Rome.
116. There is very little relating to Fenianism in Tuam diocese in the official files for the years 1876-8 at the State Paper Office, Dublin Castle.
117. MacEvilly to McCabe, 8 June 1879, DDA.

118. MacEvilly to McCabe, 21 April 1879, DDA.
119. McCabe to Kirby, 29 June 1879, *Arch. Hib.,* XXX, 1972, p.85.
120. MacEvilly to Kirby, 20 July 1879, *Arch Hib.,* XXX, 1972, p 85.
121. McCabe to Kirby, 8 August 1879, *Arch Hib.,* XXX, 1972, pp 85-6.
122. Simeoni to MacHale, 22 August 1879, quoted in O'Reilly, op. cit., II, pp 626-7.
123. Letter to Simeoni from seven parish priests of Tuam diocese, 22 August 1879, Irish College Archives, Rome.
124. Reilly, op. cit., II, p 626.
125. MacEvilly to McCabe, 2 September 1879, DDA.
126. MacHale to Simeoni, quoted in O'Reilly, op. cit., II, pp 626-7.
127. Duggan to McCabe, 2 September 1879, DDA.
128. MacEvilly to McCabe, 8 October 1879; 26 December 1879; DDA. MacEvilly to Kirby, 20 October 1879, *Arch. Hib.,* XXX, 1972, pp 87-8.
129. MacEvilly to Kirby, 24 October 1879, *Arch. Hib.,* XXX, 1972, p 88.
130. MacEvilly to Kirby, 27 October 1879, *Arch Hib.,* XXX, 1972, p 88.
131. MacEvilly to Kirby, 11 December 1879, *Arch Hib.,* XXX, 1972, pp 90-1.
132. MacEvilly to McCabe, 21 December 1879, DDA.
133. MacEvilly to McCabe, 21 December 1879, DDA.
134. McCabe to Kirby, 29 December 1879, *Arch Hib.,* XXX, 1972, p 91.
135. MacEvilly to Kirby, 13 February 1880, *Arch. Hib.,* XXX 1972, p 91.
136. MacEvilly to McCabe, 12 March 1880, DDA.
137. D'Alton, op. cit., II p 99.
138. MacEvilly to McCabe, 6 January 1881, DDA.
139. MacEvilly to McCabe, 6 March 1881, DDA. This opinion is borne out by D'Alton in his *History of the Archdiocese of Tuam,* II, p 98.
140. MacEvilly to McCabe, 23 March 1881, DDA.
141. *Freeman's Journal,* 8 November 1881.
142. MacEvilly to Kirby, 19 November 1881, Irish College Archives, Rome.
143. MacEvilly to McCabe, 14 December 1881, DDA.
144. D'Alton, op. cit., II, p 107.
145. D'Alton, op. cit., II, p 112.
146. Cf. Chapter Six, Tenant Right and Tenant League, p 96.
147. D'Alton, op. cit., pp 113-4.
148. Cf. 'The Politicisation of the Irish Catholic Bishops 1800-1850,' Oliver MacDonagh, *The Historical Journal* (March 1975), pp 37-53.

Chapter 4

1. Cf. 'The Devotional Revolution in Ireland 1850-1871', Emmett Larkin, *The American Historical Review,* Vol. 77, No. 3, June 1972.
2. Cf. Chapter Three, MacEvilly and MacHale, p 40.
3. Martin Coen, *The Wardenship of Galway.* (Galway 1967) p 172.
4. Norman, op. cit., p 16.
5. MacEvilly to Cullen, 12 July 1857, DDA.
6. *Galway Vindicator*, 30 September 1868.
7. *Irish Catholic Directory* 1857, p 204.

8. *Galway Vindicator*, 12 May 1866; Norman, op. cit., p 16.

9. *Galway Vindicator*, 12 May 1866.

10. *Galway Vindicator,* 30 September 1868; *Western News,* 20 December 1902.

11. Richard M. Lynch to MacEvilly, 15 December 1857, GDA.

12. MacEvilly to Leonard, 10 February 1858 (copy in MacEvilly's hand), GDA. From first to last, MacEvilly carefully documented the Daly affair. The Galway Diocesan Archives contain original letters, copies of letters in MacEvilly's hand and notes on events. It was as if MacEvilly had foreseen that one day the affair would be studied.

13. Leonard to Rev. Mother, Convent of Mercy, Clifden, 26 December 1857 (copy), GDA. Also a list of monies received at the profession of sisters and a list of securities.

14. Signed declaration of Peter Daly, 29 September 1852 (copy), GDA.

15. MacEvilly to Cullen, Holy Saturday, 1858, DDA.

16. MacEvilly to Leonard, 13 February 1858 (copy), GDA.

17. Daly to MacEvilly, 22 March 1858, GDA.

18. MacEvilly to Daly, 22 March 1858 (copy), GDA.

19. Letter of parish priests of the town of Galway to MacEvilly, dated 2 April 1858 and signed Mathias Joyce, P.P., G. Commins, P.P., Laurence Leonard, GDA.

20. MacEvilly to Daly, Good Friday 1858 (Draft of a letter in MacEvilly's hand), GDA.

21. MacEvilly to Daly, 9 April 1858 (copy), GDA.

22. Daly to MacEvilly, 10 April 1858, GDA.

23. MacEvilly to Daly, 13 April 1858 (copy), GDA.

24. MacEvilly to Cullen, 15 April 1858, DDA.

25. *Galway Vindicator,* 24 December 1859.

26. *Galway Vindicator,* 24 March 1860; *Galway Press,* 21 March 1860.

27. This paper replaced the *Galway Mercury.* Its first edition appeared on 17 March 1860.

28. Frs Goode and Phew to MacEvilly, 27 January 1860, Irish College Archives, Rome.

29. Document in MacEvilly's hand listing seven conditions, April 1860, GDA.

30. MacEvilly to Daly, 8 December 1861 (copy), GDA.

31. Daly to MacEvilly, 26 December 1861, GDA.

32. *Freeman's Journal*, 7 January 1862.

33. MacEvilly to Cullen, 6 January 1862, DDA.

34. *Freeman's Journal*, 7 January 1862; MacEvilly to Cullen, 6 January 1862, DDA.

35. *Galway Vindicator*, 8 January 1862.

36. *Freeman's Journal*, 7 January 1862.

37. MacEvilly to Kirby, undated, GDA. The earlier part of this letter is missing but it was obviously written at this time.

38. MacEvilly to Cullen, 12 January 1862, DDA.

39. Daly to MacEvilly, 17 January 1862, GDA.

40. *Galway Vindicator,* 22 January 1862; *Freeman's Journal*, 21 January 1862.

41. MacEvilly to Cullen, 28 January 1862, DDA.

42. MacEvilly to Kirby, 22 January 1862 (draft in MacEvilly's hand), GDA.

43. Cullen to Barnabo, 31 January 1862, quoted in MacSuibhne, op. cit., IV, p 111; also Cullen to Kirby, 31 Janaury 1862, *Arch. Hib.,* XXXII, 1974, p 53.

44. MacEvilly to Cullen, 20 February 1862, DDA.

45. Daly to MacEvilly, 24 February 1862, GDA.

46. MacEvilly to Cullen, 1 March 1862, DDA.

47. Daly to MacEvilly, 26 February 1862, GDA.

48. *Freeman's Journal*, 27 February 1862.
49. MacEvilly to Cullen, 1 March 1862, DDA.
50. MacEvilly to Daly, 7 March 1862 (copy), GDA.
51. Daly to MacEvilly, 10 March 1862, GDA.
52. Note in MacEvilly's hand, GDA.
53. Kirby to MacEvilly, 20 March 1862, GDA.
54. *Galway Vindicator*, 23 April 1862.
55. Cf. Chapter Five, The Education Question, p 83.
56. MacEvilly to Daly, 16 August 1863, (copy), GDA.
57. Daly to MacEvilly, 16 August 1863, GDA,
58. MacEvilly to Cullen, 21 August 1863, DDA.
59. MacHale to MacEvilly, 17 August 1863, GDA.
60. MacEvilly to MacHale, 21 August 1863, (copy), GDA.
61. Daly to MacHale, 30 August 1863, GDA.
62. MacHale to MacEvilly, 15 September 1863, GDA.
63. MacHale to MacEvilly, 18 September 1863, GDA.
64. B.I. Roche to MacEvilly, 3 October 1863, GDA.
65. MacEvilly to Kirby, dated October 1863 (copy), GDA; MacEvilly to Kirby, 4 October 1863, Irish Colleges Archives, Rome.
66. Minutes of the meeting of Propaganda, courtesy of M. Coen.
67. MacEvilly to Daly, 9 October 1864 (copy), GDA.
68. MacEvilly to Cullen, 11 November 1864, DDA.
69. These three conditions are attached to Daly's letter of 8 December under the comment 'Above not enough,' GDA.
70. MacEvilly to Cullen, 15 December 1864, DDA.
71. MacEvilly to Cullen, 23 December 1864, DDA; memo in MacEvilly's hand, recording the sequence of events of these days, GDA.
72. *Freeman's Journal*, 24 December 1864; *Galway Vindicator,* 24 December, 1864.
73. MacEvilly to Kirby, dated 20 December 1864, Irish College Archives, Rome.
74. MacEvilly to Cullen, 12 August 1865, DDA.
75. *Galway Vindicator,* 30 September 1868.
76. MacEvilly to Cullen, 5 October 1868, DDA.
77. Kirby to MacEvilly, 30 October 1868, GDA.
78. *Irish Catholic Directory,* 1857.
79. Desmond Bowen, *Souperism: Myth or Reality* (Cork 1970), p 129.
80. Ibid., p 130.
81. MacEvilly to Cullen, 12 July 1857, DDA.
82. MacEvilly to Cullen, 14 May 1866, DDA.
83. Norman, op. cit., pp 75-6.
84. *Galway Vindicator,* 22 March, 1871.
85. Linus H. Walker, *Fire-Tried Gold* (Galway 1974), p 336.
86. MacEvilly to Cullen, 4 November 1873, DDA.
87. Walker, op. cit., p 465.
88. D'Alton, op. cit., p 11.
89. Bowen, op. cit., p 100.
90. Ibid., p 103.
91. Cited in D'Alton, op. cit., p 68.

92. MacEvilly to Kirby, 23 September 1889, Irish College Archives, Rome.
93. Bowen, op. cit., p 130.
94. Ibid., p 135.
95. Ibid., p 135.
96. D'Alton, op. cit., p 67.
97. Cf. D'Alton, op. cit., pp 58-9.
98. Bowen, op. cit., p 131.
99. MacEvilly to McCabe, Easter Monday, 1867, DDA.
100. MacEvilly to Kirby, 8 August 1879, *Arch. Hib.,* XXX, 1972, pp 85-6.
101. The Census of 1861 gives the number as 215, out of a population of 1,434.
102. *Freeman's Journal,* 5 August, 1887.
103. Cf. Chapter Five, The Education Question, p 83.
104. D. H. Arkenson, *The Irish Education Experiment* (London and Toronto 1970) p 1.
105. MacEvilly to Cullen, 21 December 1863, DDA.
106. *Irish Catholic Directory,* 1879, p 196. Here the parochial schools are described as ''fair in number and tolerably efficient.''
107. *Tuam News,* 20 October 1899.
108. *Tuam News,* 20 October 1899.
109. D'Alton, op. cit., p 114.
110. *Connaught Telegraph,* 21 February 1891.
111. *Connaught Telegraph,* 28 February 1891.
112. *Freeman's Journal,* 18 March 1891.
113. *Connaught Telegraph,* 21 March 1891.
114. *Connaught Telegraph,* 28 March 1891. The *Telegraph* refused to print many of the objectors' letters. This was left to the *Western People,* copies of which I have been unable to obtain.
115. *Connaught Telegraph,* 11 April 1891.
116. *Connaught Telegraph,* 2 May 1891.
117. *Connaught Telegraph,* 23 May 1891.
118. *Connaught Telegraph,* 30 May 1891, 6 June 1891.
119. *Connaught Telegraph,* 24 September 1892.
120. D'Alton, op. cit., p 115.
121. *Connaught Telegraph,* 18 October 1901.
122. *Connaught Telegraph,* 2 May 1891.
123. *Freeman's Journal,* 28 January 1867.
124. *Galway Vindicator,* 29 April 1874.
125. *Galway Vindicator,* 31 October 1874.
126. *Galway Vindicator,* 3 April 1875.
127. *Galway Vindicator,* 11 October 1876.
128. *Galway Vindicator,* 17 January 1877.
129. *Galway Vindicator,* 14 February 1877.
130. *Freeman's Journal* 27 November 1902.
131. Michael J. Walsh, *The Apparition at Knock* (Naas 1955), p 3. (Hereinafter referred to as Walsh, *Knock*).
132. Walsh, *Knock,* p 15.
133. Walsh, *Knock,* p 36.
134. MacEvilly to Kirby, 13 February 1889, *Arch. Hib.,* XXX, 1972, p 91.

135. MacEvilly to Kirby, 14 June 1880, *Arch. Hib.,* XXX, 1972, p 94.
136. MacEvilly to Kirby, 14 June 1880, Irish College Archives, Rome.
137. Walsh, *Knock*, p 123; D'Alton, op. cit., p 224.
138. Details of this involvement with MacEvilly and Knock are contained in M. F. Cusack, *The Nun of Kenmare* (London 1889).
139. Cusack, *Nun of Kenmare*, pp 177-187.
140. Cusack, *Nun of Kenmare,* pp 192-3.
141. Ibid., p 285, p 295.
142. Ibid., pp 313-15.
143. Ibid., p 377.
144. Walsh, *Knock,* p 110.
145. MacEvilly to Kirby, 5 May 1889, Irish College Archives, Rome.
146. Cusack, *Nun of Kenmare,* pp 198-9.

Chapter 5

1. *Galway Vindicator*, 9 January 1864.
2. MacEvilly to Kirby, 5 January 1866, quoted in Norman, op. cit., p 190.
3. Norman, op. cit., pp 59-61.
4. Norman, op. cit., pp 52-9.
5. Akenson, op. cit., p 301.
6. Ignatius Murphy, art. op. cit., p 33.
7. Norman, op. cit., p 69; Ignatius Murphy, art. op. cit., p 34.
8. Norman, op. cit., p 71.
9. D. H. Akenson, op. cit., p 303.
10. MacEvilly to Gillooly, 20 March 1860, DDA.
11. Norman, op. cit., p 73; Akenson, op. cit., p 304.
12. Norman, op. cit., p 78.
13. Norman, op .cit., p 212.
14. Norman, op. cit., pp 213-6.
15. Norman, op. cit., p 218, states that Grey ignored the second memorial. In fact he referred it to the Commissioners of the National Board. In the Dublin Archives there is the printed reply dated 'Whitehall, 4 May 1866.'
16. Norman, op. cit., p 245.
17. Ignatius Murphy, art. op. cit., pp 38-9.
18. Norman, op. cit., pp 437-8; Ignatius Murphy, art. op. cit., p 39.
19. Akenson, op. cit., p 316.
20. Gladstone to Fortescue, 26 February 1873, quoted in Norman, op. cit., p 444.
21. *Freeman's Journal,* 2 October 1888.
22. MacEvilly to Kirby, 14 March 1892, *Arch. Hib.,* XXXII, 1974, p 36.
23. L. P. Curtis, Jr., *Coercion and Conciliation in Ireland 1880-92* (London 1963), p 391.
24. Ignatius Murphy, art. op. cit., pp 45-6; Akenson, op. cit., p 348.
25. Curtis, op. cit., p 392.
26. T. J. O'Connell, *History of the Irish National Teachers' Organisation* 1868-1968, p 272.

27. Ignatius Murphy, art. op. cit., p 42.
28. *Connaught Telegraph*, 24 October 1896.
29. O'Connell, op. cit., p 56.
30. Ibid., pp 57-58.
31. O'Connell, op. cit., p 56.
32. *Freeman's Journal*, 2 July 1898.
33. *Connaught Telegraph*, 2 August 1902.
34. Usually the subject of Model schools is treated of under primary education, since they were controlled by the National Board of Education. However, I have decided to treat of them here because it was his opposition to the Model schools that led MacEvilly directly to establishing a comprehensive system of secondary education in Galway.
35. Ignatius Murphy, art. op. cit., p 28.
36. Akenson, op. cit., p 148; Murphy, op. cit., p 28, gives May 1849 as the date of opening of the first two schools.
37. Ignatius Murphy, art. op. cit, p 28.
38. *24th Report of Commissioners of National Education in Ireland,* 1859, p 202.
39. *Freeman's Journal*, 9 January 1863.
40. *Galway Vindicator*, 9 January 1864, DDA.
41. *34th Report of Commissioners of National Education in Ireland,* 1867, p 101.
42. Ignatius Murphy, art. op. cit., p 39; Akenson, op. cit., p 353.
43. Akenson, op. cit., p 349.
44. 'The Irish Intermediate Education Act 1878,' *Irish Ecclesiastical Record,* 5 January – February 1915, p 126.
45. *Freeman's Journal*, 27 July 1885.
46. This introduction is based on Fergal McGrath, *Newman's University: Idea and Reality* (Dublin 1951), pp 73 f.
47. McGrath, *Newman,* p 468.
48. 'The University Question,' Fergal McGrath, S.J., *A History of Irish Catholicism,* edited P. J. Corish, Vol. 5, p 97.
49. McGrath, *Newman,* p 468.
50. Norman, op. cit., p 58.
51. Norman, op. cit., p 59.
52. Norman, op. cit., pp 64-5.
53. Ibid., pp 67-8.
54. MacEvilly to Kirby, 26 December 1859, *Arch. Hib.,* XXXI, 1973, p 26.
55. MacEvilly to Cullen, 24 April 1860, DDA.
56. MacEvilly to Gillooly, 13 January 1861, EDA.
57. Cullen to Kirby, 2 February 1861, *Arch. Hib.,* XXXII, 1974, p 52.
58. Norman, op. cit., pp 213-6; see above, Primary Education, p 84.
59. Norman, op. cit., p 218.
60. MacEvilly to Cullen, 6 February 1866, DDA.
61. Norman, op. cit., p 219.
62. MacEvilly to Cullen, 6 November 1866, DDA.
63. M. Morris to MacEvilly, 4 November 1866, DDA.
64. MacEvilly to Morris, 9 November 1866 (copy in MacEvilly's hand), DDA.
65. Morris to MacEvilly, 17 November 1866, DDA.
66. MacEvilly to Cullen, 18 November 1866, DDA.

67. Cullen to MacEvilly, 1 December 1866, GDA.
68. MacEvilly to Cullen, 4 December 1866, DDA.
69. Norman, op. cit., pp 236-8; McGrath, art. op. cit., p 103.
70. Norman, op. cit., pp 448-9; McGrath, *Newman*, p 492.
71. McGrath, art. op. cit., p 104.
72. Norman, op. cit., p 451; McGrath, art. op. cit., p 105.
73. MacEvilly to Cullen, 7 March 1873, DDA.
74. MacEvilly to Cullen, 25 February 1877, DDA.
75. McGrath, *Newman*, p 492.
76. *Galway Vindicator*, 1 May 1878.
77. Larkin, op. cit., p 11.
78. MacEvilly to Kirby, 19 February 1879, quoted in Larkin, op. cit., p 11.
79. *Galway Vindicator*, 26 February 1879.
80. McGrath, *Newman,* p 493.
81. McGrath, *Newman,* p 493; Larkin, op. cit., p 165.
82. Larkin, op. cit., pp 166-7.
83. Ibid., p 167.
84. Ibid., p 167.
85. McGrath, art. op. cit., p 119.
86. Ibid., p 121.
87. *I.E.R.*, Vol. II, 1897, 'Important Statement on University Question,' p 84.
88. MacEvilly to Walsh, 31 December 1897, DDA.
89. *Tuam News,* 4 March 1898.
90. *I.E.R.*, Vol. VIII, 1900, p 82, 'Resolution of Bishops on University Question,' 20 June 1900.
91. Quoted in Patrick O'Farrell, *Ireland's English Question* (London 1971), p 210, no source given.
92. *Tuam News*, 22 February 1901.

Chapter 6

1. Cf. Whyte, *Irish Party*, pp 6-12.
2. *Tuam Herald*, 1 June 1850, 15 June 1850.
3. C. Gavan Duffy, *The League of North and South* (London 1886), p 48.
4. Ibid., p 79.
5. Duffy, op. cit., p 244; Whyte, 'Political Problems', p 112.
6. *The Nation,* 28 January 1854; *Tuam Herald,* 28 January 1854.
7. *The Nation,* 28 January 1854; Duffy, op. cit., p 374; *Tuam Herald,* 21 February 1857.
8. *Tuam Herald,* 3 February 1855.
9. *Tuam Herald,* 24 January 1857. Footnote: The Independent Irish Party was founded in the wake of the general election of July 1852. The party was pledged to oppose any English administration which would not repeal the Ecclesiastical Titles Act and adopt the Tenant League programme. Following the defection of Sadlier and Keogh, the party was in disarray. The leadership passed to George Henry Moore, a friend of John MacHale, who was unseated after the 1857 election on the grounds of 'undue clerical influence.'
10. Oliver MacDonagh, art. op. cit., p 52.

11. Cf. Norman, op. cit., pp 139 ff.
12. *Galway Vindicator,* 1 March 1865.
13. *Freeman's Journal,* 9 November 1869; *Galway Vindicator,* 10 November 1869.
14. *Freeman's Journal,* 13 November 1869.
15. Ibid.
16. Cf. E.D. Steele, *Irish Land and British Politics* (Cambridge 1974), pp 312-5.
17. Cf. Chapter Two, Elections and Fenianism, p14.
18. *Galway Vindicator,* 20 December 1871.
19. *Galway Vindicator,* 20 December 1871; 6 January 1872.
20. *Galway Vindicator,* 18 June 1879.
21. *Galway Vindicator,* 25 October 1879.
22. *The Nation,* 1 November 1879.
23. *The Nation,* 8 November 1879.
24. *Galway Vindicator,* 5 November 1879.
25. MacEvilly to Kirby, 11 December 1879, quoted in Larkin, op. cit., pp 28-29.
25. MacEvilly to Kirby, 11 December 1879, quoted in Larkin, op. cit., pp 28-29.
26. Cf. Thomas Brett, *Life of Patrick Duggan, Bishop of Clonfert,* Dublin 1921. This, the only biography of Duggan, is deficient in many respects and Duggan's biography is one that merits a fuller treatment.
27. MacEvilly to McCabe, 26 December 1879, DDA.
28. *Galway Vindicator,* 14 January 1880.
29. Crown evidence for the High Court in Ireland. Affidavits of John M. Kilkelly sworn 25th, 26th February 1880; document in archives of Irish College, Rome; MacEvilly to McCabe, 16 February 1880, DDA.
30. MacEvilly to McCabe, 16 February 1880, DDA.
31. MacEvilly to McCabe, 21 February 1880, DDA.
32. MacEvilly to McCabe, 30 May 1880, DDA.
33. MacEvilly to Kirby, 21 June 1880, Irish College Archives, Rome.
34. MacEvilly to McCabe, 19 November 1880, DDA.
35. MacEvilly to McCabe, 10 December 1880, DDA.
36. Larkin, op. cit., pp 59-71.
37. Cf. F.S.L. Lyons, *John Dillon* (London 1968), pp 44-9.
38. *Galway Vindicator,* 2 March 1881.
39. *Galway Vindicator,* 9 March 1881.
40. MacEvilly to McCabe, 15 March 1881, DDA.
41. *Freeman's Journal,* 12 March 1881.
42. *Freeman's Journal,* 17 March 1881.
43. MacEvilly to McCabe, 21 March 1881, DDA.
44. Larkin, op. cit., pp 105-6; Mark Tierney, *Croke of Cashel* (Dublin 1976), pp 115-6.
45. Curtis, op. cit., p 10.
46. MacEvilly to Mother Clare, 13 November 1881, quoted in M. F. Cusack, *The Nun of Kenmare,* p 187.
47. *Freeman's Journal,* 20 October 1881; *The Nation,* 22 October 1881.
48. *Freeman's Journal,* 20 October 1881.
49. *The Nation,* 5 November 1881.
50. Larkin, op. cit., p 128.
51. MacEvilly to McCabe, 22 October 1881, DDA.

52. MacEvilly to Woodlock of Ardagh, 21 January 1882, quoted in Larkin, op. cit., p 162.

53. *Freeman's Journal*, 13 January 1882; *Tuam News*, 20 January 1882.

54. *Freeman's Journal*, 13 January 1882; *Tuam News*, 20 January 1882.

55. *Tuam News*, 27 February 1882.

56. *Connaught Telegraph*, 25 February 1882.

57. Bew, op. cit., p 190.

58. MacEvilly to Kirby, 13 May 1882, Arch. Hib., XXX, 1972, p 110; *Connaught Telegraph*, 13 May 1882.

59. MacEvilly to Kirby, 13 May 1882, Arch. Hib., XXX, 1972, p 110; quoted in Larkin, op. cit., p 163.

60. *Connaught Telegraph*, 13 May 1882.

61. MacEvilly to McCabe, 4 May 1882, DDA.

62. Ibid.

63. Larkin, op. cit., p 169.

64. Larkin, op. cit., pp 169-70.

65. Larkin, op. cit., p 171.

66. MacEvilly to Kirby, 17 June 1882, quoted in Larkin, op. cit., p 172.

67. *United Ireland*, 8 July 1882.

68. *Freeman's Journal*, 11 July 1882.

69. *Freeman's Journal*, 12 July 1882.

70. Cf. Larkin, op. cit., pp 174-7.

71. MacEvilly to Kirby , 3 August 1882, quoted in Larkin, op. cit., p 177.

72. Cf. Chapter Seven, Famine and Emigration, p 119.

73. *Tuam News*, 9 February 1883.

74. N. D. Palmer, *The Irish Land League Crisis* (New Haven and London 1940), p 64.

75. Larkin, op. cit., pp 363-4.

76. MacEvilly to Kirby, 15 May 1886, quoted in Larkin, op. cit., p 377.

77. Curtis, op. cit., pp 147-8.

78. For a detailed account see F.S.L. Lyons, *Charles Stewart Parnell* (London 1977), pp 360-70.

79. *Tuam News*, 7 January 1887; *Freeman's Journal*, 7 January 1887.

80. Cf. Curtis, op. cit., pp 174-215, et. al.

81. *Tuam News*, 22 April 1887.

82. *Freeman's Journal*, 19 February 1887.

83. Cf. Chapter Eight, Irish Party, p 138.

84. MacEvilly to Walsh, 28 August 1887, DDA.

85. Ibid.

86. MacEvilly to Walsh, 11 September 1887, DDA.

87. Cited in Curtis, op. cit., p 179.

88. Cf. Chapter Eight, The Irish Party, p 138.

89. MacEvilly to Kirby, 29 July 1888, Arch Hib., XXXII, 1974, p 17.

90. William O'Brien, Evening Memories (Dublin and London 1920), pp 420-33; F.S.L. Lyons, *John Dillon* (London 1968), pp. 100-1.

91. *Tuam News*, 13 December 1889.

92. MacEvilly to Kirby, 29 December 1889, Irish College Archives, Rome.

93. *Tuam News*, 28 November 1890.

94. W. L. Micks, *History of the Congested Districts Board* (Dublin 1925), p 16.

95. Ibid., p 132.
96. Connaught *Telegraph,* 12 November 1892.
97. Micks, op. cit., pp 104-5.
98. Joseph V. O'Brien, *William O'Brien and the Course of Irish Politics 1881-1918* (California 1976), p 102.
99. Micks, op. cit., p 103.
100. William O'Brien, *An Olive Branch in Ireland* (London 1910), p 88.
101. Micks, op. cit., p 103.
102. Miller, op. cit., p 19.
103. William O'Brien, *An Olive Branch*, p 89.
104. Joseph O'Brien, op. cit., p 107.
105. Miller, op. cit., p 19.
106. *Tuam News*, 25 February 1898.
107. Miller, op. cit., p 20.
108. Ibid., p 21.
109. Ibid., pp 21-2.
110. Joseph O'Brien, op. cit., p 112.
111. Freeman's *Journal,* 31 January 1899; *Tuam News,* 3 February 1899.
112. *Freeman's Journal,* 2 October 1899; *Tuam News,* 6 October 1899.
113. *Freeman's Journal,* 6 October 1899.
114. F.S.L. Lyons, *Ireland Since The Famine* (Fontana Edition), p 217.
115. F.S.L. Lyons, *The Irish Parliamentary Party, 1890-1910* (London 1951), pp 78-9.
116. *Tuam News*, 22 February 1901.
117. *Connaught Telegraph*, 2 August 1902.

Chapter 7

1. Bew, op. cit., pp 9-11.
2. *'Seasonal Migration and Post-Famine Adjustment in the West of Ireland,'* Cormac O'Grada, *Studia Hibernica,* XIII (1973), p 74.
3. R. B. McDowell, *The Irish Administration 1801-1914* (London and Toronto 1964), pp 177-9; Gearoid Ó Tuathaigh, *Ireland before the Famine 1798-1848* (Dublin 1972), pp 113-4.
4. McDowell, op. cit., pp 166-8.
5. Ó Tuathaigh, op. cit., p 113.
6. Cf. Ó Tuathaigh, op. cit., pp 96-7; Curtis, op. cit., pp 362-4.
7. 'The Agricultural Depression of 1859-64,' James S. Donnelly, Jr., *Irish Economic and Social History, Vol. III* (1976), pp 34-5.
8. MacEvilly to Cullen, 4 December 1861, DDA.
9. *Galway Vindicator*, 22 January 1862.
10. *Freeman's Journal,* 26 February 1862; *Galway Vindicator,* 26 February 1862.
11. *Galway Vindicator,* 26 February 1862.
12. Donnelly, art. op. cit., p 35.
13. MacEvilly to Cullen, 3 January 1863, DDA.
14. MacEvilly to Cullen, 20 January 1863, DDA.
15. *Galway Vindicator,* 24 January 1863.
16. *Galway Vindicator,* 21 January 1863; also 28, 31 January to 29 April 1863.

17. Cf. Chapter Five, The Education Question, p 83.
18. MacEvilly to Cullen, 9 March 1863, DDA.
19. MacEvilly to Cullen, 7 June 1863, DDA.
20. *Galway Vindicator,* 6 June 1863.
21. MacEvilly to Cullen, 25 June 1863; 8 July 1863, DDA.
22. MacEvilly to Cullen, 1 August 1863, DDA.
23. MacEvilly to Cullen, 11 December 1863, DDA.
24. Donnelly, art. op. cit., p 36.
25. *Galway Vindicator,* 25 January 1865.
26. Derry of Clonfert to MacEvilly, 27 January 1865, GDA.
27. *Galway Vindicator,* 28 January 1865.
28. *Galway Vindicator,* 22 January 1867.
29. *Galway Vindicator,* 26 January 1867.
30. *Galway Vindicator,* 30 January 1867.
31. *Galway Vindicator,* 6 March 1867.
32. Cf. Donnelly, art. op. cit., pp 47-9.
33. *Galway Vindicator,* 21 December 1872.
34. MacEvilly to Cullen, 5 January 1873, DDA.
35. James Donnelly in his article on the agricultural depression of 1859-64, op. cit., argues that the depression of those years was more serious than that of 1879-80.
36. N.D. Palmer, op. cit., p 97.
37. Cf. Chapter Six, Tenant Right and the Tenant League, p 96.
38. Curtis, op. cit., p 9.
39. *Galway Vindicator,* 17 January 1880.
40. MacEvilly to Kirby, 13 February 1880, *Arch. Hib.,* XXX, 1972, p 91.
41. Printed copy of the memorial, EDA; *Tuam News,* 12 January 1883.
42. Ibid.
43. Ibid.
44. R.G.C. Hamilton to MacEvilly, 8 March 1883, original in EDA.
45. *Freeman's Journal,* 17 March 1883.
46. Ibid.
47. Ibid.
48. Cf. Chapter Eight, The Irish Party, p 138.
49. *Tuam News,* 29 January 1886.
50. MacEvilly to Kirby, 6 January 1886, quoted in Larkin, op. cit., p 383.
51. MacEvilly to Kirby, 15 May 1886, quoted in Larkin, op. cit., p 383.
52. *Tuam News,* 5 February 1886.
53. MacEvilly to Kirby, 30 January 1887, Irish College Archives, Rome.
54. Cf. Chapter 6, Tenant Right and the Tenant League, p 96.
55. *Freeman's Journal,* 8 March 1888.
56. Ibid.
57. Curtis, op. cit., p 371.
58. Ibid., p 364.
59. Cf. Chapter 6, Tenant Right and the Tenant League, p 96.
60. Curtis, op. cit., p 358.
61. Ibid., pp 361-2.
62. Micks, op. cit., p 12.

63. *Tuam News,* 22 February 1895.
64. *Tuam News,* 1 March 1895.
65. *Freeman's Journal,* 23 September 1897; *Tuam News,* 24 September 1897.
66. *Tuam News,* 25 February 1898.
67. *Tuam News,* 3 June 1898.
68. *Tuam News,* 1 July 1898.
69. MacEvilly to Walsh, 13 November 1898, DDA.
70. Census of Ireland 1851, 1861, 1871, 1881, 1891, 1901; *Irish Historical Statistics, Population 1821-1971,* edited by W. E. Vaughan and A. J. Fitzpatrick (Dublin 1978), p 14.
71. MacEvilly to Cullen, 3 January 1863, DDA.
72. MacEvilly to Cullen, 9 March 1863, DDA.
73. MacEvilly to Cullen, 11 December 1863, DDA.
74. MacEvilly to Kirby, 10 March 1865, Arch Hib., XXX, 1972, p 46.
75. *Galway Vindicator,* 6 March 1867.
76. R. D. Collison Black, *Economic Thought and the Irish Question 1817-1870* (Cambridge 1960), p 206.
77. Ibid., pp 220-5.
78. Ibid., p 235.
79. *Freeman's Journal,* 29 October 1883, 10 November 1883.
80. *Connaught Telegraph,* 10 November 1883; *Freeman's Journal,* 7 November 1883.
81. *Freeman's Journal,* 9 November 1883; *Tuam News,* 16 November 1883.
82. *Freeman's Journal,* 10 November 1883; *Tuam News,* 16 November 1883.
83. *Freeman's Journal,* 14 November 1883; *Tuam News,* 16 November 1883.
84. *Freeman's Journal,* 16, 20, 21 November 1883; *Connaught Telegraph,* 24 November 1883.
85. Cf. Chapter Eight, The Irish Party, p 138.
86. *Freeman's Journal,* 25 March 1884.
87. *Freeman's Journal,* 1, 2 April 1884; *Connaught Telegraph,* 5 April 1884.
88. *Tuam News,* 23 May 1884; *Freeman's Journal,* 21 May 1884.
89. *Freeman's Journal,* 27 May 1884; *Tuam News,* 20 May 1884.
90. *Freeman's Journal,* 31 May 1884; 14, 18 September 1884.
91. *Freeman's Journal,* 14 September 1894.
92. *Freeman's Journal,* 15 June 1894.
93. *Connaught Telegraph,* 7 July 1894.
94. MacEvilly to Walsh, 30 June 1894, DDA.
95. *Connaught Telegraph,* 7 July 1894.
96. *Freeman's Journal,* 5 July 1894; *Connaught Telegraph,* 7 July 1894.
97. *Tuam News,* 16 March 1900.
98. *Connaught Telegraph,* 2 August 1902.
99. *Freeman's Journal,* 2 July 1898.
100. 'Resolutions of Bishops on Emigration,' *Irish Ecclesiastical Record,* Vol. XI, 1902, p 472.
101. *Census of Ireland,* 1901. The figures are those given for the years 1851-1901.

Chapter 8

1. Lyons, Parnell, p 122.
2. MacEvilly to Kirby, 23 May 1880, quoted in Larkin, op. cit., p 22.
3. MacEvilly to Kirby, 20 April 1880, *Arch. Hib.,* XXX, 1972, p 93.
4. MacEvilly to Kirby , 14 June 1880, *Arch. Hib.,* XXX, 1972, p 94.
5. MacEvilly to Kirby, 23 May 1880, *Arch. Hib.,* XXX 1972, p 93.
6. C. J. Woods, *The Catholic Church and Irish Politics, 1879-92 (*unpublished thesis), p 137.
7. *Tuam News,* 12 January 1883; Cf. Chapter Seven, Famine and Emigration, p 119.
8. MacEvilly to Kirby , 3 February 1883, quoted in Larkin, op. cit., p 181.
9. R.G.C. Hamilton to MacEvilly, 8 March 1883 (copy), EDA; *Freeman's Journal,* 17 March 1883.
10. *Freeman's Journal,* 17 March 1883; *Tuam News,* 28 March 1883; Cf. Chapter Seven, Famine and Emigration pp 119.
11. MacEvilly to Kirby, 30 May 1882, quoted in Larkin, op. cit., p 188.
12. MacEvilly to Kirby, 30 May 1882, quoted in Larkin, op. cit., p 188.
13. MacEvilly to Kirby, 22 July 1883, quoted in Larkin, op. cit., p 201.
14. *Freeman's Journal,* 29 October, 10 November 1883; Cf. Chapter Seven, Famine and Emigration, p 119.
15. *Freeman's Journal,* 21 November 1883; *Connaught Telegraph,* 24 November 1883.
16. *Tuam News,* 14 March 1884.
17. *Tuam News,* 30 May 1884; *Freeman's Journal,* 31 May 1884.
18. MacEvilly to Kirby, 13 July 1884, quoted in Larkin, op. cit., pp 239-40.
19. Larkin, op. cit., p 239.
20. MacEvilly to Kirby, 13 July 1884, quoted in Larkin, op. cit., p 240.
21. 'The Maamtrasna Massacre,' Impeachment of the Trials, a pamphlet by T. Harrington, M.P. (Dublin 1884); Woods, op. cit., pp 183-4.
22. *Freeman's Journal,* 12 August 1884.
23. MacEvilly to the lord lieutenant; *Freeman's Journal,* 14 August 1884.
24. *Freeman's Journal,* 25 August 1884.
25. *Freeman's Journal,* 29 August 1884.
26. *Freeman's Journal,* 30 August 1884.
27. The Harrington Papers in the National Library attest to Harrington's endeavours and to his interest in the case, which he also pursued assiduously in the public press.
28. Curtis, op. cit., pp 41-43.
29. *Freeman's Journal,* 29 October 1884.
30. *Freeman's Journal,* 25 October 1902; *Tuam News,* 31 October 1902.
31. *United Ireland,* 4 October 1884.
32. MacEvilly to Kirby, 26 October 1884, quoted in Larkin, op. cit., p 245.
33. 'Joseph Chamberlain, Parnell and the Irish "central board" scheme, 1884-5,' C.H.D. Howard, *I.H.S.,* Vol. VIII, 1952-3, p 321.
34. MacEvilly to Gillooly, 16 November 1884, EDA.
35. MacEvilly to Gillooly, 5 January 1884, EDA.
36. Croke to Walsh, 17 May 1885, DDA.
37. *Freeman's Journal,* 6 May 1885; *Tuam News,* 8 May 1885.
38. MacEvilly to Manning, 7 July 1885, quoted in Larkin, op. cit., p 295.
39. *Tuam News,* 3 July 1885.

40. *Connaught Telegraph,* 25 July 1885.
41. *Freeman's Journal,* 27 July 1885.
42. MacEvilly to Kirby, 18 October 1885, Irish College Archives, Rome.
43. MacEvilly to Kirby, 4 November 1885, quoted in Larkin, op. cit., p 339.
44. *Freeman's Journal,* 7 September 1885; *Tuam News,* 11 September 1885.
45. *Freeman's Journal,* 26 October 1885; *Tuam News,* 30 October 1885.
46. *Freeman's Journal,* 27 October 1885; *Tuam News,* 30 October 1885.
47. MacEvilly to Kirby, 2 December 1885, quoted in Larkin, op. cit., p 343. *Arch Hib.,* XXXII, 1974, p 6.
48. MacEvilly to Kirby, 15 May 1886, quoted in Larkin, op. cit., p 377.
49. *Tuam News,* 11 June 1886.
50. *The Irish Times,* 15 June 1886.
51. MacEvilly to Kirby, 19 June 1886, quoted in Larkin, op. cit., p 378.
52. Walsh to Kirby, 16 June 1886, quoted in Larkin, op. cit., pp 378-9.
53. *Tuam News,* 7 January 1887; *Freeman's Journal,* 7 January 1887.
54. Quoted in Curtis, op. cit., p 179.
55. *Freeman's Journal,* 14 April, 20 April 1887; *Tuam News,* 22 April 1887.
56. Quoted in Patrick O'Farrell, op. cit., p 191, no source given; MacEvilly to Kirby, 22 April 1887, Irish College Archives, Rome.
57. Cf. Chapter Six, Tenant Right and the Tenant League, p 96.
58. *Tuam News,* 26 August 1887; Patrick J. Walsh, *William J. Walsh, Archbishop of Dublin* (Dublin 1928), p 297.
59. Original letter, 23 November 1887, Harrington Papers, National Library; *Connaught Telegraph,* 26 November 1887; *Freeman's Journal,* 25 November 1887.
60. *Freeman's Journal,* 5 November 1887.
61. *Freeman's Journal,* 17 December 1887.
62. *Freeman's Journal,* 20 December 1887.
63. *The Tablet,* 31 December 1887.
64. Vincent Alan McClelland, *Cardinal Manning* (London 1962), p 192.
65. P. J. Walsh, *William J. Walsh, Archbishop of Dublin* (London 1920), p 318.
66. Letter to Cardinal Rampolla, signed by five Irish bishops, including MacEvilly, dated 19 January 1888, Archives of Propaganda, Fide Rome.
67. *Connaught Telegraph,* 28 January 1888.
68. *Connaught Telegraph,* 4 February 1888.
69. *Connaught Telegraph,* 5 May 1888.
70. Lyons, *John Dillon,* pp 93-4; *Freeman's Journal,* 31 May 1888.
71. MacEvilly to Kirby, 27 November 1887, Irish College Archives, Rome.
72. *Tuam News,* 6 July 1888.
73. Duggan to Walsh, 8 July (1888), DDA.
74. *Freeman's Journal, 25 August 1888; Tuam News,* 31 August 1888.
75. MacEvilly to Kirby, 22 November 1888, Irish College Archives, Rome.
76. MacEvilly to Kirby, 10 December 1888, *Arch Hib.,* XXXII, 1974, p 18.
77. MacEvilly to Kirby, 29 December 1889, *Arch Hib.,* XXXII, 1974, p 23. MacEvilly to Gillooly, 25 August 1890, DDA.
78. MacEvilly to Walsh, 20 November 1890, DDA.
79. MacEvilly to Walsh, 30 November 1890, DDA.
80. MacEvilly to Walsh, 30 November 1890, DDA.

81. *Tuam News,* 5 December 1890; *Connaught Telegraph,* 6 December 1890.
82. *Tuam News,* 19 December 1890.
83. *Tuam News,* 19 December 1890; *Irish Catholic,* 20 December 1890.
84. *The Irish Catholic,* 20 December 1890.
85. MacEvilly to Kirby, 30 December 1890, Irish College Archives, Rome.
86. Lyons, *Irish Party,* p 38.
87. MacEvilly to Kirby, 8 February 1891, Irish College Archives, Rome; *Arch Hib.,* XXXII, 1974, p 29.
88. MacEvilly to Gillooly, 8 January 1891, EDA.
89. *Tuam News,* 13 February 1891; *Freeman's Journal,* 16 February 1891.
90. *Freeman's Journal,* 21 November 1890.
91. *Tuam News,* 5 December 1890.
92. *Tuam News,* 26 December 1890.
93. *Freeman's Journal,* 3 March 1891.
94. *Tuam News,* 6 March 1891.
95. Michael Davitt, *The Fall of Feudalism in Ireland* (London and New York 1904), p 660.
96. *Tuam News,* 13 March 1891; *Freeman's Journal,* 11 March 1891.
97. MacEvilly to Kirby, 22 March 1891, Irish College Archives, Rome.
98. MacEvilly to Kirby, 16 June 1891, Irish College Archives, Rome.
99. Copy of document signed by MacEvilly, DDA; *Freeman's Journal,* 3 July 1891.
100. MacEvilly to Kirby, 22 October 1891, Irish College Archives, Rome.
101. MacEvilly to Walsh, 30 January 1892, DDA.
102. Lyons, *Irish Party,* p 38.
103. MacEvilly to Kirby, 15 March 1892, Irish College Archives, Rome.
104. MacEvilly to Walsh, 15 February 1892, DDA.
105. Lyons, *Irish Party,* p 38.
106. *Freeman's Journal,* 24 June 1892; *Tuam News,* 1 July 1892.
107. *Freeman's Journal,* 28 June 1892; *Connaught Telegraph,* 2 July 1892.
108. MacEvilly to Kirby, 26 June 1892, Irish College Archives, Rome.
109. *The Irish Catholic,* 9 July 1892; *Connaught Telegraph,* 9 July 1892.
110. *Connaught Telegraph,* 9 July 1892.
111. MacEvilly to Walsh, 3 July 1892, DDA.
112. 'Ireland as it is, and as it would be under Home Rule' (Letters written by a special correspondent between March and August 1893); *Birmingham Daily Gazette,* pamphlet.
113. *Freeman's Journal,* 9 August 1892.
114. *Tuam News,* 15 July 1892.
115. MacEvilly to Walsh, 3 July 1892, DDA.
116. *Tuam News,* 26 July 1895.
117. *Freeman's Journal,* 20, 22, 23, 27 July 1895; *Tuam News,* 2 August 1895.
118. *Freeman's Journal,* 29 July 1895; *Tuam News,* 2 August 1895.
119. 'The machinery of the Irish parliamentary party in the general election of 1895,' F.S.L. Lyons, *I.H.S.,* Vol. VIII, 1952-3, p 139; Lyons, *John Dillon,* pp 164-8.
120. MacEvilly to Walsh, St. John's Day, 1896, DDA.
121. MacEvilly to Walsh, 3 December 1897, DDA.
122. *Freeman's Journal,* 29 September 1900.

123. Lyons, *Irish Party,* p 89.

124. Cf. Chapter Six, Tenant Right and the Tenant League, p 96.

125. *An Claidheamh Soluis*, 18 March 1899.

Chapter Nine

1. MacEvilly to Kirby, 29 August 1888, Irish College Archives, Rome.

2. MacEvilly to Kirby, 22 November 1888, Irish College Archives, Rome.

3. Brett, op. cit., p 187; *Freeman's Journal*, 19 August 1896; *Tuam News,* 21 August 1896.

4. MacEvilly to Kirby, 29 December 1894, Irish College Archives, Rome.

5. D'Alton, op. cit., p 116.

6. Ibid.

7. *Freeman's Journal*, 28 November 1902.

8. *Tuam News*, 28 November 1902; *Freeman's Journal,* 28 November 1902.

9. *Tuam Herald,* 29 November 1902.

10. *Tuam News,* 5 December 1902; *Freeman's Journal*, 3 December 1902.

11. For a scholarly view, see J. H. Whyte, *Church and State in Modern Ireland 1923-1970* (Dublin 1971).

12. See for instance, Patrick O'Farrell, *Ireland's English Question* (London 1971).

13. See Emmett Larkin, *The Roman Catholic Church and the Creation of the Modern Irish State 1878-1886* (Dublin 1975).

Sources

I. Primary Sources

A. Manuscript Collections
- i   Dublin Diocesan Archives
- ii   Elphin Diocesan Archives
- iii   Galway Diocesan Archives
- iv   National Library of Ireland
- v   State Paper Office of Ireland
- vi   Private Collections

B. Official Publications
C. Contemporary Newspapers and Periodicals
D. Contemporary Books and Pamphlets

II. Secondary Sources

A. General Works
B. Published Essays and Articles in Journals and Periodicals
C. Unpublished Works

I. Primary Sources

A. Manuscript Collections:

i Dublin Diocesan Archives
Letters and documents of Paul Cullen, archbishop of Dublin 1852-1878.
Letters and documents of Edward McCabe, archbishop of Dublin 1879-1885.
Letters and documents of William Walsh, archbishop of Dublin 1885-1921.

ii Elphin Diocesan Archives
Letters and documents of Laurence Gillooly, bishop of Elphin 1858-1921.

iii Galway Diocesan Archives
Letters and documents of John MacEvilly, bishop of Galway 1857-1881.
Letters and documents referring to the dispute with Peter Daly.

iv National Library of Ireland
Journal of W. J. O'Neill Daunt
Letters of William Monsell, Baron Emly
Letters of G. H. Moore
Larcom Papers
Diary of William Woodlock
The collected papers of J.F.X. O'Brien
The collected papers of Timothy Harrington
Letters of T. P. Gill

William O'Brien Papers
Parnell Papers
Propaganda Fide, Rome, Papers (1857-73), microfilm.

v **State Paper Office of Ireland**
Fenian Papers 1865-1879

vi **Private Collections**
Copies of unpublished letters and documents made available to me by the following:
Dom Mark Tierney, O.S.B.: From Kirby Papers, Irish College archives, Rome; Persico Papers and other documents from archives of Propaganda Fide, Rome; Croke Papers.
Fr Martin Coen, M.A.: From Kirby Papers, Irish College archives, Rome.
Padraig O Tuairisc: From Kirby Papers, Irish College archives, Rome.

B. **Official Publications:**
Parliamentary papers:
1857-8, XXVI. Galway Town corrupt practices. Minutes of evidence.
1866, Galway Town Petitions.
1872, XLVIII, Galway County Petition.
1874, LIII, Galway Town Petition.
First Report of the Commissioners appointed to enquire into the Municipal Corporations in Ireland 1835.
Reports of the Commissioners of National Education Ireland 1859, 1867, 1883, 1884, 1885, 1895, 1901.
Census of Ireland 1851-1901.
Court of Queen's Bench (Ireland). Report on the action for libel – *Rev. Robert O'Keeffe P.P. v Cardinal Cullen.* (London 1874).

C. **Contemporary Newspapers and Periodicals:**

An Claidheamh Soluis	*Irish People*
Connaught Telegraph	*Irish Times*
Freeman's Journal	*The Nation*
Galway Express	*Tuam Herald*
Galway Mercury	*Tuam News*
Galway Press	*The Tablet*
Galway Vindicator	*United Ireland*
Irish Catholic	*Western News*

Irish Catholic Directory 1857-1901.
Irish Ecclesiastical Record, Vol. II, 1897; Vol. VIII, 1900; Vol. XI, 1902.
The Irishman 1871.

D. **Contemporary Books and Pamphlets:**
'Ireland as it is, and as it would be under Home Rule' (62 letters written by the Special Correspondent of the *Birmingham Daily Gazette* between March and August 1893), a pamphlet.
BLUNT, Wilfred S., *The Land War in Ireland* (London 1912).
My Diaries, Part One, 1888-1900 (London 1921).

	My Diaries, Part Two, 1900-1914 (London 1921).
BRADY, W. Maziere,	*The Episcopal Succession in England, Scotland and Ireland 1400-1875,* 3 Vols. (Rome 1876).
BUTT, Isaac,	'Irish Municipal Reform,' a pamphlet (Dublin 1840).
CULLEN, William,	*The History of the Irish National Teachers' Organisation* (Belfast 1876).
CUSACK, M. F.,	*The Nun of Kenmare* (London 1889).
DUFFY, C. Gavan,	*My Life in Two Hemispheres,* 2 Vols. (London 1898).
	The League of North and South (London 1886)
DAVITT, Michael,	*The Fall of Feudalism in Ireland* (London and New York 1904).
FAHEY, J.,	*The History and Antiquities of the Diocese of Kilmacduagh* (Dublin 1893).
GREGORY, Sir William	*An Autobiography,* ed. Lady Gregory (London 1894)
HARRINGTON, Timothy C.,	*Maamtrasna Massacre,* a pamphlet (1884).
HEALY, John,	*Maynooth College 1795-1895* (Dublin 1895).
LUCAS, Edward,	*The Life of Frederick Lucas M.P.,* 2 Vols. (London and New York 1860.
McCARTHY, Michael J. F.,	*Five Years in Ireland 1895-1900* (London 1902).
O'BRIEN, William	*An Olive Branch in Ireland* (London 1910).
	Recollections (London 1910).
	Evening Memories (Dublin and London 1920).
O'DONNELL, F. H.,	*History of the Irish Parliamentary Party,* 2 Vols. (London 1910).
O'REILLY, Bernard,	*John MacHale, His Life, Times and Correspondence,* 2 Vols. (New York and Cincinnati 1890).
O'ROARKE, Rev. J.,	*The History of the Great Irish Famine of 1847* (Dublin 1875).
PURCELL, Edmund S.,	*Life of Cardinal Manning,* 2 Vols. (London 1896).
SOCIETY OF FRIENDS,	*Distress in Ireland 1846-47* (Dublin 1852)
SULLIVAN, A.M.,	*New Ireland* (Glasgow 1882).

II. Secondary Sources

A. General Works:

AKENSON, D.H.,	*The Irish Education Experiment: The National System of Education in the Nineteenth Century* (London 1970).
BEW, Paul,	*Land and the National Question in Ireland 1858-82.* (Dublin 1978).
BLACK, R.D.C.,	*Economic Thought and the Irish Question 1817-1870* (Cambridge 1960).
BLAKE, Robert,	*The Conservative Party from Peel to Churchill* (London 1970).
BOWEN, Desmond,	*Souperism: Myth or Reality?* (Cork 1970).

187

	The Protestant Crusade in Ireland 1800-70 (Dublin 1978).
BRETT, Rev. T.,	*Life of Patrick Duggan, Bishop of Clonfert* (Dublin 1921).
BUTLER, Dom C.,	*The Vatican Council 1869-70*, ed. Christopher Butler (London 1962).
COEN, Martin,	*The Wardenship of Galway* (Galway 1967).
CULLEN, L.M.,	*An Economic History of Ireland since 1660* (London 1972). ed. *The Formation of the Irish Economy* (Cork 1969).
CURTIS, L.P. Jr.,	*Coercion and Conciliation in Ireland 1880-92* (Princeton 1963).
D'ALTON, Monsignor E.A.,	*History of the Archdiocese of Tuam*, 2 Vols. (Dublin 1928).
EDWARDS, R. Dudley and Williams, T. Desmond (ed.),	*The Great Famine* (Dublin 1956).
EGAN, P.K.,	*The Parish of Ballinasloe* (Dublin 1960).
FENTON, Seamus,	*It All Happened,* Reminiscences (Dublin 1958).
HAMMOND, J.L.,	*Gladstone and the Irish Nation* (London 1938).
HURST, Michael,	*Parnell and Irish Nationalism* (London 1968).
JOYCE, P. J.,	*John Healy, Archbishop of Tuam* (Dublin 1931).
LARKIN, Emmett,	*The Roman Catholic Church and the Creation of the Modern Irish State 1878-1886* (Dublin 1975).
LEE, Joseph,	*The Modernisation of Irish Society 1898-1918* (Dublin 1975).
LESLIE, Sir S.,	*Herbert Edward Manning, His Life and Labours* (London 1921).
LYONS, F.S.L.,	*Ireland Since the Famine* (London 1971).
	The Irish Parliamentary Party 1890-1910 (London 1951).
	The Fall of Parnell (London 1964).
	John Dillon (London 1968).
	Charles Stewart Parnell (London 1977).
MacCAFFREY, J.,	*History of the Catholic Church in the Nineteenth Century,* 2 Vols. (Dublin and St. Louis 1909).
McCAFFREY, L.J.	*Daniel O'Connell and the Repeal Year* (University of Kentucky 1966).
McCLELLAND, V.A.	*Cardinal Manning, His Public Life and Influence 1865-1892* (London 1962).
McDOWELL, R.B.,	*The Irish Administration 1801-1914* (London and Toronto 1964).
McGRATH, F.,	*Newman's University: Idea and Reality* (London 1951).
MacSUIBHNE, P.,	*Paul Cullen and His Contemporaries 1820-1902,* 5 Vols. (Naas 1961-77).
MICKS, W. L.,	*History of the Congested Districts Board* (Dublin 1925).

MILLER, David W.,	*Church, State and Nation in Ireland 1898-1921* (Dublin 1973).
NORMAN, E.R.,	*The Catholic Church and Ireland in the Age of Rebellion 1859-1873* (London 1965).
O'BRIEN, Conor C.,	*Parnell and His Party 1880-1890* (Oxford 1957).
O'BRIEN, Joseph V.,	*William O'Brien and the Course of Irish Politics 1881-1918* (California 1976).
O'CONNELL, T.J.,	*History of the Irish National Teachers' Organisation 1868-1968* (Dublin 1968).
O'FARRELL, Patrick,	*Ireland's English Question* (London 1971).
Ó'FIAICH, Tomas,	*Má Nuad* (Má Nuad 1972).
Ó'TUATHAIGH, G.,	*Ireland Before the Famine 1798-1848* (Dublin 1972).
PALMER, N.D.,	*The Irish Land League Crisis* (New Haven and London 1940).
STEELE, E.D,	*Irish Land and British Politics* (Cambridge 1974).
TIERNEY, Mark,	*Croke of Cashel* (Dublin 1976).
THORNLEY, David,	*Isaac Butt and the Home Rule Party* (London 1964).
VAUGHAN, W.E., and Fitzpatrick A. J. (ed.),	*Irish Historical Statistics, Population 1821-1971* (Dublin 1978).
VINCENT, John,	*The Formation of the Liberal Party 1857-1868* (1966).
WALKER, Linus H.,	*Fire-Tried Gold* (Galway 1974).
WALSH, Michael J.,	*The Apparition at Knock* (Naas 1955).
WALSH, Patrick J.,	*William J. Walsh, Archbishop of Dublin* (Dublin 1928).
WHYTE, J.H.,	The Independent Irish Party 1850-9 (Oxford 1958). *Church and State in Modern Ireland 1923-70* (Dublin 1971).

B. **Published Essays and Articles in Journals and Periodicals:**

COOKE, A.B. and Vincent, J.R.,	'Ireland and party politics 1885-7, an unpublished Conservative memoir, *I.H.S.,* Vol. XVI, 1968-9.
CORISH, P.J. (ed.),	'Irish College Rome: Kirby Papers 1862-1883,' *Archivium Hibernicum,* Vol. XXX, 1972.
	'Irish College Rome: Kirby Papers 1836-1861,' *Archivium Hibernicum,* Vol. XXXI, 1973.
	'Irish College Rome: Kirby Papers 1884-1894; Addenda 1852-1878, *Archivium Hibernicum,* Vol. XXXII, 1974.
	'Political Problems 1860-1878,' *A History of Irish Catholicism* (general editor Patrick J. Corish), Vol. 5 (Dublin 1967).
COUSENS, S.H.,	'Emigration and Demographic Change in Ireland 1851-61,' *Economic History Review,* 2nd Serv. XIV (1962)

'The Regional Variation in Population changes in Ireland 1861-1881,' *Economic History Review*, XVII (1964-5).

DONNELLY, James S. Jr., 'The Agricultural Depression of 1859-64,' *Irish Economic and Social History*, Vol. III (1976).

HARKNESS, D.A.E., 'Irish Emigration,' *International Migrations*, Vol. II (New York 1931).

HOPPEN, K. Theodore, 'Tories, Catholics and the General Election of 1859' *The Historical Journal*, Vol. XIII, 1970.

HOWARD, C.H.D., 'The Parnell Manifesto of 21 November 1885 and the Schools Question,' *English Historical Review*, Vol. LXII, 1947.

'Joseph Chamberlain, Parnell and the Irish 'central board' scheme 1884-5,' *I.H.S.*, Vol. VIII, 1952-3.

HURST, Michael, 'Ireland and the Ballot Act of 1872, *'The Historical Journal*, Vol. VIII 3 (1965).

LARKIN, Emmett, 'The Roman Catholic Hierarchy and the Fall of Parnell,' *Victorian Studies* (Indianapolis), Vol. IV, No. 4 (June 1961).

'The Roman Catholic Hierarchy and the Destruction of Parnellism,' *Review of Politics*, XXV, No. 2 (April 1963).

'Launching the Counter Attack,' Part II of above, *Review of Politics*, XXVIII, No. 3 (July 1966).

'The Devotional Revolution in Ireland 1850-75,' *The American Historical Review*, Vol. 77, No. 3, June 1972.

LYONS, F.S.L., 'The machinery of the Irish Parliamentary Party in the General Election of 1895,' *I.H.S.*, Vol. VIII, 1952-3.

McCAFFREY, L.J., 'Home Rule and the general election of 1874 in Ireland,' *I.H.S.*, 1954.

MacDONAGH, O., 'The Politicization of the Irish Catholic Bishops 1800-1850,' *The Historical Journal* (March 1975).

McGRATH, Fergal, 'The University Question,' *A History of Irish Catholicism*, Vol. 5, VI (Dublin 1971).

MURPHY, Ignatius, 'Primary Education,' *A History of Irish Catholicism*, Vol. 5, VI (Dublin 1971).

Ó FIAICH, Tomas, 'The Clergy and Fenianism,' *I.E.R.*, Vol. 109 (Jan-June 1968).

'The Patriot Priest of Partry Patrick Lavelle: 1825-1886,' *Journal of the Galway Archaeological and Historical Society*, Vol. 35, 1976.

Ó GRÁDA, Cormac, 'Seasonal Migration and Post-Famine Adjustment in the West of Ireland,' *Studia Hibernica*, XIII (1973).

'Some Aspects of Nineteenth-Century Irish

	Emigration,' in *Comparative Aspects of Scottish and Irish Economic History 1600-1900,* ed. L. M. Cullen and T.C. Smout.
O SUILLEABHAIN, Seamus V.,	'Secondary Education,' *A History of Irish Catholicism,* Vol. 5, VI (Dublin 1971).
STEELE, E.D.,	'Cardinal Cullen and Irish Nationality,' *I.H.S.,* Vol. XIX, No. 75, March 1975.
TIERNEY, Mark,	'A short-title calendar of the Papers of Archbishop Thomas William Croke in Archbishop's House, Thurles,' *Collectanea Hibernica* 1970.
WHYTE, J. H.,	'The influence of the Catholic Clergy on Elections in Nineteenth Century Ireland,' *English Historical Review,* LXXV, 1960.
	'The Appointment of Catholic Bishops in Nineteenth Century Ireland,' *Catholic Historical Review,* April 1962.
	'Political Problems 1850-1860,' *A History of Irish Catholicism,* Vol. 5, II and III (Dublin 1967).
WOODS, C. J.,	'Ireland and Anglo-Papal Relations 1880-85,' *I.H.S.,* XVIII, No. 69 (March 1972).
	'The Politics of Cardinal McCabe, Archbishop of Dublin 1879-1885,' *Dublin Historical Record,* XXVI, No. 3 (June 1973).

C. **Unpublished Works:**

WOODS, C.J.,	*The Catholic Church and Politics in Ireland, 1879-92* (Ph.D. Thesis, University of Nottingham 1968).

Index

People

Places

General

Archbishop MacEvilly Family Tree

Walter & Winnifred MacEvilly[1]

William MacEvilly m. Sarah Boland[2]
b. 1786 d.1872 — b. 1786 d. 1886

John	Jeremiah	Walter	James	Mary	Ellen	Winnifred
	Archbishop of Tuam b. 1816 d. 1902	m. Sarah Goram (Connemara)	m. McHale / m. Joyce		m. G. Gibbons Louisburgh No issue	m. O'Toole[3]
	Priest		No issue			

Sarah[4] m. Kelly — Maria m. Nicholson

m. MacEvilly Ballintubber

Eileen[5]	Margaret	Pat	John	Jerry	Walter	William	Michael
m. Johnston	m. Keary Bohola	m. Scanlon	m. Treacy				

James	Matthew	John	Julia	Sarah	Eileen	Nora
m. Scott	m. Mason	m. O'Mahony	m. McGough	m. Waugh	m. Dunne	

1. Walter and Winnifred had 2 sons and 2 daughters. Brother of Archbishop Patrick went to USA. Sister of Archbishop married Gibbons, Partry – antecedents of Cardinal Gibbons, USA.
2. Sarah Boland's brother, a priest, drowned while swimming.
3. 5 sons and 3 daughters were born to William & Sarah MacEvilly. Fr. O'Toole, P.P., Kilmeena, son of Winnifred. Fr. Patten, Westport, also related.
4. Also twins who died young. Kellys, Octagon, Westport & Ryans, Westport related.
5. Pat, Jerry, William went to USA. Walter killed in Boer War. Michael died while studying for priesthood.